BASIC MOVEMENT
EDUCATION FOR CHILDREN
Rationale and Teaching Units

BASIC MOVEMENT EDUCATION FOR CHILDREN
Rationale and Teaching Units

Foreword by Joan Tillotson

Bonnie Cherp Gilliom
The Ohio State University

▲
Addison-Wesley Publishing Company
Reading, Massachusetts
Menlo Park, California • London • Don Mills, Ontario

This book is in the
ADDISON-WESLEY SERIES IN PHYSICAL EDUCATION

ISBN 0-201-02377-6
EFGHIJKLMN-AL-787654

I was walking through a hazy mist along the seashore when this outerspace creature with an English accent appeared and confronted me with this question: "Blimey! Aren't they leaving out the self?"

One is constantly amazed by his own dreams. An analyst would have fun with some of mine, if I had the courage to engage such a person. Usually I remember dreams for a very short period of time, but this one had special significance for me. I realized, after awakening with a start, that the dream creature had explicitly stated a semi-submerged discomfort that I had been feeling for some time: the ingredient most lacking in our elementary school programs has been the "self."

The dream had significance not only for me, but also for Mrs. Gilliom's work. The reader will be filled with the awareness that all of what is stated, in concrete form, relates directly to the child's *self*. Actually, that is what "basic movement education," as Mrs. Gilliom calls it, is all about: guiding, assisting, helping children identify themselves as moving, feeling, thinking, and sharing individuals who can, indeed, find true identity in a movement class. This is what education should be all about . . . but so often the self is of secondary importance to the content to be learned.

There will be readers of this book who are unable, at first, to see the self woven through the content. Yet once they launch into the lessons, CHILDREN pop out all along the way, moving to be seen, heard, and praised as individuals. This is one of the beauties of movement experiences as spelled out in this book. Children are moving to learn more about movement as content and more about themselves as individuals. Children are discovering their own ways to move effectively, efficiently, and expressively. And through the process identified throughout the lessons, children are learning how to learn, and, furthermore, are enjoying the experience.

This book, the first of its kind, is unique reference material. Its uniqueness lies in its double-barrelled approach. The rationale (Part One) fills the need for a scholarly, comprehensive, definitive statement of basic movement education. The teaching units (Part Two) fill the need for an example of theory translated into practice in the most specific, detailed, sequential way. Through selected movement problems, the subject matter and the process of physical education are "uncovered" by the child rather than "covered" by the teacher.

To me, this book is a jumping-off place . . . for beginning teachers who are desirous of some rather specific ideas to present to children and for experienced teachers who will question, experiment with, discard, or revise to suit the needs of their children. If some teachers begin to use the printed daily experiences in an inflexible manner, they will soon find that children differ. Some children will need to move quickly through various phases. Some will need and want to refine movement before going on, while others will be happy discovering new movement experiences daily. Thus teachers will need to jump about, using the materials purposefully, and developing new and exciting ideas of their own, with the help of creative children. What more meaningful way of learning and teaching is there?

Mrs. Gilliom has completed a most valuable tool for those of us who have been involved in movement education for twelve or more years. Her contribution will be of extreme value to those in teacher training, who will benefit especially from the guidelines for curriculum development in Part One. Elementary school classroom teachers and specialists who are ready to go beyond the first steps in exploration will find the teaching units in Part Two especially helpful in moving to an in-depth problem-solving process with their children. I trust, along with Mrs. Gilliom, that all teachers of children will assume the ready position with this book as a guide, and then JUMP.

Joan S. Tillotson
Consultant in Movement Education
Northeast Regional Supplementary
Education Center, Plattsburgh, N.Y.

This book is addressed chiefly to prospective, beginning, and experienced teachers of elementary school physical education—both specialists and classroom teachers who are responsible for the physical education of the children in their self-contained classes. Although intended primarily as a textbook in methods of teaching physical education, the book includes a three-year curriculum (Part Two) which will be of most value to teachers already in the field of elementary education. The comprehensive rationale for adding basic movement education to existing physical education programs (Part One) is appropriate, however, for teachers at any level—preschool through adult education.

After more than a decade of growing emphasis on the study of movement per se as a core content area in physical education, many teachers have acquired a vague awareness of the values of basic movement education. Perhaps they have read one stimulating article or perhaps they have seen one thought-provoking demonstration in which children were delighted with their own creative physical responses to movement problems, were freed to work at their own ability levels, and were totally absorbed in the business of becoming physically educated. Yet when these teachers returned to their classes to try out what they had seen, too often they were quickly stymied. After three lessons of exploring space, what next? Too often they were frustrated. After years of teaching and learning physical education by the standard explanation-demonstration-practice cycle in a highly controlled setting, they did not find it easy to cope with the drastic shift in teaching behaviors—and courageous new teaching behaviors are needed to create the free environment which is necessary for the basic movement portion of physical education. Superficial changes in content and method will not suffice if basic movement education is to free children to become responsible, intellectually autonomous individuals . . . individuals with a life-long yen for creative physical activity . . . individuals with an enhanced self concept. This book has been written to give guidance to the stymied and the frustrated by suggesting a specific theoretical approach to curriculum design.

Two most important tasks face teachers who are ready to add basic movement education to their existing physical education programs. The first is to identify a *structure of foundational knowledge* of movement—that which is worth knowing about and that which is worth experiencing in order to know. The second task is to identify a *process* of becoming physically educated—that which will make what is learned one's own, the giant leap from merely required, blindly copied learning to wanting to discover and use the foundational knowledge of movement.

Part One: Rationale

Chapter 1 stresses the need for *individualization* in teaching and defines basic movement education as a highly individualized approach to teaching the foundational structure and process portion of physical education.

Chapter 2 deals with the *content of basic movement*. It postulates that by answering the two questions of how man moves and why man moves, one may arrive at a structure for the knowledge of movement. Criteria for selecting structural content themes are proposed, examples of appropriate organizing themes are given, suggestions for developing other thematic organizations are made, and sequencing for spiral development of skills, knowledge, and attitudes is stressed. With examples taken from the teaching units in Part II, guidelines for teachers are set forth for organizing the new knowledge into a three-level hierarchy of concepts, main ideas, and facts. Again with examples taken from the teaching units in Part II, guidelines for teachers are set forth for establishing realistic, behavioral objectives for children—knowledge objectives; physical, social, and thinking skill objectives; and attitude objectives. A teacher's attitude of unconditional positive regard for his students is proposed as the starting point from which a healthy classroom atmosphere may grow.

Chapter 3 deals with the *process of becoming physically educated*. An application of principles of learning drawn from many schools of psychology is given through examples from the units. Definitions of discovery, inquiry, problem solving, and the process approach to learning are proposed, with emphasis on the act of discovery and a classification of problem types. Process criteria are proposed for teaching and learning basic movement education: for the statement of major problems presented to all the children, for developing subproblems by and for individual children, for nurturing creativity in all children, and for selecting learning activities to fulfill the objectives in all three areas—knowledge, skills, and attitudes.

Chapter 4, "Talks with Teachers," should really be read first, as it reflects the enthusiasm of the field test teachers who tried out the teaching units in Part II. It reports their wide range of teaching strategies, although all were using the same unit materials. Many practical and imaginative suggestions for implementing a basic movement education program are made, and the values of adding basic movement education to existing physical education curricula are especially well expressed by those who were doubters in the beginning.

Part Two: Teaching Units

Specific, detailed teaching units for any three consecutive grades in the elementary school are included as one of many possible interpretations of basic movement education. They may be used in a vast variety of ways—studied as one interpretation of the content of basic movement, or analyzed for their deliberate discovery and problem solving techniques, or scanned as one person's synthesis and application of the work of movement theorists, curriculum theorists, and learning theorists. Perhaps some teachers will want to begin by teaching from them almost "as is," as a means of bridging the theory-practice gap more quickly. The field test teachers did this—and found within two weeks that they were gaining the confidence to modify, to adapt, to change, to teach individuals instead of classes, to learn from their students, and to rely less on the units and more on their accumulated knowledge of children and their needs.

It is the author's hope that this text will encourage teachers to add basic movement education to their physical education curricula—not because someone has written out three years of lesson plans for them but because they recognize, hold in high esteem, and want to pass on the values of becoming movement-educated and movement-appreciative individuals.

Columbus, Ohio   B. C. G.
February, 1970

ACKNOWLEDGMENTS

I wish to thank the teachers and administrators in the following school systems for field testing and evaluating the basic-movement problem-solving units included in this book:

System	School	Test Teachers
Bexley Public Schools Columbus, Ohio	Montrose School	Cathy Bennett Karen Lustig
Columbus Public Schools Columbus, Ohio	Maryland School	Ann Schlessman
	Medary School	Onabel McFarland Craigen Wall
	Sharon School	Dorothy Dilworth Karen Egelhoff Diane Osterwise
School District #13 South Huntington, New York	Maplewood Elementary School	Ruth Gregg
Setauket Public Schools Setauket, New York	Three Village School	Jean Berger
Syosset Public Schools Syosset, New York	Village School	Mary Conklin
	South Grove Annex	Dierdre Breslin Eileen Marino
Upper Arlington Public Schools Columbus, Ohio	Barrington School	Maurice Angle
	Windermere School	Irv Mitchell

A preliminary version of the first level of problems in the units was also field tested by twenty-five teachers in the Cleveland, Ohio, area who used my television series, *Physical Education for Doers and Viewers,* broadcast by WVIZ-TV. Appreciation is expressed both to the Cleveland teachers and to the members of the advisory committee for the TV series, who motivated my interest in basic movement conceptualization and problem design. Members of the committee were: Anita Aldrich, Naomi Allenbaugh, Jane Fink, Margie Hanson, Chalmer Hixson, Hayes Krueger, Aileen Lockhart, Bette Logsdon, Robert McLaughlin, Heidie Mitchell, and Carolyn Rasmus. Joan Tillotson, Heidie Mitchell, and Cathy Bennett were most helpful in final evaluations of this book.

I am also indebted to my husband, M. Eugene Gilliom, whose work in curriculum design in the social studies so closely parallels and frequently motivates mine in the field of physical education. Opal Border and Gregor and Julia Gilliom deserve our heartfelt thanks for bringing both of us joy and peace of mind while we go about our tasks.

PART I RATIONALE

Chapter 1   Escape from Little Boxes   3

Basic Movement Education Illustrated   4

Chapter 2   Structure: The Content of Basic Movement   6

  In search of structure   6

In Search of Structure in Physical Education   6

  The structure of how man moves   6

    Criteria   6

    Scope: The organizing themes to be revisited   7

    Movement variables related to themes   7

    Sequence: The order of introducing themes   7

    Depth: Developing interrelated major themes   8

  The structure of why man moves 11

Teacher's Guidelines for the Structure of Basic Movement 11

  The concept 12

  The major ideas 12

  The facts 12

Children's Objectives in Studying Basic Movement 15

  Knowledge objectives and check lists 15

  Skill objectives 16

  Attitude objectives 16

Chapter 3   Process: Becoming Physically Educated   18

  In search of process 18

Points of Agreement in Learning Theories 19

Discovery as Process: Problem Solving as Technique 21

  Definitions 21

  Bruner's hypotheses about the act of discovery 21

  Libby's classification of problem types 22

Criteria for Designing Problems (Learning Activities) 23

  Criterion 1: Major problems—presented problems with no standard methods
for solving them 23

  Criterion 2: Subproblems—examples of problems that exist with no standard
methods for solving them 24

  Criterion 3: Productive thinking—reasoning and imagining 25

  Criterion 4: Creativity—nature and nurture 25

  Criterion 5: Multiple objectives—problems for knowledge, skill, and attitude
development 27

Chapter 4 Teaching Strategies: Talks with Teachers   29

    Background of field testing 29

  Instructions for Using the Units 29

    How a beginning grade level teacher uses a problem 30

    How a middle grade level teacher uses a problem 31

    How a last grade level teacher uses a problem 32

  Flexible Usage of Units Suggested by Field Test Teachers 33

    Question one (before field testing): Alternating or integrating 33

    Question two: Grade level placement 34

    Question three: Time needed for basic movement education 35

    Question four: Time needed for each set of problems 36

    Question five: Space needed for basic movement education 36

    Question six: Discipline 36

    Question seven: Verbalizing and demonstrating 37

    Question eight: Appropriate dress 39

    Question nine: Equipment 39

    Question ten: Evaluation 42

  Teachers' Personal Reactions 43

  At the end of the first week 43

  At the end of six weeks 44

  At the end of the program 45

    Children's responses 45

    Reactions to basic movement as content 46

    Reactions to discovery and problem solving as technique 46

Summary of Part I: Rationale   47

PART II TEACHING UNITS

Calendar of Basic Movement Education Units 50

Unit 1 Where Can You Move? (Space)   51

First Set of Problems   Moving in Self Space and in General Space 53

Second Set of Problems   Moving in Different Directions 64

Third Set of Problems   Moving at Different Levels 74

Fourth Set of Problems   Moving in Different Ranges and by Changing Shapes   84

Fifth Set of Problems   Moving in the Air (Flight) 93

Sixth Set of Problems   Moving in Different Pathways 102

Unit 2   What Can You Move? (Body Awareness)   109

Seventh Set of Problems   Moving Different Body Parts   110

Eighth Set of Problems   Changing Relationships of Body Parts (Meeting and Parting)   117

Ninth Set of Problems   Review—Moving the Body in Space   124

Unit 3   How Do You Move? (Force, Balance, Weight Transfer)   132

Tenth Set of Problems   Creating Force—Weak and Strong   133

Eleventh Set of Problems   Absorbing Force   142

Twelfth Set of Problems   Moving On-balance and Off-balance (Gravity) . .   150

Thirteenth Set of Problems   Transferring Weight (Rocking, Rolling, Sliding) .   158

Fourteenth Set of Problems   Transferring Weight (Steplike Movements) . .   167

Fifteenth Set of Problems   Transferring Weight (Flight) and Review—Force, Balance, Weight Transfer   175

Unit 4   How Can You Move Better? (Time, Flow)   181

Sixteenth Set of Problems   Moving at Different Speeds   182

Seventeenth Set of Problems   Moving in Response to Different Rhythms (Pulse Beats)   190

Eighteenth Set of Problems   Moving in Bound or Free Flow and Creating Movement Sequences   197

Nineteenth Set of Problems   Moving in Response to Phrases and Creating Movement Sequences   204

Twentieth Set of Problems   Creating Movement Sequences as a Review of Basic Movement   214

Bibliography   221

Little boxes on the hillside, little boxes made of ticky tacky,
Little boxes, little boxes, little boxes all the same.
There's a green one, and a pink one, and a blue one, and a yellow one,
And they're all made out of ticky tacky, and they all look just the same.

And the people in the houses all go to the University,
And they all get put in boxes, little boxes all the same.
And there's doctors and there's lawyers and business executives,
And they're all made out of ticky tacky, and they all look just the same.

And they all play on the golf course and drink their martini dry,
And they all have pretty children, and the children go to school.
And the children go to summer camp and then to the University,
And they all get put in boxes, and they all come out the same.

And the boys go into business and marry and raise a family,
And they all get put in boxes, little boxes all the same.
There's a green one, and a pink one, and a blue one, and a yellow one,
And they're all made out of ticky tacky, and they all look just the same.

—Malvina Reynolds*

Teachers and teachers-to-be who value *individuality* rather than *sameness* in their students often request practical help in designing curricula aimed at freeing boys and girls from their identical little boxes. Traditional physical education is as guilty as other subject fields in trying to force all children—the large and the small, the alert and the lethargic, the fat and the thin, the adept and the inept—into the same stereotyped behavior with all children doing the same thing at the same time. Frequently the stereotyped "good movement" taught by classroom teachers with little background or interest in physical education, in addition to following the philosophy of sameness for all, is ticky tacky in content. Those few children who fit the ticky tacky boxes thrive within them, love the games and dances, but gain little in movement ability and understanding. Many other children, those five- or six-year-old physical education dropouts one so often sees standing passively in the corners of the school yard, learn to hide in the little boxes. One thing these children learn is how to escape. Is this behavior that physical education programs should produce? Should avoiding physical activity or dropping out be an end result of physical education? The curriculum materials presented in this book are an example of one beginning step away from thoughtless sameness equalling success and thoughtful differentness equalling failure. That beginning step is to add the study of basic movement to existing physical education programs.

The major purpose of this book is to encourage teachers *to add basic movement education to their existing physical education programs*. The secondary purpose is to present as succinctly and practically as possible one interpretation of basic movement, with a "new" approach to content and methodology. Although the term "new" is used, it should be kept in mind that basic movement content has been taught in some schools in this country for over ten years, and that problem solving, the "new" method, is older than any other technique of teaching. The "new" approach to *content* is based on the proposition that there is an *undergirding body of knowledge* relevant to all the traditional content areas of games and sports, dance, and gymnastics. The "new" approach to *methodology* is based on the proposition that the *process of discovery* and the *techniques of problem solving*—the techniques of having children discover their own mental and movement solutions to carefully stated problems—are the most effective ways of improving movement in general. "If physical education is to make a *real* contribution to the total education of each student, it must do more than give him a few isolated skills, most of which can be used only in specific,

---

*   Words and music by Malvina Reynolds. Copyright © 1962 by Schroder Music Co. (ASCAP) Used by permission.

recreational situations." [Broer, 8]* If physical education is to make any contribution at all, it must do much more than give a child an in-school opportunity to play the games he would learn on his own.

A great deal of confusion and misunderstanding has arisen about basic movement education. The following three points of view illustrate the range of divergent but inaccurate opinions of what the "new" basic movement education is.

- *Teacher 1.* "Basic movement is just another method of teaching the same old thing . . . let children explore movement until they discover the *right way* to pitch a soft ball . . . eventually they will find that the way I used to explain and demonstrate it is the right way . . . the new method takes more time, but children remember what they've learned longer."

- *Teacher 2.* "No, I don't think basic movement is a method of teaching. I think it is primarily an attitude toward movement . . . it is movement for the sake of movement, for the sake of experiencing the joy of movement . . . there is really no other content . . . a teacher merely encourages the child to feel good about his random movements and about himself . . . there are no quality standards and specific skill development becomes a lost art."

- *Teacher 3.* "From what I've heard, basic movement is all content—pure knowledge content . . . principles of human movement, physical laws of motion, and things like that . . . children could learn it in a classroom and never move an inch away from their desks . . . preparing for a future populated by big-headed, shriveled-bodied people, I guess."

The above opinions reflect a vague awareness of some of the values of adding basic movement to existing programs, but each is too narrow an interpretation, thus leading to a lack of appreciation for the multi-faceted worth of basic movement. Problem solving *is* emphasized, joy in movement *is* important, a knowledge content *is* presented to give structure to the field; yet in the above shortsighted views, the movement content has been overlooked, and the interrelatedness of the various values has not been comprehended. Basic movement is the foundational *structure and process portion* of physical education. The structure of human movement is delineated in Chapter 2. The process of becoming physically educated through movement experiences is discussed in Chapter 3.

Basic movement education illustrated

Two avenues have been chosen to illustrate in this book a more comprehensive view of basic movement education. First, in Part I, a rationale for adding the study of basic movement to existing physical education programs is discussed. The structure and process portion of physical education is examined and guidelines are suggested for teachers who are developing new units in basic movement.

The second avenue, in Part II, is the inclusion of very detailed, well tested teaching units in basic movement with problem solving as the primary methodology. The four units provide a comprehensive coverage of basic movement, the "new content" least understood by most teachers. The relationship of these basic movement units to the more traditional units in games, dance, and gymnastics is one of undergirding and supplementing the total physical education curriculum, not of replacing it.

The units are designed for use in any three consecutive grades in the elementary school: K-1-2, 1-2-3, 2-3-4, 3-4-5, or 4-5-6. Since a problem-solving approach to content is employed, it is appropriate for both teachers of kindergarteners and teachers of fourth graders to use the beginning grade level of the materials successfully. The third grader will solve the problems at his own level of movement skill and cognition. The kindergartener will

---

* All references are listed in the Bibliography.

do the same. Occasionally, the third grader's response will not surpass that of the kindergartener, yet he will not fail.

One self-imposed question has given the author some concern: "Will making available such detailed lesson plans amount only to spoonfeeding?" These units are offered to teachers as one of many resources to be used in developing their own curricula. They are an attempt to synthesize for teachers the work of movement theorists, curriculum theorists, and learning theorists into a practical plan which teachers can modify and use with confidence and which, hopefully, will motivate their interest in the primary sources. Movement theorists (Laban, Brown, Simpson, Allenbaugh) have identified foundational knowledge which is only vaguely understood by most classroom teachers and specialists. Curriculum theorists (Taba, Goodlad) have built sophisticated systems designs which in their comprehensiveness are often impractical for teachers to apply conscientiously. Learning theorists (Bruner, Bloom, Wertheimer) have proposed effective, efficient, economical ways to develop in children high-level problem-solving abilities which require great change in teaching and learning behavior—change frequently not even attempted, as a result of insecurity on the part of the teacher. Thus the answer might be a qualified "yes" to spoonfeeding a predigested mixture of theory and experience to those who want to swallow it whole. An unqualified "no" answer to the self-imposed spoonfeeding charge is premised on the belief that the professional teacher will never blindly accept a packaged curriculum—a curriculum designed without the designer's knowing the idiosyncrasies of individual teachers who will use it, their specific school environments, or the needs of the individual children they teach.

It is hoped that every teacher will use the units in his own way—study them as an interpretation of the new content, analyze them for their deliberate discovery and problem-solving technique, perhaps even begin by teaching from them almost "as is" as a means of bridging the theory-practice gap more quickly. To have a teacher adopt these units uncritically and use them in the same way year after year, however, would negate the entire effort. Although children might emerge partially from their identical ticky tacky boxes, the teacher would be slamming down the lid of his own box, locking inside all the creative teaching potentiality he has.

STRUCTURE: THE CONTENT OF BASIC MOVEMENT

Chapter 2

The curriculum of a subject should be determined by the most fundamental understanding that can be achieved of the underlying principles that give structure to that subject.

—Jerome S. Bruner, 1963

In Search of Structure

Jerome Bruner's oft-quoted proposition, "that the foundations of any subject may be taught to anybody at any age in some form," resulted in a flurry of activity by educators in all fields. Their task: to take a new view of their knowledge foundations in order to skeletonize them into powerful basic themes simple enough for a youngster of five to grasp, yet potent enough to organize vast amounts of data. Once such themes were identified, theoretically a curriculum could be designed in which the themes could be visited over and over again throughout the school years. Through regular planned revisitations, children could come to understand each theme in ascending levels of abstraction, complexity, and sophistication. At each revisitation, more flesh could be added to the skeleton, more relationships within the structure and with other subject areas could be perceived. Nearly everyone is aware of the new math which has resulted from this search. In physical education, the search for structure has resulted in the identification of a body of knowledge which has come to be known as basic movement.

Basic movement education, for purposes of this book, *is defined as the foundational structure and process portion of physical education which is characterized by the experiential study of*

1   *time, space, force, and flow as the elements of movement,*
2   *the physical laws of motion and the principles of human movement which govern the human body's movement, and*
3   *the vast variety of creative and efficient movements which the human body is capable of producing through manipulation of movement variables.*

In search of structure in physical education

How does man move? Why does man move? The answers to these two fundamental questions can provide a structure for the knowledge content of basic movement. Indeed, a structure obtained from answering the questions is appropriate for all of physical education with units in basic movement serving to introduce the structure to children at an early age.

The Structure of How Man Moves

• *Criteria.*   The "how man moves" question can be partially answered through children's experiential study of the nineteen themes to be developed in Part II of this book. Two major criteria were used in selecting the themes:

1   Knowledge obtained from studying the themes must be applicable to any specific skill, game, dance, or sport to be learned in physical education and to all other movements which life might demand of the learner.
2   Themes must be powerful enough to merit repeated visitations over a minimum of three years* with continual broadening and deepening of knowledge occurring at each visitation.

Each time a theme is repeated, knowledge previously attained should be manipulated to fit new tasks, and the manipulations themselves should be evaluated.

---

*   The problems in this book are designed for a span of three years; thus the criterion was established for three years. In testing, however, a span of eight years with the same themes proved the themes were broad enough for further use.

- *Scope: The Organizing Themes to be Revisited.*   The following themes are those selected for the basic movement units in this book, and they are listed in the order in which they are developed in the units. They reflect Laban's [41, 42] research findings in analyzing human movement elements, the curricular interpretations of his work by his many followers such as Russell [65] in dance and Pallett [55] in gymnastics, and the accumulated findings of Scott [69], Broer [8], and others in delineating the physical laws of motion and the principles of human movement.

Unit One. Where can you move? (space)

Moving within self space and into general space (alone, with others, and in relationship to static and moving objects).*

Moving in different directions.

Moving at different levels.

Moving in different ranges and by changing shapes.

Moving in air (flight).

Moving in different pathways.

Unit Two. What can you move? (body awareness)

Moving different body parts.

Changing relationships of body parts (to each other and to objects in space)

Unit Three. How do you move? (force, balance, weight transfer)

Creating force.

Absorbing force.

Moving on-balance and off-balance (gravity).

Transferring weight (rocking, rolling, and sliding on adjacent parts).

Transferring weight (steplike movements on nonadjacent parts).†

Transferring weight when flight is involved.

Unit Four. How can you move better? (time, flow)

Moving at different speeds.

Moving rhythmically (to pulse beats).

Moving in bound or free flow.

Moving rhythmically (to phrases).

Creating movement sequences.

---

*   These relationships apply to all the themes and are developed in the set of problems for each theme.

†   The term "steplike movements" does not limit activity to foot-to-foot movements; instead, stepping on a variety of body parts is stressed.

- *Movement Variables Related to Themes.*   The number of movement variables which can flesh out this skeletal structure of themes is enormous. For example, in developing the last theme, "creating movement sequences," the children are all asked to perform a set sequence. Each child is then asked to vary one or more aspects of the sequence. His movement repertoire, from which he can draw for creating his own variation, includes one hundred specific movement variables previously studied and experienced in movement. By raising each variable to the hundredth power, one still does not exhaust the possible number of movement variables, because each one can be further broken down into more specific dimensions. A child, although he is never asked to verbalize or reproduce on paper the total structure given to these movement variables, should be able to demonstrate in movement his understandings of the structure. Movement Chart III (pages 212–213) outlining the one hundred variables experienced by children through the study of the units is reproduced on the next page in abbreviated form.

- *Sequence: The Order of Introducing Themes.*   The organizing themes listed above and on page 51 are arranged in the order that they are introduced in the units, but this does not imply a hierarchy of themes or a natural, developmental sequence of themes. All of the themes are interrelated, and conceivably one could shuffle them in any way and still build a logical curriculum around them. The sequence shown was selected primarily on the basis of vocabulary—on words which would be most easily understood

Movement Chart I

My body	moves	in space	in time and with force	and with flow . . . .

Body parts
1 Head
2 Neck
3 Etc., to 25.

Body surfaces
26 Front
27 Back
28 Sides

Body shapes
29 Curved
30 Straight and narrow
31 Straight and wide
32 Twisted

Body relationships: body part to body part
33 Near to each other (curled)
34 Far from each other (stretched)
35 Rotation of one part

Relationship of body parts to objects: on, off, over, around, across, under, near to, far from
36 Walls, floor
37 Boxes, benches, beams

Manipulating
38 Balls—bouncing, catching, tossing, pushing
39 Ropes, hoops, etc.

Relationship of one person to another or others
40 Near to
41 Far from
42 Meeting
43 Parting
44 Facing
45 Side by side
46 Shadowing
47 Mirroring
48 Leading
49 Following

By transfer of weight
50 Steplike actions
51 Rocking
52 Rolling
53 Sliding
54 Flight

By balancing (active stillness)
55 Balancing weight on different body parts
56 Balancing on different numbers of parts (4, 3, 2, 1)

Division of space
57 Self space
58 General space

Dimensions of space
59 Directions
60 Forward
61 Backward
62 To one side
63 To the other side
64 Up
65 Down
66 Levels
67 High
68 Medium
69 Low
70 Ranges
71 Large
72 Medium
73 Small
74 Planes
75 Pathways (floor or air)
76 Straight
77 Curved
78 Zigzag

Time
79 Speed
80 Slow
81 Medium
82 Fast
83 Accelerating
84 Decelerating

85 **Rhythm**
86 Pulse beats
87 Phrases

Degrees of force
88 Strong
89 Medium
90 Weak

Qualities of force
91 Sudden, explosive
92 Sustained, smooth

Creating force
93 Quick starts
94 Sustained, powerful movements
95 Held balances

Absorbing force
96 Sudden stops on-balance
97 Gradual absorption ("give")

Dimensions of flow
98 Free flow
99 Bound flow

100 **Movement sequences.**

Smooth series of movements.

Beginning and ending.

Preparation, action, and recovery smoothly linked.

Transitions.

by children when spoken by a teacher as stimuli for thoughtful movement. One of the objectives of basic movement education is to develop a functional movement vocabulary—a "doing" vocabulary, not a verbalizing vocabulary. The same kind of care must be taken in introducing new movement vocabulary words (the words used to stimulate movement responses in children) as is used in building a foreign language vocabulary. In both cases, no natural sequence or hierarchy is implied because a child is introduced to the movement meaning or foreign word for "space" before he is introduced to the movement meaning or foreign word for "balance." However, once a sequence of themes (each with its own new vocabulary) has been chosen, a *carefully planned system of repetition* should be used by which a child can effectively master the linguistic stimuli. In these units, each new structural word is used at least three times in the set of problems (one theme) in which it first appears, then is repeated at least once in the next set of problems, and then is repeated again at least five more times in ensuing problems. Thus teachers choosing to use the movement problems in the book in a sequence different from the one presented would do well to check the words used to stimulate movement variables as some of them may not have been previously introduced and reinforced. To sum up, the themes themselves may be studied in any order, but the problems stated in the units are designed for sequential use, especially at the first level of the three consecutive grades. Teachers of children who have had at least a year's experience in using the functional movement vocabulary may want to change the sequence to fit the needs of students who may be movement poor in one of the areas.

• *Depth: Developing Interrelated Major Themes.*   Students who have successfully completed three consecutive years of basic movement education or who demonstrate a readiness for more depth before completing the three-year program need to have additional themes to work on. These additional themes are not really new if a comprehensive structure has been previously introduced. Instead, the additional themes should stress relationships between themes. The simplest way to select such additional themes is to pick out problems which have been used in studying one theme, and use them again while studying a different theme. Often just one problem, repeated in relationship to almost any other theme, can lead to a whole series of learning activities. For example, in Problem 72 in the units, the children are asked to keep their hands on the floor in one spot while they move their feet around in different ways. This problem is posed in the context of studying balance. With very little adaptation it could be profitably repeated in relationship to:

    space—levels, ranges, shapes, pathways,

    body awareness—different body parts, changing relationships of body
       parts,

    force—creating force, absorbing force, qualities of force,

    weight transfer—steplike movements, rocking, rolling, sliding,

    flight—leading into or following the balance,

    time—speeds, to pulse beats, to phrases,

    flow—free flow, bound flow,

    sequences—alone, with one person, in a small group, matching, mirroring,

    equipment—on a balance beam, bench, box, using a wall, within a hoop,
       etc.

In the above example, the relationship between the one requirement (hands on floor, feet moving) and one after another of the themes could be developed in three to thirty class periods. To spend many weeks on just a hands down problem would lead to boredom, however, and would neglect many other valuable activities. The above method of devising new themes is recommended only for short periods of time.

For planning an additional year or years of work and for maintaining a balanced program, it is suggested that teachers construct a number of different yet logical *models of the structure of movement,* such as the one that appears in Fig. 2–1.

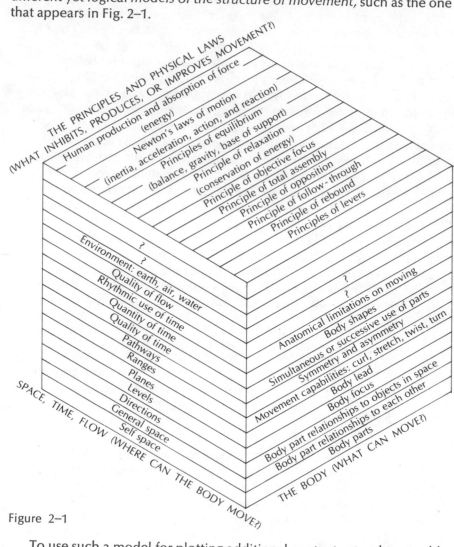

Figure 2–1

To use such a model for plotting additional content, a teacher would select one statement from each of the three sides, and use that three-way relationship as the new major theme to be studied in all its variability. The next major theme would be another selection of three statements, and so on.

By taking out any one cube of the model, a more complex interrelationship is isolated than any developed in the curriculum in Part II. The cube then becomes a theme to be developed in depth. For example, by taking the cube marked in Fig. 2–1, the theme becomes *balancing* in *self space* on *different body parts,* an idea worthy of several days of work and one a future gymnastics coach might cherish.

To give another example, suppose "principle of follow through" instead of "balance" had been selected from the base of the model. The theme then becomes *following through* with *different body parts* in *self space.* Intensive study of this theme could make future coaches of all the ball games equally happy. More importantly, a child or an older and more experienced student is given the opportunity to discover his own ways of moving efficiently and effectively and of demonstrating in movement his current grasp of the cognitive structure of movement. Structure strengthening results from relating the elements of the structure in different ways.

If one were to construct different yet logical models of the structure of movement and use all the cubes as themes to be studied, one would have at hand enough content themes for a lifetime of study.

How does man move? is a question that cannot be answered by any three-dimensional model. First, the knowledge content to answer "how" has more than three dimensions. Second, there are "how" answers beyond the knowledge content—"how" as it is affected by the physical, social, and emotional maturity of the mover and as it is permeated by his value system. The search for structure, however, is limited to knowledge content—finding that which is worth knowing.

The Structure of Why Man Moves

The other fundamental question around which the basic themes of movement may be structured is "Why does man move?" Philosophers in physical education categorize the purposes of man's movement behavior in different ways. Camille Brown [9] suggests movement behavior can be classified as (1) coping, (2) expressive, or (3) communicative. Naomi Allenbaugh [1] conceptualizes the answer to this question in four ways:

1 Man moves to survive.
2 Man moves to understand his environment.
3 Man moves to adjust to and to control his environment.
4 Man moves to communicate.

Only one core concept, *"movement for environmental control,"* has been selected for development in the following units, and it stands at the top level in the hierarchy of knowledge in physical education. Other concepts, however, could have been selected which would pass the test of relevancy to all of physical education. In fact, other concepts will inevitably be developed to a degree in the execution of the units, but a systematic revisiting of them is not planned. For example, children *will* communicate as they move and *will* think about new ways to improve or to vary their nonverbal self expression. They *will* gradually learn to interpret more accurately the movement messages sent by their peers. Such learning could be broadened by interspersing lessons in dance-making after sequence formation has been studied.

In summarizing this discussion on the structure of knowledge as the basis for selecting content for the curriculum, we return to Bruner. "To learn structure, in short, is to learn how things are related." The "things" in the basic movement curriculum in Part II are the elements of movement, the physical laws of motion, the principles of human movement, and the variability of human movement for different purposes. *To know basic movement,* to relate these "things" to each other and to knowledge from other disciplines in a meaningful way, is one long-range aim of physical education.

Teacher's guidelines for the structure of basic movement

Teachers who are unfamiliar with basic movement will find the knowledge content outlined in the Introduction to each set of problems (each theme) in Part II under Content Structure (for teachers). This content is the same for kindergarten teachers and for sixth grade teachers just as it is the same for the child in his first year or his third year of studying basic movement. It delineates one structure of the knowledge content, which teachers may accept or modify. Children, while never required to verbalize this structure, will be immersed in it while thinking and moving. Graduated, concrete, problem-solving experiences in movement are designed to illustrate the structure. Problems are introduced, then returned to again and again with a spiral of differing subproblems designed to widen the relationships of previously acquired knowledge and to suggest movement solutions for new tasks.

The following example of Content Structure (for teachers) is taken from the introduction to the sixth set of problems and is focused on the theme of "Moving in different pathways." It is the last theme to be studied in the unit on space, and is preceded by study of moving in self space and general space, moving in different directions, levels, and ranges, moving by changing shapes, and moving in the air (flight).

Unit One

Where can you move? (space)

Sixth set of problems / Organizing theme: Moving in different pathways

Content structure (for teachers)

Concept

Movement for environmental control.

Major ideas (review)

1   Man moves to control his environment; a child moves to discover and to cope with his environment.

2   The body is the instrument of movement and can be used in a vast variety of ways.

3   **Space,** force, time, and flow are the elements of movement.

4   **Space** is the medium of movement.

5   The dimensions of space are directions, levels, planes, and ranges.

Major ideas (new)

6   The **pathway** the body takes is one spacial movement variable which can be consciously manipulated.

Selected facts

1   While traveling, the body makes floor pathways of straight or curved lines.

2   While traveling, the body also carves a pathway in air space.

3   Isolated body parts (e.g., foot, hand, head) as well as the whole body describe floor and air pathways.

4   A zigzag pathway is a combination of straight lines with sharp turns to change directions.

Notice, in the above example, the hierarchy in levels of knowledge, each of which serves a different function in instruction and learning:

1   the basic concept,

2   the major ideas,

3   the selected facts (specific descriptive information).

The three-level hierarchy of knowledge as developed for each theme in the units is based on Hilda Taba's [73] definitive work in curriculum development.

The Concept

"Movement for environmental control" is a high-level abstraction which encompasses and has the power to organize large amounts of specific data. It is one answer to the fundamental question of why man moves. It is the single concept around which all the lessons for all grade levels in this book are focused. If one subscribes to Bruner's proposition "that the foundations of any subject may be taught to anybody at any age in some [intellectually honest] form," then stating such an abstract concept for kindergarteners becomes realistic. A kindergartener is not expected to master this basic concept in all its complex relationships, but he is capable of an elementary comprehension of it through concrete movement experiences. His understanding of the concept is to be continually developed through successive studies of each theme and is to be broadened and deepened through repetition of the same themes in three successive grades. The spiral development of this one concept, "movement for environment control" is central to the three years of basic movement education outlined in this book.

The Major Ideas

Major ideas are those generalizations which serve as the basic foci for planning and study. They support development of the concept. Look again

at the major ideas in the Content Structure (for teachers), page 12. The first
five major ideas have been previously introduced and are being revisited.
Although they are not listed for every set of problems, they pertain to every
lesson and should provide a continuous focus. The sixth generalization
is the new theme. "The pathway the body takes is one spacial movement
variable which can be consciously manipulated." Here is the focus for the
sixth set of problems. What kinds of movement experiences will develop this
theme? An example of just one problem a teacher could pose to children in
their first year of basic movement follows:

> **"Moving into general space, see how many ways you can
> make a curved pathway on the floor."**
>
> Some movement variables:
>
> Large curves, small curves (range previously studied).
>
> A curve to one side, a curve to the other side (direction
> previously studied).
>
> Curves while moving forward, backward, or sideways
> (direction previously studied).
>
> High curves, low curves (level previously studied).
>
> Different body shapes while making a curved pathway
> (shapes previously studied).
>
> (If children don't discover the relationships on their own,
> subproblems may be posed while they are moving to
> broaden the scope of their movement solutions.)

In the units, eight problems are centered around the pathway theme, and
all eight of them are appropriate for use at all three consecutive grades. For
the first of the three grades, twenty-five subproblems are also listed as
"bumpers" for children who have run out of ideas for discovering
relationships—discovering "new" ways to make a curved pathway on the
floor. Twenty-eight subproblems are listed for the second of the three
grades, and fifteen more subproblems are listed for the last grade.

Among the experiences planned for the whole set of problems on
pathway are:

> Moving in different pathways while avoiding collisions.
>
> Making sharp turns in zigzag pathways.
>
> Demonstrating (half of the class demonstrates for the other half) the
> variety of zigzag pathways possible.
>
> Making sharp changes of direction on drum beats.
>
> Discussing the use of knee flexion for quick change of direction.
>
> Bouncing a ball in curved and straight pathways.
>
> Bouncing a ball near to an obstacle, then zigzagging away quickly.
>
> Drawing air pathways with different body parts.
>
> Using different pathways to connect several held balances.
>
> Mirroring a partner's movements.
>
> Making a movement sequence of curves and zigzags in small groups.
>
> Demonstrating and evaluating the movement sequences.

The major idea on pathway variability is a generalization to be grasped
through a multitude of approaches. There is no "right" or stereotyped
pathway to be followed, no "right" or stereotyped movement to be
performed. Thus, no child can fail. Every child should begin to deduce
from his experiences such practical data as how to vary his pathway to avoid
collisions on the playground, how to avoid his guard in basketball, how to
slide safely into third in baseball, how to perceive when to pass another car

when driving, how to maneuver himself adroitly when getting out of the back of a crowded elevator with his arms full of packages. Such is the practicality of teaching generalizations, and the above list merely scratches the surface. How many more practicalities can you list? How many "teachable moments" can you identify for pointing out the practicalities?

One cannot forego generalizing—the perversity of human nature is such that one does generalize. Yet, typically, physical education prepares students inadequately for skillful, conscious elevation above the level of the specific. The major ideas (generalizations) outlined at the beginning of each theme characterize the nature of movement and transcend particular skills and specific dance, games, and gymnastics activities. One's understanding of the essence of movement ultimately is largely dependent upon his comprehension of these ideas. Students who grasp the major ideas should accordingly have a deeper understanding of the higher-level concept previously discussed: movement for environmental control.

The Facts

The third level of knowledge consists of specific facts. Traditionally, physical education curricula have been fact-oriented rather than idea-oriented. Courses have been designed by conscientious teachers to expose students to and drill them in vast amounts of factual detail—thousands of rules for a wide scope of simple games, relays, and dances; minute, analytical details for the "right" way to perform fundamental and specialized motor skills, all the way down to the placement of the big toe. A student's success in such a course has been measured by his ability to absorb and regurgitate these facts and his ability to perform movement skills in exactly the way they were demonstrated.

Yet facts tend to become obsolescent, new rules are devised, and new styles of specialized skills evolve. In addition, research has shown that approximately eighty per cent of disconnected facts are forgotten within two years. [Taba, 74] Thus it is highly questionable whether curricula which stress an accumulation of specific, isolated facts are as efficient and as effective as one could legitimately expect.

Despite the abuse of facts in teaching, they are essential to an understanding of major ideas (generalizations). As William James [37] has suggested, no one sees farther into a generalization than his knowledge of detail extends. Facts assume their greatest significance and durability, moreover, when used in the molding of major ideas. Major idea and concept development has been conspicuously lacking in many elementary physical education programs.

Using the pathway example again, the facts are simple definitional statements. They provide descriptive information, a vocabulary framework to illustrate, explain, and develop the major ideas. They define floor pathway and air pathway. They name curves, straight lines, and zigzags as the three main pathways to be studied. Experienced teachers in the curriculum may later substitute other facts in light of their own knowledge and interests. They may expand the number of problems for each theme or rephrase problems to bring in more relationships. They may, after becoming secure in a new field, restructure it in a way that is more appropriate for the kind of students they teach, or, better yet, restructure it for individuals.

In conclusion, the Content Structure as outlined in three levels of knowledge is for the teacher's enlightenment. Children are not expected to remember all the specific facts introduced to develop the major ideas. Children need verbalize neither the major ideas nor the concept. Their interpretation of facts leading to generalizations which in turn support concepts is to be *demonstrated in movement rather than in verbalization*. Verbal evaluations, however, of their own movements and the movements of others may serve as a method of reinforcement.

Children's objectives in studying basic movement

The Objectives (for children) in studying each theme are found on the same page with Content Structure (for teachers) and parallel it in terms of children's behavior to be achieved. The following are the objectives for the study of pathway.

Unit One

Where can you move? (space)

Sixth set of problems / Organizing theme: Moving in different pathways

Objectives (for children)

Children need to understand (knowledge)

1 That while moving they produce pathways they can recognize both on the floor and in the air.

2 That the two main kinds of pathways are curved lines and straight lines.

3 That zigzags are combinations of straight lines with sharp turns to change direction.

4 That mirroring a partner's movements is done by facing him and doing the same movements he does, as if looking in a mirror (e.g., both lean north, one leaning to his right, and the other leaning to his left).

Children need to learn how (skill)

1 To control consciously the pathway of the body on the floor and in the air while moving in a wide variety of ways.

2 To change direction quickly and with sharp turns when moving in a zigzag pathway.

3 To travel in a wide variety of pathways while manipulating a ball.

4 When working with a partner in mirroring movements, to adjust the speed and complexity of their own movements to those of their partners.

Children need to become (attitude)*

1 Willing to listen to problems, to think about them, and to seek increasingly more skillful, thoughtful, and original ways of solving them through movement.

2 Willing to carry tasks through to completion.

3 Increasingly self-motivated, self-determined, and self-disciplined, so that each individual appreciates his own self-worth.

4 Appreciative of others like and unlike themselves.

5 Willing to help and to work with others.

6 Success-oriented in movement, so that they appreciate and enjoy movement.

---

* The attitude objectives stated are broad and cannot be achieved quickly; therefore they are the same for the entire three-year period.

Knowledge Objectives and Check Lists

Notice that the knowledge objectives above are really only at the definitional framework level. The interrelationships to be perceived are so numerous they are not listed in the objectives, but instead are delineated in a Checklist of Quality Factors at the end of each problem in the units. For example, Problem 37, "Moving into general space, see how many ways you can make a curved pathway on the floor," is followed by these objectives (which have become evaluation criteria):

Checklist of quality factors for Problem 38

☐ Moving in a wide variety of ways in curving pathways. Suggested minimums:
Beginning grade—6 ways, including varying the range, level, and direction of the movement.
Middle grade—12 ways, including locomotion on different body parts.

Last grade—14 ways, including moving backward and in different body shapes.

☐ Avoiding collisions with others by using the general space well.

☐ Continuing to be well distributed over the floor space.

When children demonstrate these factors, go on to Problem 39.

The terms "beginning grade," "middle grade," and "last grade," are used, since the materials are adaptable to any three successive grades.

Skill Objectives

Notice, too, that the skill objectives do not designate specific skills. For example, "to control consciously the pathway of the body on the floor and in the air while moving in a wide variety of ways" is an objective which can be fulfilled through use of all the named locomotor skills on the feet (running, walking, jumping, hopping, leaping, galloping, sliding, skipping), or all of the named locomotor skills on different body parts (e.g., rolling, crawling, walking on the hands). Some, if not all of these specific named skills will be performed by each child as he searches for new ways to make pathways, and chances are that he will throw in a few completely unorthodox movements of his own because he is exploring and because they "feel good." Moreover, the very young child with advanced skills such as cartwheels may take great delight in exploring pathways he can take while cartwheeling. His classmate, having never been taught to cartwheel and never before having wanted to try a cartwheel, may nevertheless become intrigued by the thought of getting his feet up high while exploring pathways. The self-teaching power of a youngster who is motivated should never be underestimated or discouraged. His concept of what he is ready to try is so much more valid than any textbook chart of physical developmental characteristics that safety precautions by teachers should be very rare. By stressing thinking skills, by requiring thoughtful control of the body's movements, by allowing each child to move in his own ways at his own ability level, the teacher can help a child become success-oriented in movement. This is another long-range aim of basic movement. When specific skills are taught in other units of the total physical education program, the child with experience in basic movement should approach them without fear, with an appreciative and honest realization of his own capabilities, and with a learned readiness to tackle new movement tasks.

Attitude Objectives

The attitude objectives are extremely important, and an awareness of them must permeate the atmosphere of every lesson. The modification of attitudes and feelings is one of the most difficult tasks in education. "Because feelings are learned by imitation, the extension of feelings and sensitivities requires a living laboratory." [Taba, 73] Direct teaching to change sensitivities and feelings seldom succeeds. An individual must do his own examining and changing. Each class period should thus become a living laboratory experience in which each child has the opportunity to be freely, happily, deeply, and acceptantly *himself*. The teacher's attitude in this laboratory is best characterized by a warm caring for each child—a nonpossessive caring in which a child's expressions of his "bad," fearful, or negative feelings are accepted as well as his expressions of "good," positive, social feelings. A climate of unconditional positive regard allows more learning to occur than an atmosphere of "I accept and care for you only if you do exactly as I say." Read the attitude objectives again in this light. How does a teacher behave when he wants his children to develop sensitivities and integrated feelings about themselves and their relationships with others? Carl Rogers [63] has described the *conditions* which either a therapist or a teacher should provide for significant learning to take place. These conditions are:

1   The teacher is a unified, or integrated, or *congruent* person . . . in his relationship with students he is exactly what he is—not a facade, or a role, or a pretense . . . He not only means exactly what he says, but also his deepest feelings match what he is expressing.

2   The teacher creates a safe climate of *unconditional positive regard* for each child, giving the child permission to have his own feelings and experiences and to find his own meanings in them.

3   The teacher is experiencing an accurate *empathetic* understanding of the child's world as seen from the inside, sensing it as if it were the teachers' own, yet never losing the "as if" quality.

4   The child is aware of the teacher's congruence, positive regard, and empathy . . . these conditions must, to some degree, be communicated to the child.

The significant learnings that can take place in a school atmosphere created by the above conditions parallel the changes which Rogers lists as results of client-centered therapy:

The person comes to see himself differently.
He accepts himself and his feelings more fully.
He becomes more self-confident and self-directing.
He becomes more the person he would like to be.
He becomes more flexible, less rigid, in his perceptions.
He adopts more realistic goals for himself.
He behaves in a more mature fashion.
He changes his maladjustive behavior.
He becomes more acceptant of others.
He becomes more open to the evidence, both to what is going on outside of himself, and to what is going on inside of himself.
He changes in his basic personality characteristics, in constructive ways.

Evidence derived from empirical research supports the above statements. That such learnings are significant can hardly be questioned. The teacher of basic movement is in an excellent position to free the minds of children, to nurture their creativity and independence and self-confidence. The freedom from having to find the one and only "right" answer to a movement problem provides, by itself, a rich opportunity for teachers to begin building an atmosphere in which modifications of attitudes and feelings may occur.

PROCESS: BECOMING PHYSICALLY EDUCATED

Chapter 3

Basic movement education, as defined in Chapter 2, is the *foundational structure and process portion of physical education* which is characterized by the experiential study of . . . movement. Thus far, only *foundational structure* has been discussed. In this chapter, the *foundational processes* of becoming physically educated will be explored. Teaching and learning *about* physical education is not the focus of the chapter; becoming physically educated is. George Angell [3] has stated the focus well by saying that physical education ". . . is not a fact or a set of facts. It is a response—a series of responses—that initiates motion, that frees men from inertia, that expresses life in unlimited variations. Physical education is self education, the discovery of self through bodily movement, the discovery of one's unlimited capacity to express love, beauty, freedom, discipline, meaning—anything that seems beyond verbal explication." Interestingly, Angell points to basic movement education as a real step in the direction of implementing his process-oriented definition of physical education.

Muska Mosston in his delineation of teaching styles places strong emphasis on process: "The education of the free, independent person must be a freeing process, a process so deliberately and elegantly developed that the students' dependency on the teacher gradually diminishes until the free student emerges." [52] To set the stage for a discussion of the freeing process of becoming physically educated, it would be well to consider Mosston's description [52] of the end product of such a process—the free man.

What kind of person is the student who knows how to select and produce the desirable physical responses? What kind of person is the student who approaches the maximum limit of the emotional development channel? Is he not a person with a relatively clear self concept, who can re-establish his emotional stability in the face of new circumstances of decision making? And what kind of person is the one who knows how to perform in new social interaction? Who is the person who knows how to observe, gather information, judge, and draw conclusions, to think and evolve new ideas?

Who is the person manifesting these admirable qualities? He is a free man. It is the free man whose unique individuality is sought and developed. It is the free man whom a free society wishes to produce through its education—education for a society of independent people. Independence implies the ability to make choices among convictions; it connotes the strength to act and pursue the chosen convictions. It requires the courage to be different and to accept the different. Independence requires the ability to interact with others so that they, too, remain independent. Independence means that one can learn to be free—free of physical limitations, oppressive social forces, emotional prisons, and intellectual dogmatism.

Through what processes does one become free? Through what methodologies does one stimulate children to learn? Through what processes does learning occur? Does motor learning differ in process from cognitive, perceptual, or verbal learning? How dependent on thinking skills is motor learning? Although full discussion of these intriguing questions is beyond the scope of this book, some of the assumptions underlying the development of the basic movement education units will be presented.

In Search of Process

Conceptions of the learning process vary—they have in the past, they will in the future. No single set of psychological theories can provide the answers to learning questions in general nor to motor learning, cognitive learning, or self realization issues specifically. In the past, the major theories (conditioning, connectionism, Gestalt, field, psychoanalytic, functionalism) associated with the great names (James and Hall, Guthrie and Hull, Thorndike, Watson, Dewey, Freud, Judd) tended to be bandwagon issues. Teachers felt obliged to choose between Hall's recapitulation theory or Thorndike's transfer of learning, between concern for cognitive process or concern for the individual. Often the rigidity of living and teaching according to one set of psychological principles became so restrictive that the principles to which the diligent teacher had adhered were thrown out entirely when they could not be applied successfully in every case. Today, educators are wisely searching out the complementary characteristics of the major theories and are developing methodologies that use the different psychologies collaboratively.

Points of agreement in learning theories

Hilgard [35] has attempted to identify points of agreement among most learning theories. The following list includes both Hilgard's principles of learning* upon which most learning theorists agree and examples from the basic movement units of the application of these principles.

Learning Theory Commonalities

1   Individuals need practice in setting realistic goals for themselves, goals neither so low as to elicit little effort nor as high as to foreordain to failure. Realistic goal-setting leads to more satisfactory improvement than unrealistic goal-setting.

2   Active participation by a learner is preferable to passive reception when learning, for example from a lecture or a motion picture.

3   Meaningful materials and meaningful tasks are learned more readily than nonsense materials and more readily than tasks not understood by the learner.

4   There is no substitute for repetitive practice in the overlearning of skills (for instance, the performance of a concert pianist).

Examples from the Units

1   Most major problems are stated "How many ways can you . . .?" Within the subproblems (given while children are working on the major problem) are subtle reminders that each child is expected, first, to explore many ways to solve the problem and, second, to discover one or two ways that are the best for him. In this way, he sets his own goal . . . he will not fail. If the teacher observes signs of a child's setting goals too low for his abilities, he does not step in and set higher goals for the child. Instead he talks with the child attempting to have him explain why he has set that particular goal. Often the child's reasoning will be sound. If he simply cannot think of a better solution, subproblems can be given as clues to more skilled or more original solutions.

2   Although one generally thinks of a physical education period as an active participation period, numerous studies have shown that through lack of equipment (necessitating much waiting for turns) and through long explanation-demonstration periods (of either new skills or of new games or dances), less than one half of a physical education period is used by an individual in active participation. In field testing the basic movement units, when children were standing still only when introductions and major problems were given, the average passive reception time in a 20-minute lesson was approximately three minutes.

3   The cognitive structure of movement, introduced in bite-size increments and returned to in different settings, gives meaning to the tasks in the units. Should a student not understand a problem, he has the time and the opportunity to go to the teacher immediately for clarification. The teacher, as manager of the learning situation, must be a keen observer, perceptive of felt difficulties in children. Since the teacher is not on center stage explaining and demonstrating and actively directing everything, he has the time to give individual problems his full attention.

4   The training of pre-Olympic performers is not the goal of basic movement education, yet there are skills of three kinds to be learned: (1) movement skills, (2) thinking skills, and (3) social skills. Repetitive practice in all three types of skills is built into the units. Examples of movement skills to be overlearned are balancing, changing direction quickly, accelerating, decelerating, transferring weight, curling and stretching, twisting and turning, manipulating objects, etc. Examples of thinking skills to be overlearned are grouping and categorizing specific information into classes, applying known data or principles to produce new movements, and evaluating their own and others' movement sequences.

---

*   From *Theories of Learning*, by Ernest Hilgard. Copyright © 1956 by Meredith Corporation. Reprinted by permission of Appleton-Century-Crofts, as paraphrased.

Learning Theory Commonalities

Examples from the Units

Examples of social skills to be learned include developing ideas through interaction with others in twos, fours, or the total group, becoming more appreciative of others' creative efforts in movement whether it is like or unlike their own, creating and organizing one's own systems of getting out and putting away equipment and of choosing partners or small groups quickly and in a socially appropriate way. Repetitive, spiral practice is required if such skills are to be overlearned.

5   Information about the nature of a good performance, knowledge of his own mistakes, and knowledge of successful results, aid learning. Tolerance for failure is best taught through providing a backlog of success that compensates for experienced failure.

5   Since no single model of a good performance exists in basic movement education, one must take care not to expect a preconceived response to problems (see pages 22–23). Mistakes are nearly always caused by a child's misunderstanding the problem, and the teacher should rephrase the problem for the individual child. Knowledge of successful results is attained through frequent demonstrations by several children of several different solutions. Brief analyses of the solutions by the class adds to the understanding of why a particular solution is a successful one—not "the right one", however. Usually another work session should follow demonstration-evaluations so that the children may experiment further after having received new ideas. Lavish but honest praise from a teacher while children are at work is a strong stimulant for further creative effort. "Well tried" to those on the low ability levels is an honest compliment.

6   Transfer to new tasks will be better if, in learning, the learner can discover relationships for himself, and if he has experience during learning of applying the principles within a variety of tasks.

6   Nearly all the subproblems (problems to be stated while children are moving) are clues for discovering relationships. These subproblems should not be given too soon after statement of a major problem—if students can discover them without the clues, they are demonstrating their increasing thinking skills. Applying the principles to a variety of tasks is the heart of the basic movement education program—cognitive reconstruction demonstrated in movement. The skeletal framework is given by the teacher in introductions. The student, while solving major problems, is fleshing out the skeleton by applying principles to a variety of tasks.

7   Spaced or distributed recalls are advantageous in fixing material that is to be long retained.

7   As stated in Chapter 2, all new facts are returned to at least eight times in each year of the program. The main ideas and concepts are returned to in spiral fashion over the three-year span.

8   A motivated learner acquires what he learns more readily than one who is not motivated. Learning under intrinsic motivation is preferable to learning under extrinsic motivation.*

8   Intrinsic motives to be cherished include the joy of movement, the joy of creation, the joy of discovery, the joy of independence, the joy of being a successful performer (of testing one's cognitive solutions in physical responses and finding they work well), the joy of reaching for more difficult solutions, the joy of discovering new problems as well as new solutions. Beside the powerful chain reaction of intrinsic motivation-achievement-appreciation of self worth-motivation, etc., the extrinsic motive of pleasing the teacher pales in significance. While the competitive drive and the need for recognition exist, more learning will accrue if the competition is with oneself, and if the recognition is of knowing that one is about to go on to another level in the ladder of successful experiences.

---

*   The above 8 points of agreement among learning theorists are a compilation of 10 of the 14 commonalities identified by Hilgard which are particularly applicable to physical education.

Every major psychological position has left a residue of useful ideas and procedure. The above commonalities only scratch the surface. Until a comprehensive science of man is developed, teachers would do well to look to all psychologies for gleaning their own personal guidelines in more depth.

Recently, an upsurge of interest has occurred among educators in the "discovery–inquiry–problem-solving–process approach" to learning. This syndrome of slogans, each of which has its own subtleties and complexities of thought, is in danger of either being rejected as nothing more than educational jargon or of becoming a popular new bandwagon, accepted on face value without giving thought to the underlying processes.

Joseph Schwab [68] warns of the danger of jumping aboard a new sloganized position without understanding it: ". . . a slogan is . . . a complex and highly qualified idea which has been stripped of its complexities and bereft of its qualifications. A slogan is like the victim of a mad scientist in a horror movie: brains removed and replaced by a dime store computer."

Since problem solving is the primary methodology selected for the units in basic movement, the process of problem solving and its corollary, creative thinking, need to be more fully examined.

Discovery as process: problem solving as technique

A focus on *discovery through problem solving* is not new in education. It has enjoyed cyclical fame and attention over the centuries. A recent example can be found in the 1942 Yearbook of the National Society for the Study of Education where Brownell [12] deplored the *neglect* of problem solving. Today, 28 years later, interest in problem solving is greater than ever before.

To provide a rationale for using problem solving as the primary methodology for basic movement education, this section will include: a) definitions, b) Bruner's hypotheses about the act of discovery, and c) Libby's classification of problem types. Later in this chapter, the criteria for problems stated in the units will be presented, followed by an analysis of the problems.

Definitions

Discovery is, in its essence, a matter of rearranging or transforming evidence in such a way that one is enabled to go beyond the evidence so reassembled to additional new insights. [Bruner, 3]

Inquiry is a disciplined movement from a starting point and by a pathway to an appropriate end. [Schwab, 68]

Problem solving is original thinking, an individual's technique of productive thinking, his technique of inquiry, which is characterized by (1) a focus on an incomplete situation, (2) the freedom to inquire, and (3) the drive to put together something new to him, on his own, to make the incomplete situation into a complete one.

The process approach to learning implies placing as much value on developing the ability to think and to act autonomously and productively as on content; as much value on self-realization as on the acquisition of knowledge.

Bruner's Hypotheses about the Act of Discovery

Jerome Bruner [13] has formulated four hypotheses on the act of discovery. These hypotheses* served as the underlying philosophy in developing the basic movement units.

1   I would urge now in the spirit of an hypothesis that emphasis upon discovery in learning has precisely the effect upon the learner of teaching him to be a constructionist, to organize what he is encountering in a manner

---

*   Reproduced by permission.

not only designed to discover regularity and relatedness, but also to avoid the kind of information drift that fails to keep account of the uses to which information might have to be put. It is, if you will, a necessary condition for learning the variety of techniques of problem solving, of transforming information for better use, indeed for learning how to go about the very task of learning. Practice in discovering for oneself teaches one to acquire information in a way that makes that information more readily viable in problem solving. So goes the hypothesis. It is still in need of testing. But it is an hypothesis of such important human implications that we cannot afford not to test it—and testing will have to be in the schools.

2   The hypothesis that I would propose here is that to the degree that one is able to approach learning as a task of discovering something rather than "learning about" it, to that degree will there be a tendency for the child to carry out his learning activities with the autonomy of self-reward or, more properly, by reward that is discovery itself.

3   It is my hunch that it is only through the exercise of problem solving and the effort of discovery that one learns the working heuristic of discovery, and the more one has practice, the more likely is one to generalize what one has learned into a style of problem solving or inquiry that serves for any kind of task one may encounter—or almost any kind of task.

4   Let me suggest that in general, material that is organized in terms of a person's own interests and cognitive structure is material that has the best chance of being accessible in memory.

Libby's Classification of Problem Types

Clearly, there are many different styles or techniques of problem solving. In addition, many different types of problems exist to be solved. Libby's [44] identification of problem types, which follows,* was a useful tool in establishing criteria for the movement problems in the basic movement curriculum.

1   The problem is given (is known) and there is a standard method for solving it, known to the problem-solver (student, experimental subject) and to others (teacher-experimenter) and guaranteeing a solution in a finite number of steps.

2   The problem is given (is known) but no standard method for solving it is known to the problem-solver, although known to the others.

3   The problem is given (is known) but no standard method for solving it is known to the problem-solver or to the others.

4   The problem itself exists but remains to be identified or discovered (become known) by the problem-solver, although known to the others.

5   The problem itself exists but remains to be identified or discovered (become known) by the problem-solver and by the others.

6   The problem itself exists but remains to be identified or discovered (as in 4 and 5) and there is a standard for solving it, once the problem is discovered, known to the problem-solver and to others (as in 1).

7   The problem itself exists but remains to be identified or discovered, and no standard method for solving it is known to the problem-solver, although known to the others (as in 2).

8   The problem itself exists but remains to be identified or discovered, and no standard method for solving it is known to the problem-solver or to others (as in 3).

---

*   Reproduced by permission.

Problem-solving behavior involves the evocation of relatively uncommon responses. [Maltzman, 47] Thus Type 1 problems, which are most often used in physical education as well as in other subjects, are really pseudo-problems. They positively disallow the uncommon response. The kindergartener is given a rhythmic and motor pattern analysis of the skip, then is given the "problem" of skipping exactly the right way. His teacher knows the standard method; the child knows the standard method. The teacher may subscribe to the problem solving approach but in reality disallows it.

In a Type 2 or Type 6 problem, again by the teacher's knowing the standard method for solving it, the child is frequently given so many cues to discover the "right" way that he never goes beyond the information given. This may result in a guided discovery approach to learning, not in true problem solving.

Types 3, 4, 5, 7, and 8 call for original thinking. No standard methods for solving the problems are known; creative thinking is required; unique solutions are allowed. Whenever problem solving is referred to in this book, only Types 3, 4, 5, 7, or 8 are regarded as real problems to be attacked.

With these definitions, hypotheses, and problem types in mind, let us now turn to the criteria for problems in the units—to the process criteria.

Criteria for designing problems (learning activities)

Part II of this book, the basic movement education curriculum, is composed primarily of *objectives* and of *movement problems* for children to solve. The problems comprise the technique by which the objectives may be attained. The following list of major criteria for movement problems (the learning activities) is followed by a discussion of each of them.

1   Major problems (the numbered problems in the units) must be Type 3 problems: presented problems with no standard method for solving them known to the problem-solver or to others.

2   Subproblems, although printed, must be *examples* of Type 8 problems: the problems exist but remain to be identified or discovered, and no standard methods for solving them are known to the problem-solver or to others.*

3   Problems must require productive thinking, and both imagining and reasoning must be encouraged as processes for solving problems.

4   For the purpose of nuturing creativity, problems must be stated:

a) so that a multiplicity of solutions is available in a wide scope of ability levels so that all children may succeed, and

b) so that the growth resulting from success in solving problems becomes an intrinsic motivation for children to attain higher levels of creativity.

5   All learning activities (problems and subproblems) must be chosen for their power to meet the objectives in all three areas—knowledge, skills, and attitudes.

A brief discussion of each of the five criteria used for developing the problems in the curriculum follows, and is included to assist and encourage teachers to formulate their own problems and to devise their own curricula, based on the needs of their students. Special emphasis is placed on Criterion 4—the nurture of creativity.

Criterion 1: Major Problems—Presented Problems with No Standard Methods for Solving Them

The 600 major problems which appear in bold type in the curriculum (200 for each of the three grade levels) must be seen by both teacher and

---

*   The printed subproblems are to be presented by teachers to individuals or to a whole class only after a period of activity in which the subproblems might be independently discovered. Children will provide many more subproblems than have been given as examples.

students as having no standard method for solving them and no single solution as the one-and-only "right" solution. Even the comparatively "better" and "best" solutions exist only for individuals. Teachers, of course, can solve the problems cognitively and physically. The important point to remember is that neither child nor teacher views the teacher's methods or solutions as ones to be mimicked. To avoid this mimicking, teachers should hold their own demonstrations to a minimum. There are times when teacher demonstrations are appropriate, as will be pointed out on page 37, but demonstrations for the purpose of imposing a standard method of solution is a negation of real problem solving and can discourage innovation and creativeness on the part of children. The major problems, sans demonstrations, are specifically designed to encourage a child to be inventive, to go beyond the given, to think creatively—regardless of how modest or how unoriginal to others the child's own creation may seem. Through careful feeding of small doses of the structure of movement, teachers provide children with the "stuff" with which to create. Beyond that, the child must not be required to use it in a preordained way.

Usually all class activity should come to a halt, and the brief, concise statement of the problem should be heard and comprehended by all children. After setting the children to work, a teacher must learn to do absolutely nothing for the next few moments. It is too early to praise . . . it is too early to offer variable cues . . . it is too early to condemn. Those first few moments of grappling with a new problem are exclusively the child's. When he is ready to turn to the teacher as a resource person, he may. The teacher is not only the most important source of data available to his students, he is also a source of emotional stability and security as well. When the teacher observes a child's creative work coming to a halt, he should be ready with subproblems gleaned from other children or from the units—problems that exist but which may never need to be stated.

Criterion 2: Subproblems—Examples of Problems that Exist with No Standard Methods for Solving Them

The several thousand subproblems which appear in regular type in the curriculum are not necessarily problems to be presented by the teacher. They are examples of problems which exist but which remain to be identified or discovered by the students. Subproblems, too, have no standard methods for solving. The inventive child will discover most of the printed subproblems and many, many more. This will be evidenced by his solutions or by his experimentation. At what point does the teacher present these printed subproblems to the class? Perhaps never—if a rich variety of responses to the major problem is forthcoming. Perhaps often—to an individual child who has difficulty in conceiving the cognitive structure of movement. Perhaps often—to the whole class if the teacher perceives an opportunity to reinforce a structural theme in a new situation. The observant teacher will also recognize the subproblem that needs to be presented as a major problem, and will stop the class and present it as a major learning activity.

Usually, subproblems are presented in a conversational tone, *while* children are moving and are actively engaged in major problem solving. If the subproblem is addressed to the entire group, the tone of voice should make it clear that the given subproblem is a suggestion, one that *some of the students* may want to experiment with. Others who have already discovered the subproblem may wish to ignore it, and others who are deeply involved in a solution of their own may want to hear it but postpone working on it until a later time.

If, as is more usual, the subproblem is presented to an individual, then as Polya [58] states, "The teacher should put himself in the student's place, he should see the student's case, he should try to understand what is going on in the student's mind, and ask a question or indicate a step that could have occurred to the student himself." The teacher asks it discreetly, naturally. He fosters the independence of the child's work, not the illusion of independence.

Criterion 3: Productive Thinking—Reasoning and Imagining

To produce an acceptable movement solution to a problem, what must a child do? He must first think productively, and then express his thoughts in movement. He must "realize" the problem by seeing that the inner structure of the situation is incomplete. He must doubt his current secure cognitive structure of movement and his physical ability to produce movements acceptable to himself. The doubt, the structural strain, the tension in the thinker-mover, is the prime motivational force for action. Getzels [27] points out that ". . . structural strains produce tensions in the thinker, and vectors are set up determining the steps to be taken to transpose the incomplete situation into one that is structually complete." Cognitive dissonance, a disjunction, a juxtaposition of two or more "truths" that don't jibe, an itch to be scratched—by whatever name it is called, the doubt is a necessity to real problem solving. The doubt prods the child to find a multiplicity of movement responses instead of just one. Can he find a better way *for him* to solve it?, a way that makes him feel better?, a way that combines many things he has learned and is uniquely his?, a way that is efficient?, or especially communicative? "Ugly" trial and error learning is not the intent in asking for a multiplicity of movement responses in many of the stated problems. Instead, structure strengthening through manipulation of many movement variables is the intent. Productive thinking need not and, if continued, will not lead to a single solution.

The steps taken to transpose an incomplete situation into one that is complete vary widely from individual to individual. At the two ends of a continuum of processes of problem solving are, at one extreme, the serious, step-by-step, scientific, logical acts of reasoning, and at the other extreme, the nonlogical "playfulness" in thinking—the as yet unexplained flights of fancy, flashes of intuition, divergent thinking processes that so often characterize the truly creative thinkers. This paradox is well stated by Getzels [27]:

Despite the self-evident need for conscious effort and rationality in problem-solving, the development of reality-orientation and logic with age, and the required training in reflective forms of reasoning in school, mature creative thinking and innovative problem-solving entail, at least in some degree, a regression to playfulness, fantasy, and the arationality of primary process and childlike modes of thought.

Both reasoning and imagining must be allowed, indeed must be fostered by the teacher if productive thinking is a goal.

Criterion 4: Creativity—Nature and Nurture

Mature creative thinking and innovative problem solving are long-term goals in a basic movement education program. The problems man faces today have been created primarily by man's own creativeness, and much more creativeness will be required if present problems are to be transcended by solutions. Mooney and Razek [50] place high priority on "the need to know more about man's creativeness and to develop his creativeness in ever-increasing proportions of the population."

"What is creativity?" is, indeed, a question being investigated by scholars from many fields. In attempting to answer it, the characteristics and the products of creative people (small children to adults) are being tentatively identified and the role of creativity in conceptual cognitive theories is being developed.

Among the characteristics of creative people identified by McGuire, Getzels and Jackson, Burkhart, Maslow, Torrance, Guilford and others are:

high degree of intellectual capacity,
outgoing independence,
appreciation of cognitive matters, independence, autonomy,
self discipline,
ethical consistency,
constructive nonconformity,
unusual sensitivity to problems,
unusual abilities to synthesize and to make intuitive jumps,
goal orientation,
willingness to take calculated risks,
playful, humorous discposition,
high level of curiosity about many things,
divergent thinking,
rich fantasy life,
ability to take off from a stimulus rather than to latch on to it.

MacKinnon [46] summarized the characteristics of a creative individual by "his high level of effective intelligence, his openness to experience, his freedom from crippling restraints and impoverishing inhibitions, his esthetic sensitivity, his cognitive flexibility, his independence in thought and action, his high level of creative energy, his unquestioning commitments to creative endeavor, and his unceasing striving for solutions to the ever more difficult problems that he constantly sets for himself."

Although the need for creative people in today's society exists without question, society in general and schools in particular foster few if any of the characteristics just outlined. Torrance [77] suggests that it is easy to spot the creative child: just look for the kid with the wild ideas, with the abundance of questions (many of which may seem to be irrelevant), who pays attention only when he wants to, and whose own humor delights him. Getzels and Jackson's [28] conclusion that parents and teachers do not value the creative child as highly as the high IQ child is not surprising, for living with him is not easy.

In addition to his relatively poor image regardless of his rather high achievement, emotional stability, and intelligence levels, the creative child has a series of cultural blocks to clear if his special giftedness is not to be squelched, again by society in general and by schools in particular. Among these are the uniquely middle class American cultural values of success (you must never fail in this land of plenty, don't take risks, do it the company way) and of peer orientation (be more concerned about classmates' evaluations than about any authority figure's evaluations). Torrance [77] lists other inhibiting cultural influences such as sanctions against questioning and exploring, misplaced sex role interpretation (boys shouldn't be too sensitive), divergency equated with abnormality (the screwball, the mad genius), the work-play dichotomy, emphasis on appearing to be rather than actually being, and overemphasis on a limited number of talents rather than on a diversity of talents.

How can teachers help soften the tyranny of the cultural forces bearing down on the creative child, or on any child for that matter? The characteristics of the creative person listed previously surely are more descriptive of every kindergartener than they are of every adult. What can teachers do to preserve and nurture creativity, the one type of giftedness that is found to a degree in all students, but that is particularly susceptible to society's diseases in general and to restrictive classroom environments in particular.

Torrance believes that creativity cannot be left to chance, that the neglect and abuse of creative talent must be stopped. This neglect and abuse takes the form of over-success orientation which has as a corollary no risk taking, no mistakes allowed. His advice to compensate for this in schools is to *find more ways in which children can succeed . . . first, by posing problems with a multitude of correct responses and second, by using the resulting growth to motivate them to higher levels of creative functioning.*

What teaching techniques can be used for nurturing creative talents in all children? The following questions are ones all teachers should ask themselves regularly.

Do I recognize and acknowledge potentialities? Am I constantly looking for and fostering these signs of creativity?

> Intense absorption in listening, absorbing, doing.
> Intense animation and physical involvement.
> Challenging ideas of authorities.
> Checking many sources of information.
> Taking a close look at things.
> Eagerly telling others about one's discoveries.
> Continuing a creative activity after the scheduled time for quitting.
> Showing relationships among apparently unrelated ideas.
> Following through on ideas set in motion.
> Manifesting curiosity, wanting to know, digging deeper.
> Guessing or predicting outcomes and then testing them.
> Honestly and intently searching for the truth.
> Resisting distractions.
> Losing awareness of time.
> Penetrating observations and questions.
> Seeking alternatives and exploring new possibilities.

Am I respectful of questions and ideas?

Do I ask provocative questions (not only for reproduction of information given)?

Do I recognize and value originality (or do I discredit an unfamiliar idea)?

Do I try to develop elaboration ability in my students? Too often creative ideas are dropped simply for lack of opportunity or desire to elaborate them.

Do I give my students the opportunity for unevaluated practice and experimentation?*

Criterion 5: Multiple Objectives—Problems for Knowledge, Skill, and Attitude Development

Hilda Taba [74] has suggested that it is useful to think of a curriculum as a *system of teaching somebody something by some process.* Thus far, the "somebody" has been defined as children in any three consecutive grades in the elementary school. The "something" has been defined as the foundational structure of movement. The "some process" from the child's point of view has been described in this chapter as individual problem solving.

The "system" of teaching consists of the following planning steps:

1   determining the objectives to be attained.
2   selecting and organizing the content.
3   *devising and organizing the learning experiences to be provided.*
4   formulating and organizing teaching strategies.

The criterion proposed here is that "all learning activities (problems and subproblems) must be chosen to fulfill the objectives in all three areas— knowledge, skills, and attitudes." It is the guideline for step 3 above.

While selecting and organizing learning experiences (problems and subproblems), one should constantly review the three areas of objectives—

---

*   These six questions are a restatement of the topics of six out of eleven workshops Torrance [77] has developed for the improvement of teachers' skills in nurturing creativity.

knowledge, skills, and attitudes. All three areas are of equal value. Learning experiences (problems) should be chosen for their power to meet the objectives in all three areas. Frequently, learning experiences are devised to implement only one of the three areas of objectives. In physical education, physical skill development has long been the overpowering area of objectives. In other subject areas, specific, factual knowledge has been the strong emphasis with almost no learning experiences designed for skill and attitude development.

The structure of human movement outlined in Chapter 2 provides the major source material for devising problems that will extend knowledge. It is also the major source material for devising problems that will improve motor skills. The process of discovery outlined in this chapter is the source material for devising learning activities that foster development in thinking skills. However, neither structure nor process can help in devising learning activities that foster social skills and attitudes. The means for reaching these two important categories of objectives lie entirely outside the area of knowledge and problem solving.

Opportunity for social skill and attitude development, as yet unaccounted for in the designing of problems, must be carefully interwoven throughout the program. Although individuality is most highly valued, the need for successful interaction with others in today's rapidly shrinking world cannot be overlooked. Again, bite-sized increments of group work should be planned. It is a long jump from the earliest problem in which one child learns to respect another child's self space to the sophisticated problem calling for a group effort in creating and evaluating a complex movement sequence. The intervening steps must be carefully planned and interspersed regularly.

A discrete series of problems for attitude development does not exist; every problem and especially every subproblem must be communicated to children in a manner conducive to the nurture of the stated attitude objectives. At the end of Chapter 2, the importance of establishing a classroom atmosphere of unconditional positive regard was discussed. The attainment of such an atmosphere is a condition for the teacher's stating of all problems.

Thus problems must be designed and threaded throughout the program to fulfill all three kinds of objectives: knowledge, skills (thinking, social, and physical), and attitudes.

Now that objectives have been stated, content selected and organized, and learning experiences devised and organized, step 4 of Taba's system (formulating and organizing teaching strategies) remains to be accomplished. In the following chapter, teaching strategies based on actual field testing of the basic movement education units in Part II will be explored.

Any curriculum guide, to be sound and usable, must be based on actual in-school practice. In-school testing of the teaching units in Part II was especially needed because, to the best of the writer's knowledge, no other comprehensive written units exist that use a structure and process approach to physical education. Thus no cross checking could be done. In this chapter, the reactions of test teachers will be reported. The wide variety of strategies for adding basic movement education to existing physical education programs which emerged from the field test should provide practical guidelines for teachers who are ready to add a new dimension to their programs.

Background of Field Testing

Fifteen teachers in public elementary schools in Ohio and New York volunteered to field test the basic movement education units at different grade levels. Seven were classroom teachers with no previous experience in basic movement education; five were elementary school physical education specialists with little or no previous experience in basic movement education; the remaining three specialists had had years of experience in teaching movement education. Inner city schools, middle-class schools, and wealthy suburban schools were included as a means of trying out the units in a variety of school environments. The amount of time scheduled for physical education varied widely—some schools had daily 20-minute periods and, at the other extreme, two schools provided for only one 30-minute physical education period per week.

Instructions for using the units

The test teachers used the units however they wished, and fifteen different patterns of usage emerged. Teachers using the units for the first time were urged to follow this minimum procedure in preparing each lesson:

1 Study the Content Structure (for teachers).
2 Determine whether Objectives (for children) are appropriate for your class.
3 Read Tips for Teachers:

   a) collect or improvise equipment needed for the lesson, storing it in a place accessible to children,

   b) determine when to introduce vocabulary to children in the classroom.
4 Select movement problems to be stated during the lesson.

Three examples follow that illustrate (1) how a beginning grade level teacher used a problem she had selected from the left-hand column, (2) how a middle grade level teacher used both left-hand and middle columns, and (3) how a last grade level teacher used all three columns.

How a Beginning Grade Level Teacher Uses a Problem

Teachers of beginning grade levels (K, 1, 2, 3, or 4) should usually use only the problems in the left-hand column. An example follows.

MAJOR PROBLEM 72

Beginning Grade

"On the signal, find a self space and try to keep your hands on the floor in one spot while you move your feet around in different ways."

". . . . Can you find ways to take some of your weight on your hands while your feet are moving around? . . . are your hands part of your base of support? . . . how many places can you take your feet? . . . into different levels? . . . have you tried different ways of jumping or hopping your feet around as well as running them around your hands? . . . how many different ways can your feet meet and part? . . . have you tried to have your stomach up toward the ceiling part of the time? . . . can you keep moving s-m-o-o-t-h-l-y all the time? . . . how strong can you make your arms so that gravity won't pull you down? . . . how many ways can you move if your base of support is very big? . . . hands far apart, and at least one foot far from your hands? . . . how many ways can you move if your base of support is very small? . . . hands close together, and at least one foot close to your hands? . . . find a way to move in which you are very stable, very much on balance."

Note: The major problem, in bold-face type, is to be stated by the teacher while the children are still.

Note: The subproblems, in light type, are to be stated by the teacher, while children are working on the major problem, only if needed to "bump" individuals or the group into finding more structural relationships within the major problem.

How a Middle Grade Level Teacher Uses a Problem

Teachers of the middle grade levels (1, 2, 3, 4, or 5) should usually give the entire beginning level problem again (as indicated by the "repeat" instructions) and then add to it the problems in the middle column.

MAJOR PROBLEM 72

Beginning Grade	Middle Grade

"On the signal, find a self space and try to keep your hands on the floor in one spot while you move your feet around in different ways."

(Then use the subproblems as they are needed.)

". . . Can you find ways to take some of your weight on your hands while your feet are moving around? . . . are your hands part of your base of support? . . . how many places can you take your feet? . . . into different levels? . . . have you tried different ways of jumping or hopping your feet around as well as running them around your hands? . . . how many different ways can your feet meet and part? . . . have you tried to have your stomach up toward the ceiling part of the time? . . . can you keep moving s-m-o-o-t-h-l-y all the time? . . . how strong can you make your arms so that gravity won't pull you down? . . . how many ways can you move if your base of support is very big? . . . hands far apart, and at least one foot far from your hands? . . . how many ways can you move if your base of support is very small? . . . hands close together, and at least one foot close to your hands? . . . find a way to move in which you are very stable, very much on-balance."

▶ Repeat all material from Beginning Grade, and then add this major problem:

"Now, keep both hands on the floor and see how many ways you can get one or two feet higher than your head."

(Then use the subproblems as they are needed.)

". . . When both feet are off the ground, are you balanced on your hands for just a second? (not unless the body weight is over the hands) . . . explore different ways of getting your hips up high while your hands remain on the floor, taking some or all of your weight . . . try changing the width of your hand placement on the floor again . . . find a way in which you feel most stable, most on-balance . . . have you found several ways to balance in which you can hold very still with at least one foot at a high level? . . . have you tried moving from one balance to another very s-m-o-o-t-h-l-y?"

(Expect and allow great variation in the students' abilities to maintain balance even momentarily on the hands. If children are not pushed to go beyond their abilities, they will explore safely and without fear.)

Note: The major problem, in bold-face type, is to be stated by the teacher while the children are still.

Note: The subproblems, in light type, are to be stated by the teacher, while children are working on the major problem, only if needed to "bump" individuals or the group into finding more structural relationships within the major problem.

Note: All words in parentheses are suggestions to teachers, not words to be spoken by teachers.

How a Last Grade Level Teacher Uses a Problem

Teachers of the last grade levels (2, 3, 4, 5, or 6) should usually give the beginning and middle level problems again (as indicated by the "repeat" instructions) and then add the problem in the right-hand column.

MAJOR PROBLEM 72

Beginning Grade	Middle Grade	Last Grade

"On the signal, find a self space and try keeping your hands on the floor while you see how many ways you can move your feet around them."

(Then use the subproblems as they are needed.)

".... Can you find ways to take some of your weight on your hands while your feet are moving around? ... are your hands part of your base of support? ... how many places can you take your feet? ... into different levels? ... have you tried different ways of jumping or hopping your feet around as well as running them around your hands? ... how many different ways can your feet meet and part? ... have you tried to have your stomach up toward the ceiling part of the time? ... can you keep moving s-m-o-o-t-h-l-y all the time? ... how strong can you make your arms so that gravity won't pull you down? ... how many ways can you move if your base of support is very small? ... hands close together, and at least one foot close to your hands? ... find a way to move in which you are very stable, very much on-balance."

▶ Repeat all material from Beginning Grade, and then add this major problem:

"Now, keeping both hands on the floor, see how many different ways you can get one or two feet higher than your head."

(Then use the subproblems as they are needed.)

".... When both feet are off the ground, are you balanced on your hands for just a second? (not unless the body weight is over the hands) ... explore different ways of getting your hips up high while your hands remain on the floor, taking some or all of your weight ... try changing the width of your hand placement on the floor again ... find a way in which you feel most stable, most on-balance ... have you found several ways to balance in which you can hold very still with at least one foot at a high level? ... have you tried moving from one balance to another very smoothly?"

▶ Repeat all material from Beginning and Middle Grades, and then add this major problem:

"This time, put your head and both your hands on the floor. See how many ways you can move your feet around this base.

(Then use the subproblems as they are needed.)

".... Have you tried getting one or both feet into a high level? ... what can you do to get one or both feet as high as possible? ... look carefully at your hands and head on the floor ... what kind of base do they make? ... think about this ... would your head and hands make a better base for balancing if they were lined up in a straight row like this:

X   O   X

... or would they make a better base for balancing if they were placed in a triangle like this:

O
X   X

... why would the triangle be better? (larger area in the middle for weight to be over) ... find a good triangle position for your head and hands and see if you can get most of your weight over them ... are your hips and spine up over the triangle? ... some of you have one foot really stretched high over your triangle ... has anyone been able to balance for a short time with both feet off the ground? ... how many different ways can you balance your legs over your base? ... if you should go off-balance, what is a soft, safe way to recover your balance? (curl up, roll out to a new balance)."

(Again, much variation in ability will be evident. Praise the child who finally gets one toe over the head as much as the child who does a headstand easily.)

Flexible usage of units suggested by field test teachers

The test teachers kept logs and were interviewed periodically as a means of determining the value of the units and how flexibly they could be used. They made many suggestions which were incorporated in the units and asked valid questions before, during, and after the field test. Some of their questions and answers, outlined below, may assist a teacher in deciding whether or not to add basic movement education to his physical education program. They may also help him see some of the many different ways in which the units in Part II can be used.

No attempt has been made by the writer to impose her preconceived judgment of usage or to "take sides" when teachers had opposing answers to questions. For example, one kindergarten teacher felt most strongly that basic movement education should not be begun until the third or fourth week of school; another kindergarten teacher argued just as strongly for using basic movement education as the opening activity on the first day of school. Each teacher defended her position with valid reasoning; each developed an excellent physical education program. Many of these diverse opinions are reported in order to encourage teachers to develop their own usage patterns.

▶ *Question One (Before Field Testing): Alternating or Integrating*

Should I alternate lessons from the basic movement units with lessons from my existing physical education program or should I do the basic movement education program first and then units in games, dance, and gymnastics during the remainder of the year?

Answers (After Field Testing)

- *Teacher 1* (classroom teacher with no previous experience in movement education).   "For one's first attempt at adding basic movement education to the physical education curriculum, I would highly recommend teaching all the basic movement at the beginning of the year. There is so much for a teacher to learn about the method and content, so many relationships, not before realized, that unfold while one is teaching, such a shift in one's own teaching behavior—that, I think, one needs at least a year's experience before attempting any real integration. I did find, in teaching my usual activities later in the year, that I was using the movement vocabulary from the units, asking for more thoughtful responses from the children, and doing less command teaching."

- *Teacher 2* (classroom teacher with no previous experience in movement education).   "I alternated lessons, i.e., on Tuesdays we had problems from the basic movement units; on Thursdays, we had the activities from the program I had developed over the years. Each influenced the other, to a degree."

- *Teacher 3* (physical education specialist with no previous experience in movement education).   "I alternated units, i.e.,

    basic movement unit on space,
    regular unit on locomotor skills and games,
    basic movement unit on body awareness,
    regular unit on ball skills and games,
    basic movement unit on force, balance, and weight transfer,
    regular unit on stunts and tumbling,
    basic movement unit on time and flow,
    regular unit on dance.

This worked very well and some problem solving crept into the regular units. The ideas and concepts from the basic movement units were reinforced in the regular units."

• *Teacher 4* (specialist experienced in movement education).   "I have always felt that games, dances, and gymnastics should *emerge from* movement experiences, and any movement problems given should apply to and complement these more traditional activities. Thus I would suggest two organizational plans for different levels.

"First, in the primary grades, movement problems such as those in the units should be the core content and the organizing center. A set of movement problems should be the center of every lesson throughout the year. As culminating activities for sets of problems, the children can develop their own games and dances, or the teacher can intersperse traditional games and dances when they are directly related to the movement theme just studied.

"Second, in the intermediate grades, the more traditional units (gymnastics, lead-ups to the team sports, dance, etc.) should be the organizing center with appropriate movement problems selected to introduce the spacial concepts of the activities, the time and force requirements of specific skills, etc. This is integration at its best.

"I would recommend either alternating lessons in basic movement with lessons in the existing program or, better yet, integrating them completely rather than scheduling the total basic movement program first and all the traditional activities later."

All fifteen test teachers agreed that eventually an integration of basic movement education and the more structured activities was desirable. However, at least one year (the beginning grade) of basic movement experiences should be isolated to the degree needed for a rudimentary understanding of the structure of movement to be achieved by children.

▶ *Question Two: Grade Level Placement*

We are planning to begin to use the basic movement education units throughout our elementary school next year. For what grade levels are they appropriate?

The basic movement units in Part II were designed for use in any three consecutive grades in the elementary school:

K—1—2   or
1—2—3   or
2—3—4   or
3—4—5   or
4—5—6.

In schools that had never before offered basic movement education as a part of physical education, the following plan was suggested to implement the addition.

The first year: Beginning level problems were used in K—1—2—3—4. Beginning and middle level problems were used in 5. Beginning, middle, and last level problems were used in 6.

The second year: Beginning level problems were used in K. Beginning and middle level problems were used in 1—2—3—4—5. Beginning, middle, and last level problems were used in 6.

The third year: Beginning level problems were used in K. Beginning and middle level problems were used in 1. Beginning, middle, and last level problems were used in 2—3—4—5—6.

The fourth year and beyond: Beginning level problems were used in K.
Beginning and middle level problems were used in 1.
Beginning, middle, and last level problems were used in 2.
Teachers with experience in teaching basic movement education in grades 3—4—5—6 selected the pertinent problems from the units and integrated them into their regular programs.

Teachers at all levels were urged to "borrow" problems and subproblems from other levels whenever they thought it was appropriate. The repetition over the three-year span was intentionally built into the program as a means of revisiting content areas, and even with "borrowing" there was no negative reaction from children about the repetition.

▶ *Question Three: Time Needed for Basic Movement Education*

What percentage of physical education time should be spent on basic movement education?

The time guidelines established by the test teachers (see Table 4–1) represent the average time they spent in teaching the units in Part II. They agreed that in the future such a time breakdown would cease to be meaningful as they learned to integrate the structure and process approach into their total program.

Table 4–1

Average Amount of Time Scheduled by Test Teachers for Basic Movement Education

If taught in	In schools scheduling a daily period of physical education (20–35 minute period)			In schools scheduling 3 periods of physical education per week (20–35 minute period)			In schools scheduling 2 periods of physical education per week (20–35 minute period)		
	No. of days per set of problems	No. of days per year	% of total program	No. of days per set of problems	No. of days per year	% of total program	No. of days per set of problems	No. of days per year	% of total program
The first year of basic movement education (Beginning Grade in the Units)									
Kindergarten	5	100	55%	4	80	74%	3	60	83%
1st grade	4	80	44%	3	60	55%	2	40	55%
2nd grade	3	60	33%	2	40	36%	2	40	55%
3rd grade	2	40	22%	2	40	36%	1½	30	41%
4th grade	2	40	22%	2	40	36%	1	20	27%
The second year of basic movement education (Middle Grade in the Units)									
1st grade	4	80	44%	4	80	74%	2	40	55%
2nd grade	4	80	44%	3	60	55%	2	40	55%
3rd grade	3	60	33%	2	40	36%	1½	30	41%
4th grade	2	40	22%	2	40	36%	1½	20	27%
5th grade	1	20	11%	1	20	18%	1	20	27%
The third year of basic movement education (Last Grade in the Units)									
2nd grade	4	80	44%	3	60	55%	2	40	55%
3rd grade	3	60	33%	2	40	36%	1½	30	41%
4th grade	3	60	33%	2	40	36%	1	20	27%
5th grade	2	40	22%	1	20	18%	1	20	27%
6th grade	2	40	22%	1	20	18%	1	20	27%

▶ *Question Four: Time Needed for Each Set of Problems*

How many physical education periods should be planned for one set of problems in the units?

• *Teacher 1.*   "In planning for three 20-minute periods of physical education a week, I anticipated using one set of problems per week. That way, on Mondays I introduced a new topic and gave 2 or 3 problems, on Wednesdays I gave two or three more problems and lots of individual help and subproblems, and on Fridays, I tried to give the last two problems in the set, which turned out to be good culminating activities. Whenever possible, we tried to have brief demonstrations and evaluations of solutions to the last problems to allow for some reinforcing verbalization of what had been learned. The one week per set of problems was only a guideline, however. Frequently we would continue to work on one set of problems for several weeks. The children's interest and progressively more skillful and original solutions to problems was the deciding factor in when to go on to another theme (new set of problems). The checklist of quality factors at the end of each problem was also a help in determining when to go on to the next problem."

The average number of days recommended by test teachers to be spent on each set of problems is shown in Table 4–1.

▶ *Question Five: Space Needed for Basic Movement Education*

Where should lessons be scheduled? Is it possible to have basic movement education in the classroom?

Among the areas where basic movement lessons were taught were

a gymnasium,
half a gymnasium, with another class in the other half,
a multipurpose room,
a blacktopped schoolyard,
a grass lawn schoolyard,
a wide hall,
a classroom with desks pushed to the edges,
a stage,
a cafeteria,
a lobby.

Usually the noise level is quite low when children are involved in problem solving. Several primary teachers used the nonlocomotor problems in the classroom as a break between work on other subjects. Nearly every set of problems contains one or more problems which could be given in the classroom.

• *Teacher 1.*   "The more space, the better. However, children learn to use whatever space is available as a part of the first unit and adapt readily when changes in location must be made."

• *Teacher 2.*   "Whenever weather permits, we prefer doing the lessons outdoors. By establishing different outdoor boundaries to "general space" occasionally, we add a new variable to the study of spacial relationships."

▶ *Question Six: Discipline*

What kind of discipline can be maintained with such a permissive program?

This is an *intellectually permissive program,* not an "anything goes" program. Its long-range goal is to produce the responsible, intellectually autonomous individual, not the alienated or socially unconscious individual. The responsible, intellectually autonomous individual is one who can arrive at his own conclusions based on the relevant data—one who can discipline himself to carry out his problem solving within the complex social setting of the classroom or gymnasium. He is not working in a vacuum; he is working among fellow students and a teacher whose needs, values, and goals may differ greatly from his.

Robert E. Jewett [38] has stated that an effective use of the problem solving approach requires an intellectually permissive classroom atmosphere—an atmosphere in which the student's contribution is courteously and fairly entertained by all. The student experiences sensitive interpersonal relations and is expected to accord equally sensitive treatment to his fellow classmates. The classroom atmosphere should be one in which children are required to be intellectually responsible and socially civilized.

Only a minimum of class management rules should be set for children, with the goal of eliminating them after a period of adjusting to the new freedom. For example, in the first set of problems in the units, starting and stopping signals are introduced and practiced. However, it is hoped that they can be eliminated in time, since it is unrealistic to believe that all children will be finished with a particular problem at the same time. "Continuing a creative activity after the scheduled time for quitting" was listed by Torrance as a sign of creativity. In addition, Torrance also called for giving individuals the opportunity to elaborate their creative ideas. Therefore, the sooner a teacher can develop the security needed to eliminate the rule that "all must stop on the signal," the better. "Stop when you are finished" may be the next step.

In the same way, the starting signal may eventually be eliminated. At all times, the starting signal means that those *who are ready* may begin to solve the problem at once. Those who need to stand and think a bit first should certainly be allowed to do so.

Whatever rule changes evolve, children must be "in on" them. An intellectually permissive atmosphere implies freedom to express opinions about class management, knowing that opinions will be courteously and fairly entertained, but rigorously analyzed. A teacher must communicate this to students, explaining the procedure for establishing and revising minimum rules of socially civilized behavior. Children and teachers gain the freedom necessary for creative work through group-made rules of orderly living.

▶ *Question Seven: Verbalizing and Demonstrating*

How much verbalizing and demonstrating should be done by the children and by the teacher?

Verbalizing and demonstrating by the teacher

- *Teacher 1.* "During the year, I noticed a decrease in the amount of talking I was doing to the whole class and an increase in the amount of individual help I was giving. The general comments I was making were too often not appropriate for children involved in a variety of solutions. Only with individuals could I offer really pertinent suggestions, encourage greater variety, pose subproblems for development of higher quality movement responses, etc."

- *Teacher 2.* "Occasionally a whole class needs to be stopped for general coaching. For example, in moving balls with the feet at a low level, the whole class seemed to be involved in seeing how far and with how much force they could kick the balls. No one had thought of exploring a controlled dribble. At such a time, the teacher can turn a subproblem into a major problem—stop the class after enough time has elapsed for their original explorations, suggest the variable of using light force, even relate this to the game of soccer, which many of the children may never have seen. The teacher still fulfills the role of being the major source of movement ideas the children have never experienced or seen. Sometimes this can be done by simply joining the children in their explorations—no words at all. They see fresh new solutions being tried by the teacher and use them as take-off data for their own responses."

Demonstrating by children

Bilbrough and Jones [5] have suggested that demonstrations are given for a number of reasons, for example,

> to show something well done,
> to show something that has been improved,
> to show something new,
> to show varying responses,
> to show varying styles in performance,
> to show similarities,
> to show differences,
> to test the "seeing" powers of the class,
> and to show particular features.

The field test teachers added to the above list the advice that only teachers themselves may demonstrate a "bad" solution, and that such demonstrations are very effective in pointing up the quality factors in a good student demonstration.

Practical suggestions by Bilbrough and Jones for carrying out a demonstration include:

> all must be able to see—it is often an advantage for the class to sit down;
>
> all must be able to hear;
>
> all must pay attention—the good teacher will not go on with the demonstration unless he has everyone's attention;
>
> demonstrations should not be given too frequently—sympathetic though we are to the values of demonstration, we are equally certain that there is great value in uninterrupted practice during which children have an opportunity to learn from their own mistakes and profit from demonstrations they have previously seen;
>
> demonstrations should not last too long—sometimes the continuity of a lesson can be spoilt by this;
>
> the same child or children should not be used too frequently—over a series of lessons it is hoped that all children will have been used for demonstration purposes;
>
> demonstrations should be used sparingly at the beginning of a lesson, in cold weather, and when children are being introduced to new apparatus;
>
> demonstrations should be followed by practice, so that the lessons learnt can be applied;
>
> coaching should sometimes be done during a demonstration and sometimes afterwards;
>
> demonstrations should sometimes be used to illustrate a movement as a whole, at other times to illustrate one aspect of it;
>
> demonstrations should sometimes be carried out with one child, sometimes with two and sometimes with more (e.g., small groups, half classes, boys, or girls).

Verbalizing by children

A sharp disagreement existed among test teachers about the value of verbalizing by children. About half felt that discussion of what was seen (and understood) in demonstrations and verbal summarizing discussions at the end of every lesson were essential for attaining the knowledge objectives. The other half felt just as strongly that a minimum of verbalizing should be allowed—that here was the perfect opportunity to "allow the child whose verbalizing skills are low to shine." The children at long last are actually moving for a full twenty minutes. Attainment of objectives is amply demonstrated in movement . . . to insist on talking about movement elements is to take away the whole impact of the program."

▶ *Question Eight: Appropriate Dress*
How should the children dress for basic movement education lessons?

- *Teacher 1.*   "The children wore bathing suits under their school clothes on gym days and stripped en masse in the classroom before going to the gym. Bare feet, of course."

- *Teacher 2.*   "The girls wore shorts under their dresses on gym days. Boys merely took off their outer shirts before class. All had gym shoes." (Most frequent.)

- *Teacher 3.*   "We have regular gym uniforms."

- *Teacher 4.*   "In kindergarten! No change necessary. Bare feet work best. Girls who wear the long footed leotards slide too much in them without shoes. I had them bring a pair of regular panties to keep in their desks."

- *Teacher 5.*   "Parents were informed of the type of activity and asked to dress their children appropriately on physical education days."

- *Teacher 6.*   "Our parents objected to bare feet, so all the children were asked to keep gym shoes at school. When they were forgotten, regular shoes were permitted as opposed to slippery socks."

▶ *Question Nine: Equipment*
What kinds of equipment are needed for beginning a basic movement education program?

Table 4–2 lists the equipment needed for all the problems in the units. Equipment is listed in order of importance. Improvisation is essential in schools with a minimum of equipment on hand.

- *Some teachers' comments.* "When I first saw 'one ball per child' I almost quit. We had two balls in every classroom and that's all. The problem was easily solved, however, when we pooled our equipment and stored everything together in cardboard boxes in a closet just off the gym."

"Even with central storage, we only had half as many balls as we needed. I gave two problems at the same time—one needing balls and one without balls. The boys worked on one problem, the girls on the other, then they traded."

"When I saw the value of having one ball per child, I went to the P.T.A. They provided us with 30 of the very inexpensive colorful bouncing balls you can get at discount stores. Also, several fathers built us an assortment of sturdy, wooden jumping boxes."

"The fifth and sixth graders made our yarn balls—it only took them about 30 minutes."

"Each child brought a ball from home."

"We adapted many problems so our permanent playground equipment could be used—horizontal ladders, horizontal bars, turning bars, jungle gyms, teeter-totters, free forms, etc."

"We used dowel rods instead of hoops—worked fine."

"I sent one row of children to the multipurpose room ahead of the class to set out the equipment needed."

"We scoured the catalogues of the commercial equipment companies and were able to pick out and purchase the most imaginative and versatile new pieces of apparatus—climbers, wooden horses, slides, beams, ladders, bars, boxes—all adjustable and easy to handle."

"Our custodian made us benches and boxes that were perfect for our first and second graders. Until they were finished, we used cardboard boxes, filled with newspapers and taped shut. They were very sturdy but too heavy for the children to move. We found they could be left on the floor throughout a lesson (eliminating the children's moving them on and off) and treated as obstacles to be avoided in the problems where they weren't needed."

Table 4–2

Equipment Needed to Begin a Basic Movement Education Program

Equipment	Quantity	Ideas (improvise!)	Needed for Problems No.
Drum and beater or other starting and stopping signal	One for the teacher		Every problem
Balls that bounce	One per child		6, 7, 8, 14, 15, 16, 29, 37, 40, 55, 66, 67, 96, 98, 99, 107, 127
Yarn balls or other soft balls, such as paper balls, that do not bounce	One per child		22, 23, 24, 55, 62, 87, 88, 89, 90, 105
Large, empty, cardboard cartons	Four to eight		All problems where balls, ropes, or other small items of equipment are used. Placed around the edges of the room for easy distribution and replacement of small equipment stored in them. 105 as targets
Sturdy boxes, strong enough for a child to climb on and jump off	As many as you can collect, but a minimum of four		35, 36, 57, 69, 78, 102, 128
Low benches and/ or low balance beams	As many as you can collect, but a minimum of four		50B, 51, 73, 79, 85, 92, 128
Short ropes (2–6 feet long)	One per child		13, 17, 63, 100, 104

Equipment	Quantity	Ideas (improvise!)	Needed for Problems No.
Long rope to be suspended horizontally across the room	One or two		97, 105
Climbing rope suspended from the ceiling	One or two		92
Balloons	One per child		63
Hoops (or used bicycle tires)	One per child		83
Inclined boards hooked onto boxes or stools	One or more		78, 92
Chalk, tape, or white shoe polish for marking lines on floors or walls			74, 105
Small obstacles such as Indian pins, plastic bottles, or books	Four to eight		105

Optional equipment

Record or music for Looby Loo.
Record or music for Dry Bones.
Record: "Listening and Moving, the Development of Body Awareness and Position in Space," by Dorothy Carr and Bryant Cratty—L.P. 605, Educational Activities, Inc., Freeport, New York, 1966.
A "slinky" spring toy: 1.

Mats: as many as you can get.
Assorted rhythm instruments.
Record with an even pulse beat at a slow tempo.
Record with an even pulse beat at a medium tempo.
Record with an even pulse beat at a fast tempo.

- *Directions for making soft balls.* Yarn balls are made like pompoms for knitted caps. Wrap about 20 turns of rug yarn around a piece of cardboard 4 inches across. Carefully remove the bundle of yarn from the cardboard and tie it securely in the middle with twine. Continue to make bundles until an entire skein of yarn is used up. Tie all the bundles together in the middle and cut the ends of the loops to form a fluffy ball. More detailed instructions can be found in books that teach knitting. A less durable ball can be made very quickly by wadding up a piece or two of tablet paper and wrapping sticky tape around the wad to hold it together.

▶ *Question Ten: Evaluation*

How can I evaluate a child's progress in a basic movement education program?

Three tools for broad evaluation are provided within the units: (1) a checklist of quality factors for evaluating movement responses to *each problem,* (2) the objectives (for children) for evaluating progress at the beginning of *each set of problems* (each theme), and (3) the review set of problems for evaluating progress at the end of *each unit.*

- *Checklist of quality factors: evaluation for each problem.* This checklist follows every problem. It is composed of specific observational points for the teacher to look for, to reward with praise when seen, or to develop with more subproblems when lacking. Often a checkpoint includes an explanation for the teacher, e.g., one of the quality factors for Problem 1 is:

  ☐ Firmly held freezes—muscles tightened so arms and other body parts do not wave about. Do not expect freezes to be held longer than 10 seconds. Beyond 10 seconds, children should relax and face teacher, listening to the next problem.

Frequently, a suggested minimum number of variations to be discovered by the children is given; e.g., one of the quality factors for Problem 49 is:

  ☐ Demonstrating a variety of ways for legs to meet and part both on the floor and on apparatus (bench or beam). Suggested minimums:

  B —6 ways, including walking, running, jumping;
  M—10 ways, including one foot leading at all times, as in galloping, side stepping, or sliding;
  L —12 ways, including level change and matching arm and leg movements.

It is unrealistic to suppose that a teacher will have time to check out every student on every problem. It is more realistic and more desirable to have children check themselves out. Older children can check each other in a buddy system. It is quite realistic to expect a teacher to give some concentrated attention to each child at least once every week or two. This individual attention should focus on teaching the art of self-evaluation to the child—helping him learn to assess his own abilities, accept his own present limitations, set new goals for himself just ahead of what he can now do. The checklist of quality factors is not intended to be used to measure an individual child's progress or to compare one child with another; it is intended to give teachers a broad outline of observational points. Through these observations, teachers may subjectively decide when to go on to the next problem.

- *Objectives (for children): evaluation for each set of problems.* The second tool for broad evaluation is the list of Objectives (for children) given at the beginning of each set of problems. Before beginning a new set of problems, a teacher should adapt these objectives to fit the needs of his own class. These adapted objectives, when restated in question form, become the basic evaluation questions. They describe the behavior to be achieved through solving that set of problems. Then before leaving that set of problems, the conscientious teacher must ask himself:

Do the children understand
1
2   (The statements under
3   the knowledge objectives?)
4

Do the children know how to
1
2   (The statements under
3   the skill objectives?)
4

Have the children made any progress in becoming
1
2   (The statements under
3   the attitude objectives?)
4

Too often, asking is the end of it. When the teacher has decided that 25 children do know how to . . . but 5 don't, he moves on to the next set of problems. Since the essence of a basic movement education program is individualization, to ignore the 5 is to negate the whole approach. Going on to the next set of problems may be very desirable since each set spirals above those preceding. Perhaps the 5 will discover that which they missed when it is presented in a new context. Should they be moved ahead before they are ready too often, however, a spiral of confusion and frustration may be the result. Instead, a totally individual program can be tailored to the special needs of the few—either by following the regular program more slowly and with additional subproblems or by designing a new program.

Mosston's [52] description of the individual program in *Teaching Physical Education* is an excellent source for designing such programs.

Review set of problems: evaluation for each unit. The third tool for broad evaluation is found in the last set of problems in each unit:

Sixth set of problems—review of space.
Ninth set of problems—review of space and body awareness.
Fifteenth set of problems—review of force, balance and weight transfer.
Twentieth set of problems—review of basic movement.

Each of these review sets of problems attempts to have children demonstrate previous learning in a new setting within the structural framework. Each problem can be used as an informal device for securing evidence about teaching-learning operations to that point.

Teachers' personal reactions

The following personal responses to adding basic movement to the physical education curriculum were made by the field test teachers.

At the End of the First Week

"The children love the program and are enthusiastic about each new problem. I, however, am still very apprehensive because the approach is so new to me. I felt exactly the same way when I started the new math."

"My only insecurity is in not knowing how many solutions the children will come up with and, thus, I find myself being too quick to offer solutions to them."

"Already I have learned that the children are better at this than I am. I'm amazed at the variety of their responses."

"Thus far, I have used the unit materials only in the classroom because I am apprehensive of turning the class loose in our large gymnasium. I have no difficulty in observing in the classroom, however, so next week, we'll go to the gym."

At the End of Six Weeks

"It took me about a month to begin to develop subproblems on the spot. Now, I'm very enthusiastic about the program. The children seem to be developing a sensitivity toward each other that I have not seen in second graders before. They respect each other's space, they handle the equipment well, they have begun making up their own games at recess based on the problems we've had in class."

"Two of my children are extremely hyperactive and they haven't calmed down yet. They, more than anyone else, really seem to enjoy the continuous activity period, the freedom to be on the move—no waiting for explanations or lining up or taking turns."

"My only concern is that the children work so hard on the problems, they are exhausted after about fifteen or twenty minutes, especially on hot days. They recuperate fast, so I've learned to limit verbalizing about the problem-solving process to brief resting periods and then only when they are necessary. The children seem to think well flat on their backs!"

"I like:
each child succeeding in his own way,
the surprising creativity coming from unsuspected sources,
the listening skills which carry over to the classroom,
the foundation (especially vocabulary) which will make teaching skills so much easier,
the look on children's faces when they go to the gym—
confident, excited, motivated."

"At first, I thought there was too much repetition, but now I see that each time a movement factor is repeated it is in a different setting and that different movement responses are forthcoming."

"I especially liked the circle chart [on page 125] and have it displayed on our gym wall, enlarged and in color, accompanied by figures in movement. The children draw some figures illustrating the different themes as they study them and the display keeps growing."

"Since music is my favorite subject to teach, I have made an effort to integrate music and basic movement education. The children make up their own small group or individual dances at the end of each theme and also accompany them."

"At the beginning, I needed the security of having the units in my hand at all times when I was moving among the children during a lesson. Then, when I needed to help an individual, I could check the subproblems to see if they were appropriate. I underlined all key words in red before the lesson for easy reference."

"I've stopped carrying the book around with me and now just make one brief notecard that I tape to the drum (used for giving stopping and starting signals). At first, without the book, I inadvertently would misphrase questions, i.e., "Do this . . ." or "Who can do this?" which limited responses. Since I have learned to phrase the problems in an open-ended way, I need only a few cue words on a card while the class is going on."

Other memory aids were also devised:

"I cut out the problems I planned to give each day and kept them with me."

"Notecards—cue words for problems and an abbreviated checklist of quality factors."

"I taped a large card on the wall with the day's major problems printed on it. That way, individuals could move on to the next problem when they were ready."

"I put my drum and book on a rolling movie projector stand!"

(As teachers became more secure, they relied less and less on the printed problems and more and more on their observations of the children.)

"Tell other teachers to expect the preparation time to decrease rapidly as they get into the units. For the first week or two, I needed at least half an hour to absorb the content, adapt the objectives, and think through possible movement solutions my students might come up with. This time spent in preparation for each lesson decreased rapidly after a few weeks of experience."

At the End of the Program

At the end of the basic movement education program, the following topics were introduced in a final interview with each teacher. The answers below are composites. No negative comments have been eliminated.

▸ *How did your children respond to the basic movement education program?*

• *Kindergarten teachers.* "They loved it . . . you could tell by their faces . . . laughing together . . . joyful when they get to choose their own ways and when they get to create and are commended for their creations . . . they solve their own discipline problems by finding they will be commended . . . and it carries over into the classroom."

"This year has been like spring all the time. The children were alive, wide awake, doing things they liked to do. When they see other classes waiting in line to move, they ask why anyone should have to do that."

• *First and second grade teachers.* "The children were very enthusiastic and they had a great deal of fun while solving problems."

"I thought the children would tire of this approach, but the more familiar they became with it, the better they liked it. I often see them playing "Teacher" and making up movement problems for each other on the playground. They ask to borrow the drum nearly every day."

"They don't want to stop at the end of a class period. I'm not sure they always know or think about what they are doing, but they love it."

• *Third and fourth grade teachers.* "Most children loved it. Their only complaint was that they didn't have enough time to *talk about* what they had discovered. The demonstration-evaluation became very important to them."

"At first, the children were content only if we moved very quickly from problem to problem. Gradually, they learned to explore each problem in more depth and to select several solutions to practice until they were satisfied with them. Once this pacing was established, they enjoyed the lessons very much."

• *Fifth and sixth grade teachers.* "A few children, especially boys who are very good at softball, volleyball, basketball, and soccer, could not see the practical application of the basic movement education problems, although they enjoyed solving them. By reversing the process occasionally—by starting with the game and breaking it down into movement problems, they came to see how they could improve their performance by having a broader understanding of the component parts."

"To tell the truth, I expected them to get bored with it, but they did not. The more complex the sequences they created, the better they liked it and the more pride they took in their work."

"For some children, it was the first time in five years of physical education that they enjoyed what they were doing. Fear of failure was eliminated; the timid progressed faster than the courageous; those with high ability set new goals for themselves they didn't know existed before, e.g., perfect stillness in balancing, gathering force by concentrating on using more body parts to throw a ball harder, etc."

▶ *What is your reaction to basic movement as content?* "Emphasis on structure of movement paid off. Week by week I could see the children developing a wider scope of movement responses."

"I was reluctant to drop the five minutes of calisthenics at the beginning of each period. I've been able to get children to enjoy exercises for years, so I continued to begin each period with them for several weeks. Clearly the children preferred the movement problems, and I soon found that development of agility, balance, flexibility, and strength was not omitted from the basic movement program. Physical fitness, per se, should be listed as an attainable goal through basic movement education. I was especially impressed with rising endurance levels."

"The content was academically sound and inherently interesting to children. Since my children have had four years of a skills- and games-centered curriculum, and asked for games if we had several consecutive lessons in basic movement education, I found the best pattern for these children was half a period of basic movement problems and half a period of the regular program. Next year I will be able to integrate the two better—selecting problems pertinent to the more traditional activities taught in the second half of the period."

"The content is very clear, directly stated (especially for teachers unfamiliar with the area), and quite suitable for children. I'm not sure the lower grade children fully grasp the structure, but their movement vocabulary is much improved."

"Two areas were particularly difficult for five- and six-year-olds—the main idea of changing the range of a movement and the physical skill of making sharp turns for zigzag pathways. By returning to these again and again as subproblems, the children made some progress, but it was slow."

▶ *What is your reaction to discovery as process and problem solving as technique?* "It is ideal—the way all subjects should be taught with young children. I find myself phrasing problems and leading discussions more carefully in other subjects."

"The children no longer say 'I can't.' Everyone is moving almost all the time; everyone can produce some appropriate response. Each individual child thinks he is doing well. The *you* in 'How many ways can *you* . . .?' is very personal. Young children are great copiers . . . in this program, they've rapidly grown more independent and more creative."

"Self-discipline, skills, and self-motivation are the best outcomes of such a program. When I learned to curb my worries (I was afraid the children would hurt themselves given so much freedom) and when I stopped trying to shower the children with advice, the children responded by becoming more self-confident and much more interested in solving problems on their own."

"When some problem solving bogged down for lack of ideas, I did not hesitate to switch to guided discovery or even direct teaching for a brief period of time. After the children had learned several ways to move, we returned to the problem that had gone unexplored, and using the learned movement patterns as a takeoff point, proceeded to discover many variations of them. Especially early in the program, children need help in finding the "stuff" with which to create."

Basic movement education has been defined as the *foundational structure and process portion of physical education* as characterized by the experiential study of

1   time, space, force, and flow as the elements of movement,
2   the physical laws of motion and the principles of human movement which govern the human body's movement, and
3   the vast variety of creative and efficient movements which the human body is capable of producing through manipulation of movement variables.

In attempting to identify a *foundational structure* of movement, one asks himself both how and why man moves. In this book, the answer to "how does man move?" is divided into nineteen organizing themes. Each theme becomes the central focus for a set of movement problems for students to solve both mentally and physically. By returning to the themes in spiral fashion over a three-year period, a useful, personal, cognitive structure of movement is to be achieved by students. Control and refinement of the body's movements are to be achieved through rigorous movements experienced as the means of formulating a valid personal structure of movement.

These nineteen structural themes are organized into units of study for children under four general headings which are in the form of questions: where can you move? what can you move? how do you move? and how can you move better?

The structure of "why does man move?" is a more abstract topic, and there are many possible answers. In this book, the single answer chosen for emphasis is: man moves to control his environment. This core concept, movement for environmental control, is a high level abstraction which encompasses and has the power to organize many generalizations and vast amounts of specific data. It spans every lesson in the three-year curriculum. It may be grasped in its most elementary form by a kindergartener; it may provide a focus for a lifetime of study by a scholar in the field.

A teacher may regard the structural themes (which are also known as major ideas, or generalizations) as subdivisions of the core concept. Specific facts are then subdivisions of the major ideas. The facts are used to define, illustrate, and develop each theme. This three-level structure of (1) concept supported by (2) major ideas defined by (3) specific facts describes, for the teacher, the *knowledge content* of basic movement education. When the knowledge content is stated in open ended problem form, it becomes the *movement content* to be experienced by students, each in his own way and at his own ability level.

In establishing behavioral objectives for children, however, the development of movement skills and the attainment of knowledge about movement are not the only areas to be considered. Thinking skill, social skill, and attitude development are equally important, and specific objectives should be established in these areas.

Chapter 2 explores the *foundational processes* by which the structure can be implemented, the objectives met. There are many different theories of learning, but they do have common characteristics which this book attempts to apply. One basic process of learning is discovery; a variety of problem-solving techniques is proposed as an effective way to make discoveries. The most stimulating problems are those for which there is no standard method of solution and no single "right" solution.

Five general criteria were established for selecting and stating movement problems (the learning activities):

1   Major problems should be of the type described above.
2   Subproblems should be "bumper" problems, to be given only if students do not independently discover them. They should be given to stimulate a variety of solutions to the major problem or to sharpen the performance of a given movement solution.

3   Problems should require productive thinking, and both reasoning
    and imagining should be encouraged as processes for solving them.
4   For the purpose of nurturing creativity, problems should be stated
    so that a multiplicity of solutions is possible in a wide range
    of ability levels, so that all children may succeed, and so that the
    growth resulting from success may become an intrinsic motivation for
    attaining higher levels of creativity.
5   All learning activities (problems and subproblems) must be chosen
    for their power to meet the objectives in all three areas: knowledge—
    movement, thinking, and social skills—and attitudes.

Practical teaching strategies for implementing a basic movement
education program are recommended by field test teachers in Chapter 4.
They are applicable either to the curriculum in Part II or to one's
own curriculum.

The personal responses of the test teachers and the responses of their
children lend credence to the three proposals which have been emphasized
in this book:

1   The development of responsible, intellectually autonomous individuals
    is a major goal of education.
2   There is an undergirding body of knowledge in physical education
    which is worth knowing.
3   The process of discovery and the techniques of problem solving are
    the most effective ways to learn (both physically and mentally)
    that body of knowledge while becoming intellectually autonomous
    individuals.

The following teaching units in basic movement education contain one
interpretation and organization of the "stuff" or structure with which
movements are created and performed by children. Readers are invited to
use the units as flexibly as did the test teachers. Inevitably, teachers will
design their own curricula to meet the needs of the individual children in
their care. These units are a resource for helping teachers to help children
escape from

> Little boxes, little boxes, little boxes, made of ticky-tacky,
> Little boxes, little boxes, little boxes all the same . . . .

CALENDAR OF BASIC MOVEMENT UNITS

Themes

Unit One.   Where can you move? (space)

Moving in self space and into general space
Moving in different directions
Moving at different levels
Moving in different ranges and by changing shapes
Moving in the air (flight)
Moving in different pathways and **review of space**

Sets of problems

1st set (Problems 1–9)
2nd set (Problems 10–17)
3rd set (Problems 18–25)
4th set (Problems 26–32)
5th set (Problems 33–37)
6th set (Problems 38–42)

Unit Two.   What can you move? (body awareness)

Moving different body parts
Changing relationships of body parts
Review: space, body awareness

7th set (Problems 43–47)
8th set (Problems 48–52)
9th set (Problems 53–57)

Unit Three.   How do you move? (force, balance, weight transfer)

Creating force
Absorbing force
Moving on-balance and off-balance (gravity)
Transferring weight (rocking, rolling, sliding)
Transferring weight (steplike movements)
Transferring weight when flight is involved and
review: force, balance, weight transfer

10th set (Problems 58–64)
11th set (Problems 65–69)
12th set (Problems 70–74)
13th set (Problems 75–79)
14th set (Problems 80–85)
15th set (Problems 86–92)

Unit Four.   How can you move better? (time, flow)

Moving at different speeds
Moving rhythmically (to pulse beats)
Moving in bound or free flow
and creating movement sequences
Moving rhythmically (to phrases)
Creating movement sequences as a
review of basic movement

16th set (Problems 93–97)
17th set (Problems 98–101)
18th set (Problems 102–105)

19th set (Problems 106–124)
20th set (Problems 124–200)

The rationale underlying the teaching units can be found in the first part of this book, and specific directions on how to use the teaching units are given in Chapter 4. The reader who begins his reading here is therefore strongly urged to read at least Chapter 4.

UNIT ONE

WHERE CAN YOU MOVE? (SPACE)

Set of Problems	Dates	Theme	Equipment Needed
			Every lesson—all year. A starting and stopping signal. Suggestions: drum (1 beat to start, 2 beats to stop), tambourine, cricket, whistle. Verbal signals may be used, but since most words are spoken while children move and frequently are spoken to individuals rather than to a whole class, a nonverbal signal to be used consistently is preferred.
1		Moving in self space and in general space	One ball per child. Suggestion: Keep balls in 4 to 6 cardboard boxes. For lessons, distribute boxes around the edges of the room.
2		Moving in different directions	One ball per child, and 1 short rope (2 to 6 feet long) per child. Suggestion: Put balls and ropes in equipment boxes around edges of room.
3		Moving at different levels	One yarn ball or very soft ball per child.
4		Moving in different ranges and by changing shapes	One ball per child.
5		Moving in the air (flight)	One ball per child. As many sturdy boxes as you can collect, but a minimum of 4.
6		Moving in different pathways	One ball per child.

General objectives to stress in Unit One

Self-discipline skills—children need to learn how to

1   Listen and think while moving.
2   Respond quickly to starting and stopping signals.
3   Get out and put away equipment efficiently.

Attitude objectives to stress in all units

Attitudes—children need to become

1   Willing to listen to problems, to think about them, and to seek increasingly more skillful, thoughtful, and original ways of solving them through movement.
2   Willing to carry tasks through to completion.
3   Increasingly self-motivated, self-determined, and self-disciplined so that each child grows in appreciative self-realization.
4   Appreciative of others like and unlike themselves.
5   Willing to help and work with others.
6   Success-oriented in movement, so that they have an increasing appreciation for and enjoyment of movement.

FIRST SET OF PROBLEMS / ORGANIZING THEME: MOVING IN SELF SPACE AND IN GENERAL SPACE

Content structure (for teachers)	Objectives (for children)

Concept

Movement for environmental control

Major ideas

1. A child moves to discover and to cope with his environment.
2. The body is the instrument of movement and can be used in a vast variety of ways.
3. *Space*, force, time, and flow are the elements of movement.

Selected facts

1. Space is the medium of movement.
2. *Self space* is the immediate area surrounding the body. Its outer boundary is ascertained by stretching as far as possible in all directions and at all levels.
3. *General space* is the area surrounding self space. Its outer boundary is arbitrarily formed by walls, fences, lines, streets, buildings, or any other real or predetermined lines within which one is moving.

Children need to understand (knowledge)

1. That they move in self space and in general space. B–M–L*
2. That they can move in a vast variety of ways in self space and in general space. B–M–L
3. That they can *control* their movements in general space to avoid collisions with people and objects. B–M–L
4. That they can conscientiously use available space wisely to attain workable spacial relationships with other people or objects. M–L

Children need to learn how (skill)

1. To move in an increasing *variety* of ways in self space and in general space. B–M–L
2. To move in general space avoiding collisions with other people or objects. B–M–L
3. To respond to stopping and starting signals. B–M–L
4. To listen and think *while* moving. B–M–L
5. To get out and put away equipment efficiently. B–M–L
6. To increase *control* of ball handling. B–M–L

Children need to become (attitude)

1. Willing to listen to problems, to think about them, and to seek increasingly more skillful, thoughtful, and original ways of solving them through movement.
2. Willing to carry tasks through to completion.
3. Increasingly self-motivated, self-determined, and self-disciplined so that each child grows in appreciative self-realization.
4. Appreciative of others like and unlike themselves.
5. Willing to help and work with others.
6. Success-oriented in movement, so that they have an increasing appreciation for and enjoyment of movement.

Teaching tips for first set of problems

1. *Arrange equipment . . . before the physical education period:* One ball per child, preferably in 4 to 6 boxes around the edges of the room.
2. *Discuss movement vocabulary . . . in the classroom:*

   self space
   general space
   freeze
   bounce
   control

3. *Discuss, review . . . after the physical education period:* In regard to finding self space and using general space well, compare the work in class with other life situations . . . using space wisely on the playground, in school, at home, etc. . . . no need for pushing and crowding.

---

* The letters B, M, and L indicate the levels at which each objective should be stressed:

B = Beginning grade (K, 1, 2, 3, or 4).
M = Middle grade (1, 2, 3, 4, or 5).
L = Last grade (2, 3, 4, 5, or 6).

These abbreviations will be used throughout the book.

Introduction

"Our first theme is moving in self space and moving in general space. We will work on
1.   learning the starting and stopping signals,
2.   listening and moving at the same time, and
3.   finding many, many different ways to move in self space and in general space."

Developmental problems and expected outcomes

PROBLEM 1

Beginning Grade	Middle Grade	Last Grade
(Children sitting on floor. Explain and demonstrate your starting and stopping signal. *One tap on the drum to start; two taps on the drum to stop.* If you prefer, you may use one and two toots on a whistle or the spoken words "start" and "stop." Hand claps or a small hand cricket are good signal devices if they can be heard.)	▶ Repeat all material from Beginning Grade, and then add:	▶ Repeat all material from Beginning and Middle Grades, and then add:
"When you hear the stopping signal, you are to "freeze." Stop as quickly as possible and hold the shape you are in as strong and still as possible.	**"On the starting signal, move your hands and arms and head as many places as you can around you."**	**"On the starting signal, move your body from the waist up as many ways as you can."**
"On the starting signal, move one hand around you as many places as you can find."	(Check "freezes.")	(Check "freezes.")
(Start . . . stop . . . check "freezes" . . . are they firm and still?)	**"How many places can you take both feet and legs without having them touch the floor?"**	**"How many places can you take your body from the waist down, keeping your shoulders and head on the floor?"**
"How many places can you take one foot without having it touch the floor?"	(Check "freezes.")	(Check "freezes.")
(Start . . . stop . . . check "freezes" . . . repeat with other isolated body parts . . . two hands, one elbow, one knee, head only, etc.)		

Checklist of quality factors for Problem 1

☐ Quick, balanced stops on signal.

☐ Firmly held freezes—muscles tightened so arms and other parts do not wave about. Do not expect freezes to be held longer than 10 seconds. Beyond 10 seconds, children should relax and face teacher, listening to the next problem.

☐ Quick starts on signal.

☐ Purposeful movement to solve the problem. Does each child understand the problem? If head movement only is called for in the problem, then arms and legs should be still.

☐ Variety of movement to solve the problem. Many solutions should be sought. Hands can go many places in addition to over the head.

When children demonstrate these factors, go on to Problem 2.

Start

Freeze

PROBLEM 2

Beginning Grade	Middle Grade	Last Grade

"On this problem, you will have to <u>listen while you move</u>, because the problem will keep changing. Can you listen and think and move all at the same time?

"On the signal, start moving one hand all around you."

(Give starting signal.)

". . . Now add the other hand . . . add one foot . . . add the other foot . . . add your head . . . are you moving in many different ways?"

(Give stopping signal . . . check "freezes.")

"On the signal, <u>move as many parts of you as you can</u>, <u>as many places</u> as you can."

(Give starting signal.)

". . . Are you moving your legs? . . . can you lie on your tummy and still keep moving in many ways? . . . can you lie on your back and still keep moving in many ways?"

(Give stopping signal . . . check "freezes." Repeat problem if children have difficulty listening while moving.)

▶ Repeat all material in Beginning Grade, and then add:

"On the signal, put your <u>head on the floor</u> and see how many ways you can move the rest of your body."

(Give starting signal.)

". . . Can you get one foot high above your head? . . . how many places can you put that foot high above your head? . . . who can put two feet high above the head? . . . are there different ways to do this?"

(Some may merely lie on back with feet up . . . others may do a head stand. *Both* responses and variations between are *correct.*)

▶ Repeat all material in Beginning and Middle Grades, and then add:

"On the signal, put <u>both hands on the floor</u> and see how many ways you can move your body around your hands."

(Give starting signal.)

". . . Make your body very small and curled as you move it around your hands . . . now make your body as long and stretched as you can as you move it around your hands . . . how high can you get one or two feet above your hands?"

(Again, expect and accept great variation of ability . . . a few may do handstands. The important point is that each child should find one or more solutions to the problem.)

Listen to subproblems *while* moving

Checklist of quality factors for Problem 2

- ☐ Listening while moving.
- ☐ Variety of movement responses . . . not just one solution or the easiest solution over and over.

- ☐ Quick response to starting and stopping signals.
- ☐ Firmly held freezes.

When children demonstrate these factors, go on to Problem 3.

PROBLEM 3

Beginning Grade	Middle Grade	Last Grade

"Now that you can start and stop on signal, and listen while you move, let's explore general space. Notice the large space in this room."

(Or playground area . . . point out boundaries).

"This is called general space. On the signal, see how many places you can go in this general space without touching each other."

(Start.)

". . . . Explore the general space . . . have you been to all parts of the room? . . . to the corners? . . . to the middle? . . . look around and try to move into spaces where no one else is . . . no touching."

(Practice stopping and starting several times, checking after every stop to see if "freezes" are held firmly and to see if children are distributed fairly well throughout the general space.)

▶ Repeat all material from Beginning Grade, and then add:

". . . . Stay as far away from everyone else as you can . . . how many ways can you move? . . . not just running . . . have you tried moving backwards or sidewards? . . . slowly and fast? . . . up high and down low? . . . no touching."

(Practice stopping and starting several times, checking after every stop to see if "freezes" are held firmly and to see if children are distributed fairly well throughout the general space.)

▶ Repeat all material from Beginning and Middle Grades, and then add:

". . . . Try exploring half of the general space at a high level and the other half at a low level . . . can you get your feet high off the ground and then land softly? . . . how quickly can you explore general space when you are moving at a low level?"

(Practice stopping and starting several times, checking after every stop to see if "freezes" are held firmly and to see if children are distributed fairly well throughout the general space.)

General space

Checklist of quality factors for Problem 3

☐ Moving into all parts of the general space . . . not just into one corner or around the edges or in a circle.

☐ No collisions with others.

☐ Demonstrating the beginning of a sense of spacing . . . keeping a fairly even distribution of bodies throughout the general space while moving.

☐ Being well spaced throughout the room on the stopping signal.

☐ Continuous exploratory movement from starting signal to stopping signal.

When children demonstrate these factors, go on to Problem 4.

PROBLEM 4

Beginning Grade	Middle Grade	Last Grade

"On the signal, see how many different ways you can move in general space."

". . . . Keep thinking about different ways to move and try out all your thoughts . . . are you still moving into all parts of the room? . . . keep exploring . . . when you have tried out one way to move, then think of another way and try it out . . . no bumping or touching . . . how quietly can you move? . . . very quiet movements."

(Select three or four children who have found very unusual ways to move and who are using the general space well. Have them demonstrate. Discuss *briefly* the many ways it is possible to move in general space, then repeat the problem, encouraging variety rather than copying the demonstrators.)

▶ Repeat all material from Beginning Grade, and then add:

". . . . Find some ways to move that will take you up into the *high level of general space* . . . can you get your feet off the ground? . . . can you do something besides jumping? . . . how many ways can you get your feet up high? . . . how softly can you land?"

▶ Repeat all material from Beginning and Middle Grades, and then add:

". . . . What different things can you do to get your *whole body up off the floor* while you move in general space? . . . how high can you get? . . . and how softly can you land? . . . what different things can you do while you are in the air? . . . different things with your hands? . . . different things with your knees?"

Checklist of quality factors for Problem 4

☐ A variety of ways to move . . . minimum of four ways.

☐ Evidence of real *thought* about different ways to move . . . not just copying what others are doing.

☐ Maintaining fairly even distribution throughout the general space while moving.

☐ No collisions or falls.

☐ Middle and last grades: variety of ways to move high into the air.

☐ Soft landings.

When children demonstrate these factors, go on to Problem 5.

PROBLEM 5

Beginning Grade	Middle Grade	Last Grade

(Check spacing . . . if distribution is not even, have each child find a space of his own where he cannot reach out and touch anyone or anything.)

"This is your own space. It is called self space.

"On the signal, staying right in your own self space and not moving about the room, see how big your self space is."

(Allow a period of free exploration.)

". . . . How much self space is in front of you? . . . stretch as far as you can without falling or moving out of your self space . . . is there high space in front of you and low space in front of you? . . . how much self space do you have beside you and behind you? . . . really stretch to reach into and touch all of your self space."

▶ Repeat all material from Beginning Grade, and then add:

". . . . Use your *legs and head* as well as your arms to reach into and touch all parts of your self space in front of you . . . in back of you . . . beside you . . . down low and up high . . . never stop moving . . . reach and stretch, twist and turn . . . let an elbow or a knee lead you all over your self space."

▶ Repeat all material from Beginning and Middle Grades. In addition:

(Assign *different positions* from which self space is to be explored.)

". . . . How big is your self space when you keep both feet on the floor?"

(Explore.)

". . . . How big when you stay sitting down? . . . how big when you are lying flat on your tummy or back? . . . how big when you are balancing on one foot?"

Self space

Option

Simple game of follow the leader after full exploration. One child leads . . . the others try to mimic his movements in self space. Children may devise their own rules for choosing leaders and how long each should lead.

Checklist of quality factors for Problem 5

☐ Staying in self space . . . demonstrating an understanding of self space.

☐ Stretching to fullest extension to discover the outer boundaries of self space.

☐ Increasing stretch to the point where an additional inch of stretch would cause the child to lose his balance.

☐ Beginning to gain the kinesthetic "feel" of one's own self space.

☐ Continuous movement rather than stretch, relax, stop . . . stretch, relax, stop.

☐ Last grade: realizing that the size of self space changes when limitations (such as remaining on two knees) are imposed.

When children demonstrate these factors, go on to Problem 6.

PROBLEM 6

Beginning Grade	Middle Grade	Last Grade

(Briefly explain method of getting out balls. Suggestion to children: "Point to the box nearest you. On signal, run to it without touching anyone, get a ball, run back to a self space as far away from everyone else as possible." Do not expect children to hold the balls when they get to their self space. Allow free exploration until all are in place, then give a stopping signal before stating the problem. Practice getting out and putting away the balls quickly, without touching, several times. You may make a game of it by seeing how many counts it takes after the signal to get the balls and begin working with them in a self space or to put the balls away and return to a self space.)

"On the signal, each one of you get a ball, find a self space, and see how many different things you can do with that ball while standing in your own self space."

(Free exploration, then stop.)

"A very important word is control. Control the ball. That means you tell the ball where to go; don't let it tell you where to go. On the signal, see how many different ways you can control the ball in your own self space."

(Encourage bouncing *and* tossing *and* rolling *and* pushing the ball around self space with different body parts such as feet, head, etc. Stress controlling the ball as it stays in self space. Then give stopping signal.)

"What happens when you hear the stopping signal and the ball is in the air? Should you freeze then? No. Get control of the ball as quickly as possible, then freeze."

(Practice starting and stopping several times.)

▶ Repeat all material from Beginning Grade, and then add:

"Now, staying in your self space, work just on bouncing the ball with control."

". . . . On the signal, see how many times you can bounce the ball on the floor without losing control of it . . . count the number of your bounces."

(Allow either continuous bouncing, called dribbling, or bounce, catch, and hold.)

". . . . See if you can get one more bounce than the last time . . . have you discovered that you have more control when you push the ball down softly?"

▶ Repeat all material from Beginning and Middle Grades, and then add:

"Now work just on tossing and catching the ball with control."

". . . . On the signal, see how many times you can toss the ball into the air and catch it without going out of your own self space . . . count the number of your tosses . . . remember to stay in your own self space . . . if you are over five in your counting, try tossing the ball a little higher . . . if you are under five, try tossing the ball a little lower. *Control* that ball."

Checklist of quality factors for Problem 6

☐ Getting out and putting away balls quickly and without touching.

☐ Finding "self spaces" for working with balls which are well distributed throughout the "general space."

☐ Controlling ball manipulation to the point that children stay within their own self spaces.

☐ Freezing on stopping signal after the ball is in control.

☐ B–M–L: Moving balls in self space in many ways (minimum of 4).

☐ M–L: Increasing number of controlled bounces.

☐ L: Increasing number of controlled tosses and catches.

When children demonstrate these factors, go on to Problem 7.

PROBLEM 7

Beginning Grade	Middle Grade	Last Grade

"On the signal, move slowly into general space and see how many ways you can control the ball while you are moving."

". . . . Remember to control the ball . . . try to keep it close to you . . . it is hard to keep moving, isn't it? . . . you have to look up to see where the empty spaces are . . . have you moved all around the general space? . . . some of you have tried pushing the ball with your feet and elbows and heads . . . others are bouncing and tossing . . . try many ways to control the ball."

▶ Repeat all material from Beginning Grade, and then add:

". . . . Just *bouncing the ball* now, can you avoid bumping into others? . . . your eyes have to be in two places . . . up to see where you are going and down to control the ball . . . keep moving into all parts of general space."

▶ Repeat all material from Beginning and Middle Grades, and then add:

". . . . Just *tossing and catching* the ball now, can you toss the ball ahead of you a short distance so that you run or walk to catch it? . . . keep looking for empty spaces to move into . . . *control* the ball . . . what can you do if you are not catching it? . . . make shorter or lower tosses?"

Control the ball in general space

Checklist of quality factors for Problem 7

☐ Controlling ball manipulation while moving in general space.

☐ Gaining ability to see the ball and space where moving at the same time.

☐ B–M–L: Moving the ball in a variety of ways in general space (minimum of 4).

☐ M–L: Increasing number of controlled bounces while moving in general space without collisions.

☐ L: Increasing number of controlled tosses and catches while moving in general space without collisions.

When children demonstrate these factors, go on to Problem 8.

PROBLEM 8

Beginning Grade	Middle Grade	Last Grade

(Briefly explain method of getting partners. The first week is the best time to establish procedures for the year. Although it takes quite a lot of time, it saves much time in repeating over and over again throughout the year. Suggested rules:

Always choose the person closest to you.

Together, find a self space big enough for both.

If equipment is to be used, one partner gets it out, the other partner puts it away.

Anyone left without a partner, go stand beside the teacher at once.

Have the children practice free movement in general space, then find a partner on signal. Again, a game of how many counts it takes to get partners may be devised.)

"On the signal, get a partner. Put one ball away, so you have one ball for the two of you. Find a self space, and see how many ways the two of you can control the ball between you."

". . . . Keep thinking of different ways to move the ball back and forth . . . remember to control it . . . try to stay in your own space . . . have you tried bouncing and tossing and pushing it softly? . . . if rolling the ball is easy for you, try something a little harder."

▶ Repeat all material from Beginning Grade, and then add:

". . . . When you are controlling the ball well, *back up* a step or two . . . can you still control the ball? . . . are you aiming the ball at the middle of your partner's body? . . . isn't it hard to catch at your feet or over your head? . . . think of different ways to move the ball back and forth."

▶ Repeat all material from Beginning and Middle Grades, and then add:

". . . . How can you catch the ball better when it doesn't come right into your hands? . . . can you keep your eyes on the ball all the time and move your whole body so you can catch the ball in front of you instead of off to the side? . . . keep trying different ways to get the ball right to your partner . . . are you staying in your self space?"

Checklist of quality factors for Problem 8

☐ Getting partners quickly: understanding the social value of working harmoniously with whomever is nearest.

☐ Increasing control of ball manipulation; propelling it with just enough force to get it to partner; aiming for the middle of the partner's body, not at feet or higher than chest.

☐ Increasing control in catching the ball; watching it, moving into line with its flight so it can be caught in front of the body.

When children demonstrate these factors, go on to Problem 9.

PROBLEM 9

Beginning Grade	Middle Grade	Last Grade

"On the signal, follow me, putting the balls away as we pass the boxes."

(Lead children into a *circle,* then stop. Discuss what floor pattern they are standing in and whether they can get into this pattern again by themselves.)

A. "On the signal, move quickly into general space, find a self space as far away from everyone else as you can and freeze there."

(Starting signal . . . stopping signal. Check distribution of children throughout general space.)

B. "Now, when you hear the signal, see how quickly you can get back to the circle without touching anyone."

(Start . . . stop. Check distribution of children around the circle. Repeat A and B several times, giving children progressively less time to find well-distributed self spaces.)

▶ Repeat step A from Beginning Grade, and then add:

". . . . And freeze there in a very large shape."

(Next time a small shape, next time a low shape, a wide shape, a tall shape, etc.)

▶ Repeat step B from Beginning Grade, and then add:

". . . . Freeze on the circle in a shape that uses your space well."

▶ Repeat all material from Beginning and Middle Grades, and then add:

". . . . Make a different balanced shape each time you freeze."

(Repeat all of Problem 9, substituting other useful formations for the circle, e.g., one long line (side by side, then lined up behind one person), parallel lines, triangles, squares, rectangles, etc. Point out relationships to using space well on the playground, in games, etc.)

Option

Create games to be played in these formations.

Review of spacial relationships

When children use the space well, go on to Theme 2.

SECOND SET OF PROBLEMS / ORGANIZING THEME: MOVING IN DIFFERENT DIRECTIONS

Content structure (for teachers)	Objectives (for children)

Content structure (for teachers)

Concept

Movement for environmental control

Major ideas

1 *Space,* force, time, and flow are the elements of movement.
2 The dimensions of space are *directions,* levels, planes, and ranges.

Selected facts

1 Space is three-dimensional, as is the body. Both have height, width, and breadth.
2 The body can be related to the three dimensions of space in six named directions:

up   forward   right side
down   backward   left side

3 In this space-body relationship, the front of the body remains facing the same way; that is, in moving backward, the back leads.

Objectives (for children)

Children need to understand (knowledge)

1 That they can move in space in six general directions—up and down, forward and backward, to one side and to the other side.   B–M–L
2 That they can move in a vast variety of ways in any of these six directions.   B–M–L
3 That they can move objects through space in any of these directions.   M–L
4 That moving forward is usually the easiest way to move because of the way bodies are built.   L

Children need to learn how (skill)

1 To move in an increasing variety of ways in each direction.   B–M–L
2 To develop control of their locomotor and manipulative movements so they can change directions quickly and efficiently.   M–L
3 To develop control in manipulating balls while stationary and while moving.   B–M–L
4 To bend (curl), stretch, twist, and pull with force and with flow.   B–M–L

Children need to become (attitude)

The attitude objectives for this physical education program (see page 52) are broad and cannot be achieved quickly; therefore, they will be the same throughout the entire three years. Please review them occasionally.

Teaching tips for second set of problems

1 *Arrange equipment . . . before the physical education period:*
One ball per child.
One short rope (between 2 and 6 feet long) per child.
Balls and ropes placed in boxes around the edges of the room.

2 *Discuss movement vocabulary . . . in the classroom:*

direction	move to the other side
move forward	bend (curl)
move backward	stretch
move up	twist
move down	pull
move to one side	

Review vocabulary . . . self space, general space, control.

Introduction

"Today, we will begin to find many ways to <u>move in different directions.</u> The six main directions we can move are

forward	right side	up
backward	left side	down."

Developmental problems and expected outcomes

PROBLEM 10

Beginning Grade	Middle Grade	Last Grade

"On the signal, go as many places as you can in <u>general space, changing directions as you go</u> . . . sometimes forward, sometimes backward, sometimes sideways."

". . . . How many different directions have you gone? . . . remember not to touch anyone . . . have you moved backward yet? . . . and sideward?"

(Practice starting and stopping several times to check firm "freezes" and even spacing around the room.)

". . . . Do you have to slow down a little if you are going backward or sideward? . . . has anyone thought of going up and down while you travel in general space? . . . keep moving in different ways . . . make your back lead for a while or your side lead for a while."

▶ Repeat all material from Beginning Grade, and then add:

"Move on as many different body parts <u>as you can while you change direction."</u>

". . . . Not on your feet alone . . . have you tried hands and knees? . . . seats? . . . hands and feet? . . . flat bodies? . . . how quickly can you change direction from forward to back? . . . from side to side? . . . try going forward *and* up and down . . . backward *and* up and down . . . move to one side going up and to the other side going down."

▶ Repeat all material from Beginning and Middle Grades, and then add:

"Let's see just how <u>quickly you can change direction without falling down.</u> Every time you hear a signal, <u>change."</u>

(Drum beat, or vocal "change direction!" given every 5 to 10 seconds. You may let children take turns in calling directions to move, with the class responding. All children should face the teacher or leader so correct responses can be observed.)

Checklist of quality factors for Problem 10

☐ Moving in a variety of ways (minimum of 8) while traveling:
forward, with front of body leading,
backward, with back leading,
sideward, with either side leading,
up and down with any part leading.

☐ Stopping and starting quickly on signal.

☐ Listening and thinking while moving.

☐ Maintaining good spacing throughout general space while moving . . . no collisions even when moving backward.

If children are not demonstrating the last three factors, go back to Problems 1, 2, and 3. When children demonstrate these factors, go on to Problem 11.

PROBLEM 11

Beginning Grade	Middle Grade	Last Grade

"Do you remember last week? You worked on getting into a circle, then finding a self space out in general space. Try that again, but when you move, move sideways . . . making one side lead.

A. "On the signal, move sideways into a circle and stop."

(Start . . . stop. Check distribution on the circle and the shape of the circle.)

B. "On the signal, move sideways into general space, find a self space as far away from everyone else as you can, and freeze there."

(Start . . . stop. Check distribution of children throughout general space.)

(Repeat A and B several times, giving children progressively less time to find well-distributed self spaces.)

". . . . Keep one side leading all the time . . . I see some of you are sliding sideways on your feet . . . very good . . . are there other ways to move sideways? . . . on different parts of your body?"

▶ Repeat all material from Beginning Grade, and then add:

"On the signal, move sideways into general space (no circle). Explore all of general space while moving sideways."

". . . . Have you been to the corners of the room? . . . to the middle? . . . make sure one side or the other is leading all the time . . . watch the spacing . . . on how many body parts can you move sideways? . . . hands and feet . . . flat bodies . . . keep thinking of different ways . . . let one side lead for a while, then the other side."

▶ Repeat all material from Beginning and Middle Grades, and then add:

"On the signal, move sideways into general space and see what different things you can do with your feet as you go."

". . . . Have you tried moving sideways on just one foot (hopping)? . . . or on two feet held tightly together (jumping)? . . . or crossing one foot over the other (simple grapevine)? . . . how fast can you slide (on feet) sideways? . . . can you slide across the room with one side leading and slide back with the other side leading . . . no collisions!"

Checklist of quality factors for Problem 11

☐ Moving sideways in a variety of ways (minimum of 4) including on the feet, on hands and feet, on flat bodies.

☐ B: Moving sideways into and out of a circle . . . no collisions.

☐ M: Moving sideways in general space . . . no collisions.

☐ L: Using different kinds of footwork to move sideways . . . including sliding, hopping, jumping.

When children demonstrate these factors, go on to Problem 12.

PROBLEM 12

Beginning Grade	Middle Grade	Last Grade

"On the signal, move backward only. Can you keep your back leading all the time?"

". . . . Remember not to bump into anyone . . . can you find different ways to move backward? . . . where do you have to have your eyes when you are moving backward? . . . have you tried taking little steps and big steps? . . . have you tried moving backward on other parts of your body?"

▶ Repeat all material from Beginning Grade, and then add:

". . . . Work on the answer to this problem: can you move faster if you move forward or if you move backward? . . . show me your answer . . . which way is faster? . . . is moving forward or backward faster when you are on your hands and knees? . . . try it . . . is moving backward on hands and feet easy to do? . . . can you move on hands and feet with your tummies toward the ceiling? . . . try moving forward and backward while lying on your back and on your tummy . . . which way is backward when you are lying down?"

▶ Repeat all material from Beginning and Middle Grades, and then add:

"Think now about using general space well. Move forward until you come to a wall or a person, then switch very quickly to moving backward until you come to a wall or a person."

". . . . This is almost like a car getting into a parking space . . . forward . . . back . . . forward . . . back."

Checklist of quality factors for Problem 12

☐ Moving backward in a variety of ways (minimum of 6) without touching.

☐ Trying out locomotion on different body parts without much prompting by the teacher.

☐ M–L: Discovering that moving forward is usually quicker and easier than moving backward (especially running).

When children demonstrate these factors, go on to Problem 13.

PROBLEM 13

Beginning Grade	Middle Grade	Last Grade

(The teacher gets one rope and briefly demonstrates folding it so it is less than 3 feet long.)

"On the signal, get a <u>rope</u>, find a <u>self space</u>, and <u>pull hard</u> on both ends of the rope. See how many places you can take your stretched rope in your own self space."

". . . . Try to keep moving your rope all the time . . . keep it going . . . up, down, forward, back, side to side . . . how far from the middle of your body can you stretch your rope? . . . how far in front? . . . how far behind you? . . . keep pulling and stretching . . . can you bend your body sideward and keep stretching the rope? . . . bend backward? . . . feel how strong your muscles are as you pull on the ends of the rope."

▶ Repeat all material from Beginning Grade, and then add:

". . . . Try standing with your *feet wide apart* . . . then with your *feet close together* . . . which way can you get a stronger and longer bend in your body and stretch on your rope? . . . *sit down* and see how many places you can stretch your rope . . . high overhead and down near the floor . . . try *kneeling* . . . how far to the side can you bend your body and still keep moving the rope? . . . can you feel the tightness of your muscles when you pull hard on the ends of the rope?"

▶ Repeat all material from Beginning and Middle Grades, and then add:

". . . . Work toward a *continuous smooth flow* of movement with the rope . . . never stop . . . make one movement flow right into the next one . . . twist, turn, sit down, stand up, without ever stopping . . . can you put one or two feet on the rope and stretch it? . . . is anyone rolling over keeping the rope stretched?"

Checklist of quality factors for Problem 13

☐ Pulling strongly on the ends of a rope, demonstrating muscle tension in the arms.

☐ Bending the body as far as possible forward, backward, and to the sides while pulling on a rope.

☐ Extending the rope into all parts of self space . . . top, bottom, sides.

☐ M–L: Beginning to move with flow . . . continuous, smooth movement from starting signal to stopping signal.

When children demonstrate these factors, go on to Problem 14.

PROBLEM 14

Beginning Grade | Middle Grade | Last Grade

"On the signal, put your rope away, get a ball, find a space of your own, and work on bouncing and catching. Stay in your own self space if you can."

". . . . Remember *control* . . . you tell the ball where to go, don't let it tell you where to go . . . how many ways can you *bounce and catch*? . . . with two hands? . . . with one hand? . . . has anyone tried bouncing the ball while kneeling or sitting? . . . some of you are doing a dribble (a continuous bounce) . . . count how many bounces you can control in a row . . . next time, can you get more bounces?"

▶ Repeat all material from Beginning Grade, and then add:

"Staying in self space, work on tossing and catching only."

". . . . Remember *control* . . . toss the ball up only hard enough to catch it without moving out of your self space . . . where are your eyes? . . . looking at the ball? . . . try looking up first just before tossing the ball . . . does that help make the ball go straight up? . . . let your hands follow the ball up high . . . again, are your eyes on the ball as it comes down? . . . are you moving to stand right under where it is coming down? . . . do you pull the ball in to your body so it doesn't slip through your hands when you catch it?"

▶ Repeat all material from Beginning and Middle Grades, and then add:

"Now try bouncing the ball so hard that it goes high into the air. While it is up in the air, see what you can do under it."

". . . . Run under and back, turn around . . . clap hands . . . remember *control* . . . how can you make the ball go straight up? . . . are you pushing straight down evenly with both hands? . . . where are your hands for catching? . . . are they reaching straight up for the ball? . . . we've been working on directions today . . . can you change directions quickly to get right under the ball as it comes down? . . . think of many things to do under the ball while it is in the air."

Checklist of quality factors for Problem 14

☐ Increasing control of:
B—bounce and catch . . . either single or dribble . . . in self space,
M—toss and catch . . . two hands or one . . . in self space,
L—forceful bounce for height, simple movement under ball, *and* catch, in self space.

☐ Self discipline . . . using only the amount of force or speed that can be controlled.

When children demonstrate these factors, go on to Problem 15

PROBLEM 15

Beginning Grade	Middle Grade	Last Grade

"On the signal, try moving into <u>general space</u> while <u>bouncing the ball</u>."

(Allow either bounce and catch or dribble.)

"Go slowly and keep the ball low at first."

". . . . How softly and carefully can you bounce the ball? . . . have you found that if you bounce the ball too hard it gets away from you? . . . try moving *backward* or *sideward* while bouncing the ball . . . you can change directions while moving the ball, can't you?"

"Practice anything you like with the ball. Two rules:
1. control the ball,
2. don't bother anyone else."

(This freedom for children of choosing their own activity allows the teacher to observe what interests a child at the moment, what he thinks his abilities are, and to evaluate control development. Stop the group occasionally to allow the children to analyze, e.g., "Take a look at Tim (who is tossing and catching with both hands) . . . what do you notice about the way he is catching the ball? . . . what do you notice about the way he is throwing the ball?")

▶ Repeat all material from Beginning Grade, through the subproblems, and then add:

". . . . Now try *tossing and catching* the ball as you move into *general space* . . . pretend the ball is breakable, and you don't want to break it . . . handle it very softly and carefully . . . what three directions are you using? (body-forward, ball-up, and ball-down) . . . what two places do you have to take your eyes? (on the ball and around the room) . . . listen to hear soft steps and no balls touching the floor . . . slowly try out moving in other directions while tossing and catching . . . try going backward . . . and sideward . . . and can anyone sit down and stand up while tossing the ball?"

"Practice any kind of activity with the ball. Two rules:
1. control the ball,
2. don't interfere with anyone else."

▶ Repeat all material from Beginning and Middle Grades, through the subproblems, and then add:

". . . . Move into *general space* while using the ball . . . the only rule is that you cannot carry the ball. Keep it moving. Then *listen*:

(Start, and give signals verbally.)

". . . . Backward . . . forward . . . sideward . . . the other side . . . around in a big circle . . . around in a small circle."

(Repeat several times.)

"Practice any kind of activity with the ball. Two rules:
1. control the ball,
2. use your space wisely."

Checklist of quality factors for Problem 15

☐ Controlling ball manipulation while on the move in general space.

☐ B–M–L: Increasing number of consecutive controlled bounces on the move (minimum of 5).

☐ M–L: Increasing number of consecutive controlled tosses on the move (minimum of five).

☐ L: Quick change of direction on signal while manipulating a ball in general space.

When children demonstrate these factors, go on to Problem 16.

PROBLEM 16

Beginning Grade	Middle Grade	Last Grade

"On the signal, get a partner, put one ball away, find a space of your own, and bounce the ball between you."

(Practice getting partners quickly, if necessary.)

". . . .Stand close enough together so that one bounce will take the ball right into your partner's hands . . . are you pushing the ball out and down to the floor? . . . can your hands follow the ball down toward the floor? . . . is the ball easier to catch when it is down low, up high, or in the middle of your body? (middle)"

(Again stop to analyze one or more couples who are successfully bouncing the ball back and forth. If the children do not see it, point out the direct path of the ball. A direct path

is better than a looping path

▶ Repeat all material from Beginning Grade, and then add:

". . . . Work now on *tossing and catching.* . . . try soft, short tosses until you get ten in a row . . . then step back and try for ten more in a row . . . are there different ways you can toss the ball? . . . some are using two hands, others one hand . . . some are tossing the ball in a straight line and others are tossing the ball high so it comes down near the partner's hands . . . can you think of different ways to toss the ball *with control?*"

▶ Repeat all material from Beginning and Middle Grades, and then add:

". . . . You and your partner move slowly into *general space while tossing or bouncing* the ball back and forth . . . now you really must look many different places . . . what direction do you aim the ball? . . . right to your partner or ahead of him? . . . try bouncing or tossing the ball a little bit in front of your partner . . . keep working on moving and tossing . . . discover a way that works for the two of you."

Checklist of quality factors for Problem 16

☐ B: Minimum of 4 consecutive bounce passes in self space.

☐ B: Minimum of 10 consecutive tosses and catches in self space . . . ball doesn't touch floor.

☐ L: Beginning control of passing a ball back and forth while on the move in general space . . . minimum of 2 consecutive passes.

When children demonstrate these factors, go on to Problem 17.

PROBLEM 17

Beginning Grade	Middle Grade	Last Grade

(Children may sit down while the teacher lays out 6 to 8 ropes on the floor in a circle. Several children may assist in getting out equipment. The teacher may explain the next problem while laying out the ropes.)

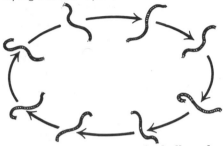

"On the signal, put away the balls and follow me around the room. Each time you go over a rope, do something different."

". . . . The problem is to keep spaced out around the room."

(Stop and start several times to check distribution.)

". . . . Can you move forward and backward and sideward over the ropes? . . . keep *thinking* about different ways to move and keep changing directions as you go. . . . relax right where you are."

(Stress spacing . . . an awareness of when to speed up and when to slow down to keep an even distribution around the circle. This concept is very difficult but should be introduced and then revisited frequently.)

▶ Repeat all material from Beginning Grade, and then add:

". . . . Can you change direction each time you go over a rope? . . . have you gone over a rope backward? . . . you may have to slow down to see where you are going . . . have you gone over a rope sideways?"

(You may see cartwheels here . . . watch spacing.)

". . . . How high can you get into the air as you go over a rope? . . . and how softly can you land?"

▶ Repeat all material from Beginning and Middle Grades, and then add:

". . . . Change direction *on the call:* everyone forward over 2 ropes in different ways . . . everyone backward over 3 ropes in as many ways as you can . . . sideways over 1 rope . . . the other side, leading over 2 ropes . . . how *quickly* can you change direction?"

(Repeat. *Option:* This may be developed into a game, with students devising the rules.)

Review: Spacing, moving in different ways in six directions, changing direction quickly.

When children use space well and demonstrate variety of movement in named directions, go on to Theme 3.

THIRD SET OF PROBLEMS / ORGANIZING THEME: MOVING AT DIFFERENT LEVELS

Content structure (for teachers) | **Objectives (for children)**

Concept

Movement for environmental control

Major ideas

1 *Space*, force, time, and flow are the elements of movement.
2 The dimensions of space are directions, *levels*, planes, and ranges.

Selected facts

1 Levels in space are areas of space in terms of high, medium, and low in relation to the body when standing.
2 The low level is defined as the area the legs *naturally* move in when one is walking . . . the area from the hips down.
3 The medium level is defined as the area the torso naturally moves in when one is walking . . . the area between the shoulders and hips.
4 The high level is defined as the area from the shoulders on up when one is walking.
5 The levels remain constant even though the whole body may move in a single level; e.g., rolling is executed at the low level.

Children need to understand (knowledge)

1 That they can move in self space or general space at three named levels: high, medium, low.　B–M–L
2 That they can move in a vast variety of ways using one, two, or three levels at a time.　B–M–L
3 That they can move objects through space at different levels.　B–M–L

Children need to learn how (skill)

1 To move in a variety of ways using one (low), two (low and medium), and three levels (low, medium, and high) at a time.　B–M–L
2 To change level *and* direction more quickly and smoothly.　B–M–L
3 To develop more control in moving balls at middle and low levels in a variety of ways.　B–M–L
4 To begin to develop control in moving balls with the feet.　M–L

Children need to become (attitude)

The attitude objectives for this physical education program (see page 52) are broad and cannot be achieved quickly; therefore, they will be the same throughout the entire three years. Please review them occasionally.

Teaching tips for third set of problems

1 *Arrange equipment . . . before the physical education period:* One very soft ball per child in equipment boxes at edges of room. (Yarn balls are ideal. Instructions for making yarn balls are on page 42. A crumpled paper ball with several strips of tape around it is quite satisfactory, although not as soft or long-lasting.)
2 *Discuss movement vocabulary . . . in the classroom:*

level	push the ball with the feet
move at a high level	kick softly
move at a medium level	shape
move at a low level	pass
combine a level and a direction	

Introduction

"Our new theme is moving many ways at different levels. The three main levels are: high, medium, low."

Developmental problems and expected outcomes

PROBLEM 18

Beginning Grade	Middle Grade	Last Grade

A. "On the signal, stand up, hold your arms straight out at shoulder level, and spin around."

(Start . . . stop.)

"Everything above your arms as you were spinning is your high level. On the signal, show me how high your high level is in self space."

". . . . Touch all of your self space that is at a high level . . . all of your self space above your shoulders . . . some of you are reaching into and touching your high level with your arms and head . . . can you get one foot or two feet into your high level?"

(Stop.)

▶ Repeat all of step A from Beginning Grade, and then add:

A. "On the signal, reach into and touch as much of your high level as you can with one or both of your feet."

". . . . Stretch that foot into *all* parts of your high level . . . good . . . some of you are standing on one foot and kicking the other foot into the high level . . . others are taking weight on your hands and moving one or two feet around at high level . . . what other ways are there?"

(Stop.)

▶ Repeat all of Step A from Beginning and Middle Grades, and then add:

A. "On the signal, see how much of your whole body you can get into the high level . . . experiment with different ways."

(Encourage soft landings on the feet, and strong use of the arms to get higher in the air. If anyone attempts a "horizontal type" jump such as a western roll or a barrel roll, have him demonstrate it to the class as a good way to get most of the body up at a high level. Stop.)

B. "Your medium level is the self space you can reach into between your shoulders and hips when you are standing. On the signal, show me how big your self space is at a medium level."

". . . . How much bending and twisting can you do at your medium level? . . . can you take your head all around your medium level? . . . what can you do with your feet and your legs at a medium level? . . . stay in your own self space . . . keep on moving and exploring."

(Stop.)

▶ Repeat all of Step B from Beginning Grade, and then add:

". . . . How much of your *medium level* can you reach into and touch with *three parts* of your body touching the floor? . . . with two parts touching the floor? . . . with four parts touching the floor."

(Moving on hands and feet will not solve this problem as children will be moving at a low level unless a very high bridge is made . . . discuss reason with the children. Stop.)

▶ Repeat all of step B from Beginning and Middle Grades, and then add:

". . . . Make a *balanced shape* with almost all of your body at the *medium level*, and *hold* it very still while you count to ten . . . then make another balanced shape."

(Have children continue to change shape and hold. Stop.)

C. "The rest of your self space is called the low level . . . all the space your legs move in when you are walking . . . everything from the hips down. On the signal, show me how big the low level of your self space is by using your legs."

". . . .How many different ways can you move your legs at the low level? . . . standing up . . . sitting down . . . lying down . . . on fronts and on backs . . . really stretch your legs to reach into all parts of your self space . . . now do you know just how big the low level of your self space is?"

▶ Repeat all of step C from Beginning Grade, and then add:

". . . . See how much of the *low level* you can touch, with any body part, from these *different starting positions:*
lying on your back,
lying on your tummy,
on hands and one knee,
on hands and one foot, tummy down,
on hands and one foot, tummy up."

(Have children suggest and demonstrate other starting positions . . . exploration of space at the low level should be free however, and not copied from the demonstrator.)

▶ Repeat all of step C from Beginning and Middle Grades, and then add:

". . . . Use *different body parts* to show *how big* the *low level* of your self space is . . . hands . . . head . . . back . . . knee . . . elbow."

(Children may devise a game of suggesting body parts for all to use.)

High level

Middle level

Low level

Checklist of quality factors for Problem 18

☐ Moving in a wide variety of ways in self space
(nonlocomotion)
at a high level (minimum of 8 ways),
at a medium level (minimum of 8 ways),
at a low level (minimum of 8 ways).

☐ Demonstrating an understanding of a person's own
areas of high, medium, and low. When a problem calls
for moving at a low level, *all* body parts should be
lower than hip level when standing.

☐ When a problem calls for moving at a medium level,
all body parts should be lower than shoulder level
when standing.

☐ Willingness to continue exploration and to find new
solutions without constant teacher direction.

When children demonstrate these factors, go on to Problem 19.

PROBLEM 19

Beginning Grade   Middle Grade   Last Grade

"On the signal, move into <u>general space</u> traveling <u>up and down</u> as you go."

". . . . Have you been to all parts of the room? . . . are you trying to keep the spacing even as you go? . . . remember not to touch anyone . . . are you changing direction, too? . . . sometimes backward, sometimes forward, sometimes sideward . . . still going up and down . . . high level, middle level, low level, middle, high . . . high to low to high . . . many ways to move . . . sometimes fast, sometimes slowly . . . all over general space."

(Stop and start several times. Check distribution throughout general space.)

▶ Repeat all material from Beginning Grade, and then add:

"On the signal, move into <u>general space</u> taking your <u>head</u> into <u>different levels</u> as you go."

". . . . Keep moving into all parts of the room . . . have you moved backward and sideward yet? . . . what different things can you do with your feet or arms when your head is at a low level? . . . remember to move your head from a high level to a low level as you go."

▶ Repeat all material from Beginning and Middle Grades, and then add:

"On the signal, move into <u>general space</u> taking your <u>feet</u> into <u>different levels</u> as you go."

". . . . Keep moving into general space . . . are you using the space well? . . . no collisions? feet high, then low in different ways . . . have you tried getting both feet into the medium level on one side or one foot on each side? . . . how many unusual jumps or kicks can you try?"

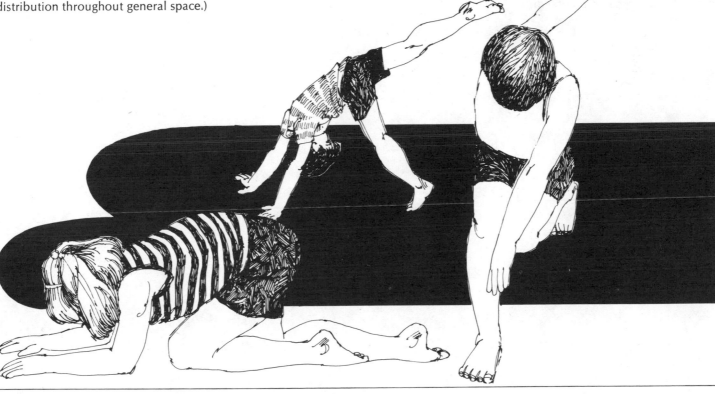

Checklist of quality factors for Problem 19

☐ Changing levels while moving through general space in a variety of ways:

B—minimum of 4 ways including changing direction,
M—minimum of 6 ways including whole body change of level and direction,
L—minimum of 8 ways including moving the feet into the high level while traveling.

☐ Using space wisely without collisions.

When children demonstrate these factors, go on to Problem 20.

PROBLEM 20

Beginning Grade	Middle Grade	Last Grade

"On the signal, move into <u>general space</u> at the <u>low level</u> only."

". . . . How many different ways can you move with your whole body at a low level? . . . keep trying different ways to move your body weight . . . can your elbows or your knees help you to move? . . . or can you move with your whole front on the floor? . . . what animal moves this way? . . . have you tried moving sideways or in a circle at a low level? . . . decide on one very unusual way to move at a low level."

(Have half the class watch the other half show their unusual ways to move, then reverse. Then repeat the problem.)

▶ Repeat all material from Beginning Grade, and then add:

". . . . Can you move at a *low level* with only *two parts* of your body touching the *floor*? . . . keep moving into general space . . . try two different parts . . . now try moving with three parts touching the floor . . . count how many different ways you can move at a low level with no more than three parts touching the floor."

▶ Repeat all material from Beginning and Middle Grades, and then add:

". . . . Try these ways of moving at a low level:
move on three parts backward . . .
move on four parts sideward . . .
move on two parts forward . . .
move on the whole body sideward . . .
find the quickest way you can move at a low level . . .
find a way to move more slowly."

Checklist of quality factors for Problem 20

☐ Moving through general space in a wide variety of ways at a low level (minimum of eight ways).

☐ Changing direction while moving at a low level.

☐ Taking weight on different body parts . . . hands, arms, elbows, knees, seats, whole bodies, heads, etc.

When children demonstrate these factors, go on to Problem 21.

PROBLEM 21

Beginning Grade	Middle Grade	Last Grade

"On the signal, see what you can do to get as much of your body as possible into the <u>high level</u> while moving into general space.

". . . . Can you get all of your body into the air? (yes) . . . can you get all of your body into your high level? (no) . . . can you get one foot or one knee into your high level? . . . how many ways? . . . can anyone get two feet into the high level?"

(Those who are ready may try a cartwheel or a mule kick.)

▶ Repeat all material from Beginning Grade, and then add:

". . . . Find ways to move in which your *seat* is *higher than* your *head* . . . your toes are higher than your head . . . your tummy is higher than any other part . . . is your tummy at the high level? (no) . . . why not?"

(Discuss the difference between moving a body part at the "high level" and moving a body part "higher than" another part.)

▶ Repeat all material from Beginning and Middle Grades, and then add:

". . . . Try to get your *head and arms as high as possible now* . . . how can you get them higher? . . . are you landing softly . . . are you using your arms and your knees to help you get more height? . . . try making a *running jump* for *height* and a *running jump* for *distance* . . . what different things can you do?"

(Select a good long jump and a good high jump. Have several demonstrations with children analyzing knee spring, use of arms, etc. Then repeat the problem.)

Checklist of quality factors for Problem 21

☐ Moving at a high level in general space in a variety of ways (minimum of 6 ways) including moving with different parts at a high level, not just the head which is naturally at a high level when walking or running.

☐ M–L: Taking part or all of the body weight on arms to get one or both feet into the high level.

☐ L: Using purposeful arm swing and knee spring to gain height or distance when jumping.

When children demonstrate these factors, go on to Problem 22.

PROBLEM 22

Beginning Grade	Middle Grade	Last Grade

"On the signal, get a yarn ball, move into general space, and see how many ways you can move the ball with control."

"... You have been working on bouncing and tossing with control ... which movement doesn't work with a yarn ball? (bouncing) ... are the yarn balls easy to toss and catch? ... can you dig your fingers into the ball to catch it? ... have you tried pushing the ball with your feet? ... or with your head? ... how many other ways can you find to move the ball softly about the room, keeping it close to you? ... have you tried changing levels? ... move the ball at a very *low level* for a while, then at a *high level* for a while."

▶ Repeat all material from Beginning Grade, and then add:

"... Still traveling in general space, move the ball at a *very low level* only ... how close to you can you keep it as you push it around? ... give very soft, gentle taps or pushes to the ball so it doesn't get away from you ... to control a ball at a low level, you need to keep it just a *little* way ahead of you ... push the ball with as many body parts as you can ... how many have you tried?"

▶ Repeat all material from Beginning and Middle Grades, and then add:

"... Now work on pushing the ball softly and in *control with* your *feet* only ... can you keep the ball very close to your feet all the time? ... which part of your foot makes the best pusher? ... your toes? ... or the inside of your foot? ... or the outside of your foot? ... try all different parts of your foot ... can you use your heel and still push the ball softly? ... can you move a little faster into general space and still control the ball? ... what two places do you have to keep looking?"

Checklist of quality factors for Problem 22

☐ Experimenting with and learning to control yarn balls in many ways. Minimums: B—four ways, M—six ways, L—eight ways.

☐ Moving a ball at a low level in a variety of ways—minimums: B—two ways, M—four ways, L—six ways.

☐ Avoiding collisions even though the eyes must be down on the ball most of the time.

☐ L—Controlling the ball at the low level with the feet: tapping or pushing it softly with the feet while running or walking; keeping the ball just slightly ahead of the running (walking) feet.

When children demonstrate these factors, go on to Problem 23.

PROBLEM 23

Beginning Grade	Middle Grade	Last Grade

"On the signal, find a self space to stay in, hold the ball in both hands, and see if you can make the ball change levels, holding on to it all the time."

". . . . Can you follow these words? Hold the ball at a high level . . . low level . . . middle level . . . are you and the ball changing levels?"

(Continue until you see that all the children understand the vocabulary.)

". . . . Find another way to hold the ball (under the chin, between the feet, behind the knee, etc.) . . . now see if you can move the ball from high level to low level to high level in many ways . . . find your favorite and most unusual way . . . when you are ready, we will look at it."

(Half the class watches the other half briefly; reverse. Discuss many ways to change level.)

▶ Repeat all material from Beginning Grade, and then add:

". . . . *Hold the ball* with your *feet* or *legs* . . . and try to follow these words: Hold the ball at a high level . . . low level . . . middle level . . . high to low very quickly . . . high to low as slowly as you can . . . hold the ball another way."

(Repeat the directions.)

". . . . How smoothly can you move from one level to another? . . . try to make continuous, flowing movements, no stops and starts or jerks . . . just keep g-o-i-n-g s-m-o-o-t-h-l-y."

▶ Repeat all material from Beginning and Middle Grades, and then add:

". . . . Staying in your own self space, see how many *different ways* you can *hold the ball* at the *high level* . . . when you find a way, *hold that shape very still for a few seconds,* then find another way . . . count the different shapes you can make, holding the ball very still at a high level . . . find at least five different ways . . . how can you get the ball even higher and still hold it? . . . how much stretch can you get with an arm or with the legs?"

Checklist of quality factors for Problem 23

☐ Demonstrating understanding of movement vocabulary . . . all should respond correctly and in a variety of ways.

☐ Using different parts of the body as the base of support . . . back, shoulders, hands, one hand and one foot, etc.

☐ Stretching to full capacity . . . "a little higher" and "a little longer."

☐ M–L: Beginning to make movement flow from one level to another.

☐ L: Holding shapes or balances *very still* for a few seconds, so they can be recognized before moving into the next shape.

When children demonstrate these factors, go on to Problem 24.

PROBLEM 24

Beginning Grade	Middle Grade	Last Grade

"On the signal, get a partner, put one of the balls away, find a self space, and see how many ways you can move the other ball back and forth between you."

". . . . Can you still make the ball go straight to your partner? . . . find ways to pass the ball to your partner at the middle level . . . can you pass it back and forth four times without losing control? . . . find ways to move the ball back and forth at the low level . . . what different body parts can you use for pushing the ball to each other at a low level? . . . can you stop the ball when it is coming to you without using your hands?"

▶ Repeat all material from Beginning Grade, and then add:

". . . . *Move* the *ball back and forth* at a *low level* using the *feet only* to push the ball and to stop the ball . . . stand close together at first and be sure to push the ball softly . . . keep the ball at a low level . . . don't let it go up high . . . when you can make the ball go right to your partner at a low level, then step back a little farther apart . . . what part of your foot doesn't work very well as a pusher? (the toes) . . . are you stopping the ball without using your hands?"

▶ Repeat all material from Beginning and Middle Grades, and then add:

". . . . When you and your partner are *passing and stopping the ball* well, try moving slowly into *general space*, still passing the ball back and forth with your feet . . . you really need control now . . . no collisions . . . move into empty spaces."

(Allow enough time for full exploration, as this will be difficult for many.)

Checklist of quality factors for Problem 24

☐ B–M–L: Ability to complete four passes at a medium or low level in a variety of ways.

☐ M–L: Controlled passing of a ball with the feet so that it stays close to the ground and goes right to a partner. Stopping a ball without using the hands (minimum of two passes and stops).

☐ L: Beginning to control passing with the feet while moving into general space (minimum of two passes).

When children demonstrate these factors, go on to Problem 25.

PROBLEM 25

Beginning Grade	Middle Grade	Last Grade

"On the signal, put the balls away, find a space of your own, and make yourself as small as possible in that space. Then listen for changes in shape."

". . . . Make a high stretched shape and hold it very still . . . freeze there . . . make a big shape at the low level and freeze . . . make a medium level shape with your head on the floor."

(Add as many variations as you and the students can devise.)

▶ Repeat all material from Beginning Grade, and then add:

". . . . A high shape with only one foot on the floor . . . a medium level shape with four parts on the floor . . . a low shape with three parts on the floor."

▶ Repeat all material from Beginning and Middle Grades. In addition:

(Give the same problem, but add slow flow between shapes as a requirement. Each shape is to flow into the next one. You will have to time your words according to student responses.)

Review of levels

When children use levels well, go on to Theme 4.

FOURTH SET OF PROBLEMS / ORGANIZING THEME: MOVING IN DIFFERENT RANGES AND BY CHANGING SHAPES

Content structure (for teachers)	Objectives (for children)

Concept

Movement for environmental control

Major ideas

1 The body is the instrument of movement; it has a *shape* or posture at any given moment.
2 *Space,* force, time, and flow are the elements of movement.
3 The dimensions of space are directions, levels, planes and *ranges.*

Selected facts

1 *Shape* is the position the body takes in space at any given instant in time. At that single moment the body is not in motion; it is static.
2 Movement is attained by a change in shape.
3 The four main types of body shapes are rounded, straight and narrow, straight and wide, and twisted.
4 *Range* is the relationship of the body to self space, denoting into how much of self space the body is extended.
5 Range relationships are near to and far from, long and short, large and small, and wide and narrow. They may be relationships of one body part to another or of body parts to other objects in space.

Children need to understand (knowledge)

1 That they can make and hold a vast variety of body shapes, including variations of rounded, straight and narrow, straight and wide, and twisted shapes. B–M–L
2 That they can control the range of their movements to fit the available space. B–M–L
3 That movements must usually be reduced in range when space is limited. B–M–L

Children need to learn how (skill)

1 To move in a wide variety of ways, both when the body is fully extended and when the available space allows smaller movements only. B–M–L
2 To "feel" full extension and the difference between larger and smaller movements. B–M–L
3 To develop control in making and holding many different body shapes, both alone and with others. B–M–L
4 To move smoothly from one shape to another (flow). M–L

Children need to become (attitude)

The attitude objectives for this physical education program (see page 52) are broad and cannot be achieved quickly; therefore, they will be the same throughout the entire three years. Please review them occasionally.

Teaching tips for fourth set of problems

1 *Arrange equipment . . . before the physical education period:* One ball per child, in boxes around the edges of the room.
2 *Discuss movement vocabulary . . . in the classroom:*

Range	Shape
near to—far from	rounded
long—short	straight and narrow
large—small	straight and wide
wide—narrow	twisted

Introduction

"Our new theme is moving in different <u>ranges</u> (<u>sizes</u>) and by changing <u>shapes</u>. <u>Range means how close one thing is to another</u>. Is your nose near to or far from your feet? Can you move your <u>nose near to</u> your <u>feet</u>? <u>Try it</u>. That makes your body into a <u>different shape</u>, doesn't it? Is it a big shape or a little shape? Now, make the <u>biggest shape</u> you can and <u>hold</u> it very still—just like a freeze."

Far from

Near to

Developmental problems and expected outcomes

PROBLEM 26

Beginning Grade	Middle Grade	Last Grade

"On the signal, move into <u>general space</u> using the <u>biggest movements</u> you can as you go."

". . . . Can you "feel" how very big you are? . . . and how big your movements are? . . . how far out are you reaching with each step or with each arm? . . . stretch and reach with every part of your body . . . can you do this at a very low level? . . . how big can you be when you are moving backward or in another direction? . . . keep moving into general space with big movements . . . change level . . . and direction as you go."

▶ Repeat all material from Beginning Grade, and then add:

". . . . Now move into *general space* using as many very *small movements* as you can . . . can you move very quickly using tiny movements? . . . try it . . . *very* small steps if you are on your feet . . . can you go very fast? . . . what is the smallest movement you can do at a *low level* and still keep moving into general space? . . . see how many different parts you can keep moving, doing small movements as you go . . . head moving, too? . . . elbows? . . . knees? . . . whole body making small movements? . . . find a movement you like that is very small, then see if you can do the same movement making it very big."

▶ Repeat all material from Beginning and Middle Grades, and then add:

". . . . Can you follow these words?"

(Direction   Level   Range)

forward . . . high . . . big movements
sideward . . . middle . . .small movements
backward . . .low . . . big movements
backward . . .high . . . small movements
sideward . . . low . . . big movements
forward . . . middle . . .big movements

(Add other variations that occur to you and the children.)

Checklist of quality factors for Problem 26

☐ B–M–L: Moving in general space in a variety of ways, including level and direction changes, while extending body parts into as much self space as possible (large range of movement). Minimums: B—six ways, M—eight ways, L—fifteen ways.

☐ M–L: Contrasting and "feeling" the difference between small and large movements.

☐ B–M–L: Using the total body, not just the arms, to increase the range of movement.

When children demonstrate these factors, go on to Problem 27.

PROBLEM 27

Beginning Grade	Middle Grade	Last Grade

"On the signal, keep moving with <u>big</u> <u>movements</u> into <u>general space</u>, but as you move, come close to someone else, then spring away and move close to another person."

". . . . Can you be very careful not to touch each other? . . . go as close as you can, then spring away . . . you will be going 'near to' and 'far from' . . . notice that sometimes you need to make your movements smaller when you are 'near to' someone and that you can make them bigger when you are 'far from' anyone."

▶ Repeat all material from Beginning Grade, and then add:

". . . . Still keep *moving close* to someone, then *spring away* without touching but . . . move *backward!*"

(Allow time for exploring this way, then:)

"Move sideways!"

(Time.)

"Move at a low level!"

(Time. And so on.)

▶ Repeat all material from Beginning and Middle Grades, and then add:

". . . . How quickly can you *change directions* as you go? . . . change direction each time you come 'near to' someone . . . for example, move forward until you meet someone, then move backward until you meet someone else, and so on . . . try *changing level* each time you meet someone . . . how quickly and smoothly can you change level?"

Checklist of quality factors for Problem 27

☐ Moving "near to" and "far from" others without collisions.

☐ Decreasing the range of movements when moving "near to" someone or whenever space is reduced enough to necessitate it.

☐ Adjusting to an environment which is constantly changing by movements of other people.

☐ M–L: Quick changes of direction to avoid collisions.

☐ L: Quick changes of level and direction to avoid collisions.

When children demonstrate these factors, go on to Problem 28.

PROBLEM 28

Beginning Grade	Middle Grade	Last Grade

"On the signal, move as quickly as you can into general space, staying as 'far from' everyone else as you can."

". . . . Keep moving quickly, using the space well . . . stay far from everyone else . . . how many different ways can you move quickly?"

(Stop.)

"Now, use only half the space."

(The teacher points out new boundaries.)

". . . . Can you still keep moving without touching? . . . do you need more control of your body in a smaller space? . . . see if you can move a little more quickly and still not touch each other."

▶ Repeat all material from Beginning Grade. In addition:

(Gradually decrease the amount of general space until students are nearly shoulder to shoulder. Then stop to discuss the need for control when space is limited: speed must be reduced, and range of movements must be smaller.)

▶ Repeat all material from Beginning and Middle Grades. In addition:

(Repeat the sequence in Problem 28 several times but with a different level or direction each time.)

". . . . Backward . . . sideward . . . at a low level . . . at a middle level."

(Use various combinations of levels and directions.)

Checklist of quality factors for Problem 28

☐ Adjusting the range of body movements to fit the available space.

When children demonstrate these factors, go on to Problem 29.

PROBLEM 29

Beginning Grade	Middle Grade	Last Grade

"On the signal, get a ball and move into **general space.** For weeks now you've **been working on different ways to bounce and toss and push balls. Now see if you can keep the ball very 'near to' you while you stay 'far from' everyone else.**"

". . . . How 'near to' you can you keep the ball while you bounce or toss or push it? . . . stay 'far from' everyone else . . . you really are controlling the ball when you keep it 'near to' you."

(Stop. Gradually decrease the amount of general space, allowing practice time after each reduction in space.)

▶ Repeat all material from Beginning Grade, and then add:

". . . . Using all the space again, *toss or bounce* the ball as forcefully as you can and still control it . . . move into general space."

(Stop. Gradually decrease space. Discuss necessity of decreasing range and force of movements when space is limited.)

▶ Repeat all material from Beginning and Middle Grades, and then add:

". . . . Still *bouncing or tossing* the balls with control, try to *follow these words:* . . . everyone 'near to' each other . . . everyone 'far from' each other . . . two's 'near to' each other . . . four's 'near to' each other . . . eight's 'near to' each other."

Checklist of quality factors for Problem 29

☐ Controlled manipulation of a ball by keeping it "near to" the body . . . low bounce and catch, low continuous dribble, small toss and catch, continuous pat bouncing in the air, dribble keeping the ball close to the feet (minimum: ball in control for two minutes).

☐ Reducing the force, range, and speed of body movements when space is limited.

When children demonstrate these factors, go on to Problem 30.

PROBLEM 30

Beginning Grade	Middle Grade	Last Grade

"On the signal, put away the balls, find a space of your own, and make several very rounded or ball-like shapes."

". . . . Show me how round you can be . . . no elbows or knees sticking out . . . find one rounded shape and freeze, then find another rounded shape and freeze . . . have you made a very small rounded shape? . . . and a very large rounded shape? . . . can you move in a rounded way *out* of your space and back *into* it? . . . try using just half of your body to make rounded shapes . . . can you make two or three rounded shapes at the same time?"

(Repeat the above sequence, substituting *twisted* shapes for rounded shapes.)

"Now see if you can make your body into many different straight and narrow shapes."

". . . . Have you tried making straight and narrow shapes at different levels? . . . can you make your straight and narrow shapes lean one way and then the other way? . . . can you move in a straight and narrow way out of your space and back into it? . . . at a low level? . . . at a high level?"

(Repeat the above sequence, substituting *straight and wide* shapes for straight and narrow shapes.)

▶ Repeat all material from Beginning Grade, and then add:

"Listen to the drum (or hand claps). On eight beats, stretch slowly until you are in as big a rounded shape as possible . . . on the next eight beats, move slowly into a different rounded shape."

(Repeat several times, adding rounded shape at a low level . . . rounded shape at a middle level, etc.)

"On eight beats, collapse slowly . . . try to melt right down to the floor."

(Repeat the above sequence, substituting *twisted shapes* for rounded shapes.)

". . . . On *eight beats:* See how far from your hands your feet can be . . . at a high level . . . see if you can make a shape with your hands and feet "near to" each other and your tummy "far from" them. . . . take the full eight beats to make a small, straight, and narrow shape . . . to make a large, straight, and narrow shape . . . to make a small, straight, and wide shape . . . to make a large, straight, and wide shape."

▶ Repeat all material from Beginning and Middle Grades, and then add:

**"On four beats, make a rounded shape with your hands and feet as "far from" each other as possible . . .
On four beats, make a rounded shape with your feet and head as "near to" each other as possible . . .
On four beats, make a rounded shape with your feet higher than your head . . .
On four beats, collapse completely."**

(Repeat the above sequence, substituting *twisted shapes* for rounded shapes.)

". . . . On *four beats,* make a shape: large range—low level . . . small range—medium level . . . straight and narrow—low . . . straight and narrow—high . . . straight and wide—medium . . . half of your body straight and narrow, the other half straight and wide . . . half rounded, half straight . . . half twisted, half rounded."

Checklist of quality factors for Problem 30

☐ Making and holding very still a wide variety of rounded shapes (minimum four), twisted shapes (minimum four), straight and narrow shapes (minimum four), straight and wide shapes (minimum four).

☐ L: Combination of shapes (minimum four).

☐ Responding realistically to "near to" and "far from" problems.

☐ M–L: Moving with control in a specified amount of time (8 beats, 4 beats).

When children demonstrate these factors, go on to Problem 31.

PROBLEM 31

Beginning Grade	Middle Grade	Last Grade

"On the signal, find a <u>partner</u> close to you and see how many <u>different shapes</u> you and your partner can make together."

(Allow time for free exploration.)

". . . . Try these different shapes: a big, rounded shape . . . another big, rounded shape . . . a small, rounded shape . . . a very long, straight and narrow shape . . . a twisted shape . . . hold it very still . . . the widest shape the two of you can make."

▶ Repeat as usual, and then have the children *form groups of four* and repeat the material from the Beginning Grade. Then add:

". . . . Two at a high level, two at a low level . . . all hands and feet "near to" each other . . . all feet as "far from" each other as possible . . . all feet higher than heads and in a rounded group shape."
(Have children hold shapes very still for five counts after they are made. Have each group demonstrate its favorite shape.)

▶ Repeat all material from Beginning and Middle Grades, and then add:

". . . . Each group choose two shapes . . . see if you can hold the first shape for five counts, then move smoothly into the second shape and hold it for five counts . . . can you keep moving back and forth very smoothly from one shape to the other holding each shape for five counts?"

Checklist of quality factors for Problem 31

☐ Making and holding very still a wide variety of shapes with one or more partners.

☐ L: Beginning to develop control in holding a shape, then moving smoothly into another shape (flow).

When children demonstrate these factors, go on to Problem 32.

PROBLEM 32

Beginning Grade	Middle Grade	Last Grade

(An adapted version of the game "Busy Bee.")

"On the signal, you and your partner find a space of your own and listen for signals."

(Example of signals.)

". . . . Face to face and rounded . . . back to back and straight . . . very long and wide . . . one big and one small . . . head to head, straight and narrow, . . . *Busy Bee.*"

(Signals can be varied. Whenever the signal "Busy Bee" is called, change partners as quickly as possible . . . and the game continues.)

▶ Before playing "Busy Bee," have the children make up a *list of* many different *shapes* for the teacher to call. Then proceed as in Beginning Grade.

▶ Before playing "Busy Bee," have the children *draw shapes on cards* to be held up instead of called. A child may then be the leader. When the child leader calls (or shows) the card "Busy Bee", he then gets a partner. The person left without a partner becomes the new leader to hold up cards, and the game continues.

Review space dimensions: direction, level, range, shape.

When children demonstrate an understanding of these space dimensions, go on to Theme 5.

FIFTH SET OF PROBLEMS/ORGANIZING THEME: MOVING IN THE AIR (FLIGHT)

Content structure (for teachers)	Objectives (for children)

Concept

Movement for environmental control

Major idea

1   Flight occurs when the body moves unsupported in space.

Selected facts

1   *Flight* is a form of locomotion involving three phases —takeoff, actual flight, and landing.
2   *Takeoff:* ankles, knees, and hips flex and then thrust against the floor to eject the body into the air; arms assist when raised forcefully in the direction of flight.
3   *Actual flight:* the shape of the body in flight can be altered by curling, stretching, or arching.
4   *Landing:* the ankles, knees and hips flex again to absorb the force of landing when the landing is made on the feet.

Children need to understand (knowledge)

1   That they can move unsupported through the air for short periods of time in many different body shapes.   B–M–L
2   That flexing ankles, knees, and hips helps produce force to get into the air.   B–M–L
3   That flexing ankles, knees, and hips helps absorb force so that they can land safely and softly on the feet.   B–M–L

Children need to learn how (skill)

1   To develop more controlled flight—takeoff, actual flight, and soft landing on the feet.   B–M–L
2   To develop control in making and holding different body shapes in flight.   B–M–L
3   To flex knees, ankles, and hips, both for takeoff and for soft landing on the feet.   B–M–L
4   To move unsupported through the air in a wide variety of ways.   B–M–L
5   To avoid collisions during flight and landing, realizing that flight takes place in space and that adequate self space is needed in the air and at the landing point.   B–M–L
6   To organize themselves into harmonious small working groups, keeping good spacing and taking turns.   B–M–L

Children need to become (attitude)

The attitude objectives for this physical education program (see page 52) are broad and cannot be achieved quickly; therefore, they will be the same throughout the entire three years. Please review them occasionally.

Teaching tips for fifth set of problems

1   *Arrange equipment . . . before the physical education period:* One ball per child . . . as many boxes (strong enough to support a child's weight) as you can collect, but a minimum of four. If you do not have regular climbing boxes, improvise with large kindergarten blocks, two empty, wooden soft-drink cases nailed together securely, cardboard boxes reinforced with wood, etc. See page 40 for examples.

2   *Discuss movement vocabulary . . . in the classroom:*

flight	flex (bend, give)
takeoff	hop
fly unsupported	jump
landing	leap
balance	

Introduction

"Today you are going to <u>fly</u>! That's right—take off, fly, and land! On the signal, stand up and try flying straight up into your own self space . . . like a helicopter going straight up. You can fly, can't you? Any time your <u>whole body</u> is in the <u>air</u>, you are flying. Try tiny bounces into the air, then bigger and bigger bounces high up into the air."

Developmental problems and expected outcomes

PROBLEM 33

Beginning Grade	Middle Grade	Last Grade

"On the signal, move into <u>general space</u>, seeing how many ways you can <u>fly</u> as you go."

". . . . How can you get your whole body up into the air? . . . find as many ways as you can to take off and *land on your feet* . . . see how long you can stay up in the air without any body part touching the floor . . . can you *push off* the floor *harder* to fly higher or farther? . . . what kinds of *shapes* can you make in the air? . . . wide shapes? . . . small shapes? . . . keep going into general space . . . moving on the floor, then flying!"

▶ Repeat all material from Beginning Grade, and then add:

". . . . Have you tried to fly in *different directions?* . . . backward? . . . sideward? . . . turning in the air? . . . have you tried landing on one foot? . . . how can your *arms* help you to fly farther? . . . try flying with your arms at your sides and then with your arms reaching in the directions you are flying . . . which works better? . . . try to feel very light while you are in the air . . . almost as weightless as an astronaut in space."

▶ Repeat all material from Beginning and Middle Grades, and then add:

". . . . Work now on *long, low flights* through the air . . . how many ways can you find to take off? . . . from one foot? . . . from two feet? . . . from a run? . . . from a walk? . . . see what all you can do with your *arms* to make your flight longer . . . explore ways to make long flights until you find the best way for you . . . practice it until you can fly a little farther than you could when you started."

(Have student demonstrations with children analyzing the movements.)

Checklist of quality factors for Problem 33

☐ B–M–L: Exploring a wide variety of ways to take off, fly, and land on the feet. Suggested minimums:

  B—four ways;
  M—eight ways including flight in different directions and making different shapes in the air;
  L—two kinds of long jumps and increase in distance jumped.

☐ B–M–L: Flexing knees, ankles, and hips for strong takeoffs.
☐ M–L: Thrusting arms in the direction of flight.

When children demonstrate these factors, go on to Problem 34.

PROBLEM 34

Beginning Grade	Middle Grade	Last Grade

"On the signal, find a space of your own and see how far up you can fly in your own self space and land softly."

". . . . Look at your knees . . . what happens to them before you take off? . . . notice that bending (flexing) your knees, ankles, and hips before you take off helps you to fly higher . . . does pushing hard against the floor with your feet help you to take off and fly higher? . . . can your arms help to get your body into the air? . . . look at your *knees* when you land . . . are they bending? . . . do you see that when knees bend your landing is softer? . . . work now on landing softly . . . try not to make a sound when you land."

▶ Repeat all material from Beginning Grade, and then add:

". . . . Find out how many *different* ways there are to *land on your feet.*"

(Free exploration. Then . . . .)

". . . . Try different ways to land on one foot . . . land on the other foot . . . land on both feet . . . land with feet far apart . . . land with feet close together . . . land with one foot in front and one foot behind."

(Suggest turning in the air, making shapes in the air, and stress landing softly, while your students work on each of the above requirements.)

▶ Repeat all material from Beginning and Middle Grades, and then add:

". . . . Try for *more height* . . . take a few little bounces before your big jump . . . does this help you feel very light? . . . can you look up at the ceiling and stretch out very long as you are going up into the air? . . . can you make other shapes with your body while you are in the air? . . . have you tried long shapes? . . . small shapes? . . . rounded shapes? . . . straight and narrow shapes? . . . twisted shapes? . . . straight and wide shapes? . . . find one unusual shape you like to make in the air and remember it . . . we will use it again in the next problem."

Checklist of quality factors for Problem 34

☐ Exploring a wide variety of vertical jumps:
   B—four ways;
   M—ten ways including different landing positions;
   L—fourteen ways including different shapes in the air.

☐ Beginning to increase height of jump by flexing knees, ankles, and hips before takeoff . . . by

extending knees, ankles, and hips to thrust strongly against the floor . . . by using arms in strong upswing.

☐ Beginning to land softly by flexing knees, ankles, and hips to absorb the force of landing.

When children demonstrate these factors, go on to Problem 35.

Takeoff

Preparation

PROBLEM 35

Beginning Grade	Middle Grade	Last Grade

"Sit down for a moment . . . ."

(They will need to rest.)

". . . . while I put out these boxes."

(Several children assist. Discuss even spacing needed for Problem 36.)

"Point to the box closest to you. On the signal, go to that box and see how many ways you can find to get on and off the box. If you fly off the box, always land on your feet."

(Allow plenty of time for free exploration without teacher prompting.)

". . . . Are you using your space well? . . . you and the others at your box work out a system so everyone has a turn and so there are no collisions."

(Stop several times. Let each group demonstrate its system of taking turns and lining up so that no collisions take place.)

". . . . Have you tried getting on from a low level? . . . feet first? . . . can you get on backward or sideward? . . . how many ways have you found to get off the box? . . . have you flown off yet? . . . soft landings."

(Have demonstrations by several children with analyses and evaluations by the rest of the class. Then repeat the problem, making different shapes in the air.)

▶ Repeat all material from Beginning Grade, and then add:

"Keep finding different ways to get on the box, but now everyone fly off the box."

". . . . Always land on your feet . . . can you 'feel' that you are flying off the box? . . . are you remembering to push off hard by bending your knees first? . . . can you make shapes in the air after you take off from the box? . . . can you change the size of the shape you make? . . . a small shape then a big shape . . . a wide shape then a narrow shape . . . a rounded shape then a twisted shape . . . keep landing as softly as possible."

▶ Repeat all material from Beginning and Middle Grades, and then add:

"Remember the shape you made in the air on the last problem (34)? Try it again, standing right where you are.

    "Now try this: Get on the box. Make that shape and hold it very still for five counts while you are on the box. Fly off and make the same shape in the air. Land softly."

(Practice until the movement sequences are smooth flowing, and until the shape on the box and the shape in the air are recognizably similar.)

Checklist of quality factors for Problem 35

☐ B: Exploring ways to get on and off boxes. Minimum, four ways.

☐ M: Exploring ways to fly off boxes. Minimum, eight ways including making different shapes in the air.

☐ L: Making a movement sequence in which the same shape is repeated on the box and in the air.

☐ Acting cooperatively in small groups at boxes so all have an equal number of turns.

☐ Using the space around the boxes wisely so there is little waiting and no crowding.

☐ Moving equipment safely and efficiently.

When children demonstrate these factors, go on to Problem 36.

PROBLEM 36

Beginning Grade	Middle Grade	Last Grade

"On the signal, follow me until we are well spaced out between the boxes."

(Stop.)

"On the next signal, go around the room seeing how many ways you can go over the boxes as you come to them. Remember what we've learned about spacing."

(Stop and start frequently to check spacing. If children are unevenly spaced have them find better spacing and begin again. This can take a game form, with the teacher trying to catch too many between two boxes. No punishment, just praise for those well spaced.)

▶ Repeat all material from Beginning Grade. Then, if boxes are low enough, add:

"This time no climbing onto boxes . . . instead fly on (spring off the floor onto the box) . . . and then fly off making different shapes in the air."

". . . . keep going around the room . . . how is your spacing? . . . you have to keep thinking whether to go slower or faster so you don't crowd the person in front of you, don't you?"

▶ Repeat all material from Beginning and Middle Grades, and then add:

"This time, get on the box any way you wish, fly off as high as possible, then move to the next box at a very low level."

". . . . again watch your spacing . . . as soon as you land, go down to a low level . . . let your landing melt right into the floor, then roll or crawl or move in some other way at a low level until you come to the next box . . . think about how much space you will need before taking off . . . is there enough so you won't land on anyone? . . . keep moving smoothly around the room . . . flying high, moving low."

Checklist of quality factors for Problem 36

☐ Adjusting movements to avoid crowding when moving in a specified pathway with a large group.

☐ M–L: Spacing so there is no waiting. (This is difficult but should be worked on until improvement is obvious.)

☐ M: Exploring ways to fly onto a box.

☐ L: Beginning to develop flow in moving from flight to low level to flight smoothly.

When children demonstrate these factors, go on to Problem 37.

PROBLEM 37

Beginning Grade	Middle Grade	Last Grade

"Your legs have worked very hard today, so let's give them a rest. On the signal, get a <u>ball</u>, find a space of your own, and <u>practice any kind of ball work</u> in your own self space . . . try to gain more control of the ball."

▶ Repeat all material from Beginning Grade, and then add:

". . . . Can you *bounce or toss* the ball from a *kneeling or sitting* position and still *catch* it? . . . try changing levels while working with the ball (example . . . kneeling to standing to kneeling while continuing to bounce the ball)."

▶ Repeat all material from Beginning and Middle Grades, and then add:

". . . . Can you *jump up* in the air *while you toss* the ball up? . . . try it . . . you and the ball both going straight up . . . try to let the ball go all the way to the floor in your hands when you catch it . . . can you feel the flow of the movement? . . . fly up and toss the ball . . . catch the ball, and let your body flow down until the ball touches the floor . . . up and down smoothly and without stopping."

Review flight and space.

When children demonstrate an achievement of the objectives on page 93, go on to Theme 6.

SIXTH SET OF PROBLEMS/ORGANIZING THEME: MOVING IN DIFFERENT PATHWAYS

Content structure (for teachers)	Objectives (for children)

Concept

Movement for environmental control

Major idea

1. The pathway the body takes is one spacial movement variable which can be consciously manipulated.

Review—Last lesson in Unit One

2. Man moves to control his environment; a child moves to discover and to cope with his environment.
3. The body is the instrument of movement and can be used in a vast variety of ways.
4. *Space*, force, time, and flow are the elements of movement.
5. *Space* is the medium of movement.
6. The dimensions of space are directions, levels, planes, and ranges.

Selected facts

1. While traveling, the body makes floor pathways of straight lines or curved lines.
2. While traveling, the body also carves a pathway in *air* space.
3. Isolated body parts (e.g., foot, hand, head) as well as the whole body describe floor and air pathways.
4. A zigzag pathway is a combination of straight lines with sharp turns to change direction.

Children need to understand (knowledge)

1. That while moving they produce pathways they can recognize both on the floor and in the air.   B–M–L
2. That two main kinds of pathways are curved lines and straight lines.   B–M–L
3. That zigzags are combinations of straight lines with sharp turns to change direction.   B–M–L
4. That mirroring a partner's movements is done by facing him and doing the same movements as he does as if looking in a mirror, e.g., both lean north, one leaning to his right, and the other leaning to his left.   B–M–L

Children need to learn how (skill)

1. To control consciously the pathway of the body on the floor and in the air while moving in a wide variety of ways.   B–M–L
2. To change direction quickly and with sharp turns when moving in a zigzag pathway.   B–M–L
3. To travel in a wide variety of pathways while manipulating a ball.   B–M–L
4. When working with a partner in mirroring movements, to adjust the speed and complexity of their own movements to those of their partners.   B–M–L

Children need to become (attitude)

1. Willing to listen to problems, to think about them, and to seek increasingly more skillful, thoughtful, and original ways of solving them through movement.
2. Willing to carry tasks through to completion.
3. Increasingly self-motivated, self-determined, and self-disciplined so that each child grows in appreciative self-realization.
4. Appreciative of others like and unlike themselves.
5. Willing to help and work with others.
6. Success-oriented in movement, so that they have an increasing appreciation for and enjoyment of movement.

Teaching tips for sixth set of problems

1. *Arrange equipment . . . before the physical education period:* One ball per child.
2. *Discuss movement vocabulary . . . in the classroom:*
   Pathways (on the floor and in the air)
   Curves, straight lines, zigzags
   Mirror movements
3. *Review general objectives for Unit 1:* Understanding the difference between moving in self space and in general space. If children need more work in this area, repeat Problems 3 (page 57), 4 (page 58), 5 (page 59).

   Listening to subproblems *while* moving. If children need more work in this area, repeat Problem 2 (page 56).

Trying to find more than one way to solve a problem. Responding quickly to starting and stopping signals. If children need more work in this area, repeat all problems, but especially Problem 2 (page 56).

Getting out and putting away equipment efficiently. If children need more work in this area, repeat Problem 6 (page 60).

Choosing partners quickly in a socially acceptable manner. If children need more work in this area, repeat Problem 8 (page 62).

Introduction

(Children sitting on the floor.)

"Today we will work on making different pathways when we move. Have you ever noticed what you leave behind you when you walk in the snow or in the sand? Yes—footprints or tracks so that you can see what pathway you took. Right where you are, can you <u>make different pathways with your fingers on the floor?</u>"

(Start—stop.)

"There are two main pathways you can make—curved ones and straight ones. Or if you put two straight pathways together with sharp corners you can make a zigzag path. Can you make <u>straight and curved and zigzag pathways on the floor</u> with one <u>hand</u> or one <u>leg?</u>"

(Start—stop.)

"This time, try making different <u>pathways in the air</u> with a <u>hand</u> or a <u>foot</u> . . . curves, straight lines, zigzags.

(Start—stop.)

Developmental problems and expected outcomes

PROBLEM 38

Beginning Grade	Middle Grade	Last Grade

"On the signal, move into <u>general space</u> to see <u>how many ways</u> you can make a <u>curved pathway</u> on the floor."

". . . . If there were snow or sand on the ground, what kinds of tracks would be behind you? . . . all curved ones? . . . can you make a big curve and then a small curve (change of range)? . . . can you make a curve to one side and then a curve to the other side (change of direction)? . . . have you tried making a high curve then a low curve (change of level)? . . . no collisions."

▶ Repeat all material from Beginning Grade, and then add:

". . . . Keep making curved pathways on the floor, but see on how many different body parts you can move."

(Free exploration. Then . . . .)

". . . . Have you tried moving on hands and feet? . . . tummies? . . . backs? . . . one foot (hopping? . . . two feet together (jumping)? . . . two hands and one foot? . . . no collisions."

▶ Repeat all material from Beginning and Middle Grades, and then add:

". . . . Try making *one side lead* on one curve and the *other side lead* on the next curve . . . do you find yourself *leaning into the curve* almost as if you were on a bicycle? . . . have you tried moving backward to make a curved pathway on the floor? . . . try making different shapes while you move in a curved pathway."

Checklist of quality factors for Problem 38

☐ Moving in a wide variety of ways in curving pathways.
  Suggested minimums:
   B—6 ways (changing range, level, direction);
   M—12 ways (including locomotion on different body parts);

  L—14 ways (including moving backward and in different body shapes).

☐ Avoiding collisions with others by using the space well.

☐ Continuing to be well distributed over the floor space.

When children demonstrate these factors, go on to Problem 39.

PROBLEM 39

Beginning Grade	Middle Grade	Last Grade

"On the signal, try moving in straight paths."

(Start—stop.)

"When you come to a wall or another person, you can't keep going straight, so you start a straight path in another direction. That is a zigzag pathway."

". . . . Keep your pathway as straight as you can . . . no curves now . . . when you make zigzags, can you make *very sharp corners* instead of curves? . . . how can you make your zigzags sharper and quicker?"

(Select one or two children who are making accurate zigzag pathways to demonstrate. Discuss flexing the knees and pushing off hard with the foot on the floor to make a sharp turn. Then repeat the problem.)

▶ Repeat all material from Beginning Grade, and then add:

". . . . Have you tried making *backward* zigzags? . . . keep your back leading all the time . . . what kinds of zigzags can you make when your *front leads* part of the time and your *back leads* part of the time? . . . can you change levels while you are zigzagging? . . . try moving up to a *high level* on the zig and down to a *low level* on the zag . . . fun . . . can you feel your *body leaning in the direction you want to go* when you make a quick turn?"

(Explore the latter.)

▶ Repeat all material from Beginning and Middle Grades, and then add:

". . . . Remember when you moved sideways in a slide? Can you zigzag while you are *sliding*? . . . try doing two or three slides with one side leading on the zig, then two or three slides with the other side leading on the zag . . . try *jumping* in a zigzag pathway . . . jumping makes it harder to make sharp turns, doesn't it? . . . try *jumping* on the zig and *running* on the zag . . . now think up one more interesting way to zigzag that we haven't tried yet."

(One half of the class demonstrates for the other half, and vice versa.)

Checklist of quality factors for Problem 39

☐ Moving in a wide variety of zigzag pathways. Suggested minimums:
  B—2 ways with sharp turns (i.e., walking and running);
  M—4 ways including changes in level and in body lead;
  L—6 ways including jumping and sliding combinations.

☐ Making sharp turns instead of curves to zigzag.

☐ Flexing knees and pushing off hard with the foot on the floor to make sharp turns.

When children demonstrate these factors, go on to Problem 40.

PROBLEM 40

Beginning Grade	Middle Grade	Last Grade

"On the signal, go get a ball and bounce the ball in a curved path on the floor. Imagine what kinds of tracks the ball would leave in the snow or sand."

". . . . Can you keep the ball bouncing (dribbling) all the time? . . . remember to control the ball . . . you tell it where to go . . . can you make curves that are very big and take you all around the room? . . . no straight lines . . . are you curving around the other boys and girls when you come to them? . . . try making smaller and smaller curves . . . can anyone stay almost in one spot and bounce the ball in a circle all the way around?"

▶ Repeat all material from Beginning Grade, and then add:

". . . . Try *bouncing the ball* in *straight lines* now . . . keep going straight until you meet a wall or a person then *zigzag away* and make another straight line . . . make those turns as sharp and quick as possible . . . now can you very carefully bounce the ball close to someone else, and then zigzag away to avoid bumping into the person you are near?"

(This will require much exploration to achieve.)

▶ Repeat all material from Beginning and Middle Grades, and then add:

". . . . Listen for the *drum beat* (or verbal signal, 'change') . . . each time you hear it, make a *sharp turn* . . . notice that you must zigzag toward an empty space, not toward a wall, or you won't be able to keep going in a straight line until you hear the next drum beat . . . keep the ball bouncing all the time . . . change . . . change . . . change."

(Gradually increase speed at which children are moving. Give change signals frequently, every 5 to 10 seconds.)

Checklist of quality factors for problem 40

☐ Controlled ball bouncing in various pathways.
   Suggested minimums:
   B—large and small curved pathways;
   M—straight-line pathways with sharp turns for zigzag pathways;
   L—sharp turns on signal.

☐ M–L: Judging available space and making sharp turns toward it to avoid collisions.

When children demonstrate these factors, go on to Problem 41.

PROBLEM 41

Beginning Grade	Middle Grade	Last Grade

"On the signal, put the balls away, find a space of your own, and staying in your own self space, see how many different parts of your body you can move in a curved pathway in the air."

". . . . Draw big curves in the air . . . try it with one hand . . . with two hands . . . has anyone tried drawing curves in the air with a foot or a whole leg? . . . could you draw curves with both legs at the same time? . . . how big a curve can you make with your head all around your self space?"

(Repeat problem, substituting zigzags in the air for curves.)

▶ Repeat material from Beginning Grade (curves only), and then add:

". . . . Try drawing some small curves in the air . . . smaller and smaller . . . can anyone draw a very big curve with an arm and a very small curve with a leg at the same time? . . . have you changed the level of your curves? . . . some high? . . . some low? . . . some at the middle level? . . . how much curving can you do with your whole body? . . . keep moving all the time."

(Repeat Problem 40, beginning and middle grades, substituting drawing zigzags in the air for drawing curves.)

▶ Repeat material from Beginning Grade and Middle Grade. Then add:

". . . . Listen for shapes and pathways:
  Big rounded shape . . . hold.
  Draw a curved pathway in the air
    until you make a small
    rounded shape . . . hold.
  Draw a zigzag pathway in the air
    until you make a straight
    and narrow shape . . . hold.
  Draw a curved pathway in the air
    until you make a twisted
    shape . . . hold."

(And so on. Repeat several times.)

Checklist of quality factors for Problem 41

☐ Describing a wide variety of curving and zigzag pathways in the air while in self space:
  B—4 ways;
  M—8 ways.

☐ Using different body parts to make pathways in the air.

☐ Seeing and feeling the difference between curved and straight lines in movement.

When children demonstrate these factors, go on to Problem 42.

PROBLEM 42

Beginning Grade	Middle Grade	Last Grade

"On the signal, get a partner, find a space of your own, and decide which one of you will be the leader first. The leader will make curves in the air with different parts of his body. The follower will try to mirror the leader. He will face his partner and try to do exactly what his partner is doing."

(Demonstrate mirroring with a child before giving the start signal.)

". . . . Leaders, you may have to *move slowly* so your followers can stay with you . . . make *big, slow movements* in your *self space* . . . followers, watch very carefully so you can mirror your partners all the time . . . have you tried making big, slow curves with your legs? . . . with your head? . . . try your best to move alike . . . as if you were one person looking at yourself in a mirror."

(Reverse the leader and follower roles, and repeat. Repeat entire problem, making zigzags instead of curves.)

▶ Repeat all material from Beginning Grade, and then add:

"Make groups of four . . . you and your partner find another couple . . . decide who will be leader first . . . now all three mirror the leader."

". . . . See which group of four can move together best . . . bend and stretch, curve and zigzag . . . move from level to level . . . think about how you can move together better . . . slowly and in your own self space."

(Choose new leaders. Repeat until all have been leader once.)

▶ Repeat all material from Beginning and Middle Grades, and then add:

"Can the four of you make a sequence of curves and zigzags in self space?"

". . . . Practice it until you can do it the same way two times . . . then we will look at it."

(Allow at least five minutes for developing a sequence . . . during the five minutes go from group to group helping children make their sequences simple enough to be repeated exactly the same way. Then have each group demonstrate twice with the total group evaluating the performance. Did the group stay together? Were the first and second demonstrations of the sequence the same? What was good about the sequence? How could it be improved?)

Checklist of quality factors for Problem 42

☐ Mirroring movements in self space. Suggested minimums:
  B—In partners . . . one child making curves and zigzags slowly and simply enough for his partner to follow; the other child watching carefully enough to duplicate the leader's movements (in reverse, as if looking in a mirror);

  M—In groups of four;
  L—In groups of four . . . producing movement sequences which can be repeated the same way.

☐ Choosing partners or fours, and deciding quickly who shall be leader.

Review of space: Direction, level, range, shape, pathways

When children's movement responses demonstrate an understanding of these dimensions of space, go on to Unit 2, Theme 7.

UNIT TWO

WHAT CAN YOU MOVE? (BODY AWARENESS)

Set of Problems	Dates	Theme	Equipment Needed
7		Moving different body parts	None required. *Optional equipment:* Record or music for Looby Loo. Record or music for Dry Bones. Record, "Listening and Moving, the Development of Body Awareness and Position in Space," by Dorothy Carr and Bryant Cratty. L.P. 605, Educational Activities, Inc., Freeport, New York, 1966.
8		Changing relationships (meeting and parting)	Minimum of 4 low benches or low balance beams (see page 40 for suggestions).
9		*Review:* Moving the body in space (Themes 1–9)	Minimum of 4 jumping boxes. One ball per child (variety of types.) *Optional equipment:* Make a large, portable movement chart (see page 125).

SEVENTH SET OF PROBLEMS/ORGANIZING THEME: MOVING DIFFERENT BODY PARTS

Content structure (for teachers)	Objectives (for children)

Content structure (for teachers)

Concept

Movement for environmental control

Major ideas

1 The body is the instrument of movement.
2 Body awareness is a critical factor in man's total physical and mental development.

Selected facts

Perception of the body includes being aware of:
1 Different body parts.
2 The relationship of one body part to another.
3 The importance of a single body part in leading movement, taking the body weight, lifting the body into the air, and moving the body in different directions, levels, or ranges.
4 The position of the body and of its parts in space.
5 The relationship of the body and its parts to objects in space.

Objectives (for children)

Children need to understand (knowledge)

1 That they can consciously move specific body parts.   B–M–L
2 That they can observe and name the parts of the body that they or others are moving.   B–M–L
3 That they can use specific body parts to lead movement,   M–L
take the body weight,   L
lift the body into the air,   B–M–L
move the body in different directions, levels, or ranges,   L
swing the body.   B–M–L

Children need to learn how (skill)

1 To bend, twist, and turn specific body parts, identifying the muscles that are stretched.   M–L
2 To hold balanced positions using specific body parts, both when moving alone and when moving with a partner.   B–M–L
3 To make different body parts lead a movement.   M–L
4 To make different body parts take the body weight or move the body weight.   L
5 To make body parts swing the body and lift the body into the air.   B–M–L

Children need to become (attitude)

1 Willing to listen to problems, to think about them, and to seek increasingly more skillful, thoughtful, and original ways of solving them through movement.
2 Willing to carry tasks through to completion.
3 Increasingly self-motivated, self-determined, and self-disciplined so that each child grows in appreciative self-realization.
4 Appreciative of others like and unlike themselves.
5 Willing to help and work with others.
6 Success-oriented in movement, so that they have an increasing appreciation for and enjoyment of movement.

Teaching tips for seventh set of problems

1 *Arrange equipment . . . before the physical education period:* None required.
Optional equipment:
Record or music for Looby Loo (beginning grade level). Record or music for Dry Bones (middle grade level). Record of "Listening and Moving, the Development of Body Awareness and Position in Space," by Dorothy Carr and Bryant Cratty (L.P. 605, Educational Activities, Inc., Freeport, New York, 1966) (for middle and last grade levels).

2 *Discuss movement vocabulary . . . in the classroom:*

Large body parts:

head	stomach	back	spine
neck	hips	front	waist
shoulders	legs	side	arms
chest			

Small body parts:

ears	forehead	forearm	feet
eyes	fingers	upper arm	heels
nose	thumb	thighs	arches
mouth	hand	knees	toes
cheeks	wrist	shins	balls of feet
chin	elbow	ankles	

Movements:

run	hold body weight
hop	move body weight
swing	

Introduction

"This week we will work on (1) knowing the names of the body parts that move, and (2) knowing what the parts of the body are doing while we move."

Developmental problems and expected outcomes

PROBLEM 43

Beginning Grade	Middle Grade	Last Grade

(This problem may be done in the classroom before going to the gym.)

"Do you know the names of the big parts of your body? See how quickly you can touch each part as I name it."

A. ". . . . How quickly can you *touch* your head? . . . your neck? . . . both shoulders? . . . your chest? . . . your waist? . . . your stomach? . . . your hips? . . . your legs? . . . your arms? . . . your back? . . . your spine? . . . your front? . . . one side? . . . the other side?"

B. ". . . . *How big* are some of your body parts? . . . run your hand down the length of your *arm* . . . where does it start and where does it stop? . . . how many different ways can you move that one arm? . . . run two hands around your *waist* . . . how big is it? . . . can you move at the waist? . . . try bending forward and backward and sideward . . . can you twist at the waist? . . . run one hand down the middle of your back . . . what do you feel? (spine) . . . how does it feel? . . . do you think it can move? . . . sit down and see if you can move your spine . . . have you tried curling up in a ball? . . . what happens to your spine? . . . feel it with your hand . . . have you tried leaning to one side? . . . what happens to your spine?"

For Section C, turn page.

▶ Quickly review the names of the large body parts, if necessary. Then repeat section A from Beginning Grade and add:

A. ". . . . How quickly can you *put your hand in front of* your head? . . . in back of your neck? . . . in front of one shoulder? . . . in back of the other shoulder? . . . in back of your chest? . . . all around your waist? . . . in front of your stomach? . . . in back of your hips? . . . in back of your legs? . . . beside one arm? . . . in front of the other arm? . . . up and down the length of your spine?"

▶ Repeat section B from Beginning Grade, and then add:

B. ". . . . *How many parts* of your body can bend? . . . see how many different ways you can bend forward . . . have you bent forward at your neck? . . . at your waist? . . . at your hips? . . . make different shapes with the rest of your body as you bend and straighten . . . now try bending backward and sideward . . . how many body parts can bend backward? . . . you can bend forward and backward and sideward at your waist . . . can you bend in all directions at your elbow? . . . why not?"

For Section C, turn page.

▶ Quickly review the names of the large body parts, if necessary. Then repeat section A from Beginning and Middle Grades and add:

". . . . Try drawing a *curved pathway* in the air with your head leading . . . with one shoulder leading . . . with the other shoulder leading . . . can you keep moving smoothly and continuously? . . . no stopping . . . move any way you want in your self space while you *think about what your spine is doing.*"

▶ Repeat section B from Beginning and Middle Grades, and then add:

". . . . Hold the rest of your body still and *see how much you can move one shoulder* . . . forward . . . back . . . up . . . down."

(Repeat the above, holding the body still and discovering the amount of movement possible in . . . .)

". . . . two shoulders . . . one foot . . . the other foot . . . the body from the hips up . . . the body from the waist down . . . one leg . . . the other leg . . . both legs held tightly together . . . both legs held far apart."

For Section C, turn page.

PROBLEM 43 CONTINUED

Beginning Grade	Middle Grade	Last Grade

C. ". . . . Run one hand down the opposite side of your body . . . have you found the *side* of your head? . . . the side of your shoulder? . . . the side of your chest? . . . the side of your waist? . . . the side of your hip? . . . the side of your leg? . . . the side of your knee? . . . the side of your ankle? . . . the side of your foot?"

(Repeat on the other side.)

Option:

Do the dance "Looby Loo." This dance is about taking a bath on Saturday night. Children may suggest other large body parts to "put in" and "take out."

▶ Repeat section C from Beginning Grade, and then add:

C. ". . . . See what *parts* of your body you can *twist or turn* . . . can you turn your shoulders sideways but keep your hips facing the front? . . . can you turn your hips sideways but keep your shoulders facing the front? . . . where is the twist? (between shoulders and hips) . . . what other parts of your body can you twist?"

Option:

Sing "Dry Bones," making up appropriate actions. Or use the record "Listening and Moving." Instructions and music are on the record.

▶ Repeat section C from Beginning and Middle Grades, and then add:

". . . . Did you know that when you bend or twist you are *stretching the muscles in parts of your body?* . . . see if you can feel your muscles stretch . . . each time *point to the muscles that are stretched:*
   bend forward at your waist, point . . .
   bend forward at your hips, point . . .
   bend back a little at your waist, point . . .
   bend sideways at your waist, point . . .
   twist your shoulders, point . . .
   twist your hips, point."

Option:

Use the record "Listening and Moving." Instructions and music are on the record.

Checklist of quality factors for Problem 43

☐ Demonstrating knowledge of the names of all large body parts.

☐ Perceiving accurately the size of large body parts.

☐ Perceiving accurately the front, back, and sides of body parts.

☐ M–L: Being conscious of body parts that will bend and twist.

☐ L: Identifying areas of muscles which *stretch* to allow bending and twisting.

When children demonstrate these factors, go on to Problem 44.

PROBLEM 44

Beginning Grade	Middle Grade	Last Grade

"Do you know the names of the small parts of your body? . . . see how quickly you can touch each part as I name it."

Head parts

A. ". . . . How quickly can you touch your nose? . . . your eyes? . . . your cheeks? . . . your chin? . . . your ears? . . . your forehead?"

▶ Quickly review the names of the small body parts, if necessary. Then repeat section A from Beginning Grade and add:

"On the signal, put one cheek and ear on the floor . . . see how many ways you can move your body around them."

(Free exploration. Then . . . .)

". . . . Make an unusual shape and hold it."

(Half the class views the other half, and vice versa.)

▶ Quickly review the names of the small body parts, if necessary. Then repeat section A from Beginning and Middle Grades and add:

"Put your forehead near your hairline on the floor . . . now how many ways can you move your body around them?"

(Free exploration. Then . . . .)

". . . . How straight above your head can you get your spine? . . . try to get the feeling that your spine goes straight up from your head."

Arm parts

B. ". . . . How quickly can you touch your upper arm? . . . your elbow? . . . your lower arm? . . . your wrist? . . . your fingers? . . . your thumb? . . . the palms of your hands? . . . the backs of your hands?"

Leg parts

". . . . How quickly can you touch your toes? . . . the balls of your feet? . . . your arches? . . . your heels? . . . your ankles? . . . your shins? . . . your knees? . . . your thighs?"

Option:

Children may play a fast moving version of "Simon Says." The teacher should be the leader to keep the movement fast.

"Get a partner near you and pick one person to be leader first . . . leaders, listen to these calls . . . followers, face your partners and mirror whatever they do."

". . . . One elbow as high as you can get it . . . one foot at the high level . . . one ear low and one knee high."

(And so on. Then reverse leader and follower roles.)

▶ Repeat section B to end of Beginning Grade, and then add:

"On the signal, get a new partner, and follow these calls":

". . . . Hands clasping your partner's ankles, freeze . . . thumbs and little fingers together, stand on one foot, freeze . . . elbows touching, stand on the other foot, freeze."

(And so on. Have couples explore different shapes with parts of arms touching. They may then devise a game of one couple demonstrating, the other couples trying to make the same shape.)

▶ Repeat section B to end of Beginning and Middle Grades, and then add:

". . . . Keeping the same partner, see how many ways you can hold on to each others' arms and turn or spin around each other . . .

(Examples: elbow swing, holding wrists, "skater's position" swing, etc.)

". . . . Change partners, and see if you can find more ways to hold on to your partner and turn."

(Repeat, changing partners frequently.)

Checklist of quality factors for Problem 44

☐ Demonstrating knowledge of the names of the smaller body parts.

☐ M–L: Being conscious of the wide amount of movements possible with the head on the floor. Minimums: M—4 ways, L—8 ways, including lining up spine with head (preparation for head stand).

☐ M–L: Holding still in a wide variety of shapes, with partners using different parts of the arms to clasp each other. Minimum: 6 ways.

☐ L: Discovering a minimum of 8 arm positions in which partners may "swing."

When children demonstrate these factors, go on to Problem 45.

PROBLEM 45

Beginning Grade	Middle Grade	Last Grade

"On the signal, move into general space moving in as many different ways as you can . . . thinking about what your legs are doing."

(A period of free exploration. Ask individual children, "What are your legs doing now?")

". . . . Are your heels or your toes coming down first? . . . can you make your heels come down first? . . . is that *walking* or running? . . . can you make your feet stay close together all the time? . . . far apart all the time? . . . what are your knees doing? . . . find ways to move in which your knees come up very high . . . in front . . . at the sides . . . can you find ways to move in which your knees do not bend very much? . . . is this easier or *harder*? . . . can you move keeping your ankles bent all the time?"

▶ Repeat all material from Beginning Grade, and then add:

". . . . See how many different ways you can *run* now . . . different ways to *move knees* (high in front and sides) . . . different ways to *move your whole legs* (kicking high in front, to the sides, to the back) . . . different ways to *move your feet* (on toes, on heels, on flat feet, toes turned in, out, and straight forward, feet crossing, and so on).

(Repeat, substituting a *hop* for a run.)

". . . . How many ways can you use your free leg when you are hopping on one foot?"

▶ Repeat all material from Beginning and Middle Grades, and then add:

". . . . *Change the range* of your run . . . big steps, little steps, middle-sized steps . . . *change directions quickly* while you are running . . . what do your legs do? (knees bend, one foot pushes hard against the floor, the other foot takes a long step in the new direction.) . . . *change the level* of your run . . . what do your legs do? . . . try going high up into the air between steps (leaping) . . . what happens to your knees and ankles? . . . soft landings (flexing prior to takeoff and upon landing)."

What are your legs doing?

Checklist of quality factors for Problem 45

☐ Being aware of what the legs are doing while moving in a variety of ways in general space. Suggested minimums:

    B—10 ways, including variations in use of feet, knees, and ankles;

    M—20 ways, including variations in use of the legs while running and hopping;

    L—awareness of leg movements when changing range direction, and level.

When children demonstrate these factors, go on to Problem 46.

PROBLEM 46

Beginning Grade	Middle Grade	Last Grade

"Staying in self space now, see how many different ways you can move your arms . . . think about what your elbows and wrists are doing."

". . . . Have you made different pathways in the air? . . . straight lines? . . . curves? . . . zigzags? . . . see how many ways you can swing your arms . . . sideways . . . forward and back . . . both arms the same direction . . . can you swing your arms in opposite directions? . . . try swinging your arms up and down . . . can any of you swing your arms so hard that they pull you up off your feet? . . . can you swing them so hard that they turn you around?"

▶ Repeat all material from Beginning Grade, and then add:

". . . . Sometimes *one part of the body leads the rest of the body* in movement. Can you make your *elbows lead* your body in rising and falling? . . . try it . . . the first part to go up is your elbow, and the first thing to come down is your elbow . . . can you make the rest of your body flow right along behind your elbow? . . . try letting your elbow lead you all around your self space."

(Repeat with other body parts leading.)

▶ Repeat all material from Beginning and Middle Grades, and then add:

". . . . Different *body parts* are also used to *hold or move your weight.* Lie down on your front and see how many ways you can use your *hands and arms* to pull your body across the floor . . . whole arms . . . elbows . . . forearms . . . hands only . . . try it lying on your *back* . . . how many ways can you find to put all of your *weight on your hands* for just a moment? . . . some of you can hold all your weight on your hands for quite a while (cartwheel, handstand, mule kick, for example)."

Checklist of quality factors for Problem 46

☐ Being aware of what the arms are doing while moving in a variety of ways. Suggested minimums:

  B—swinging arms in 6 ways, using arms forcefully enough to lift the body into the air and to turn the body;

  M—using elbows to lead movement, with all other body parts following;

  L—using arms in 4 ways to take the body weight or move the body weight.

☐ Beginning to understand that any *one body part* can be important in movement and can be used to:

  lead the movement,
  lift the body into the air,
  swing the body,

  move the body weight, or
  take the body weight.

When children demonstrate these factors, go on to Problem 47.

PROBLEM 47

Beginning Grade	Middle Grade	Last Grade

"On the signal, find a <u>self space</u>, make a <u>shape</u> in which your <u>arms are important</u> and <u>hold</u> it very still. Then listen for new shapes."

". . . . Make your legs important, hold . . . make your front important, hold . . . make your knees important, hold . . . make your shoulders important, hold . . . make your elbows important, hold . . . make your back important, hold . . . make your side important, hold."

(And so on.)

▶ Repeat all material from Beginning Grade, and then add:

". . . . *Make and hold a shape* with: two hands and two feet on the floor . . . one shoulder on the floor . . . stomach close to, but not touching the floor . . . one ear close to one knee . . . chest higher than head . . . waist as high as you can get it . . . hips higher than any other part."

▶ Repeat all material from Beginning and Middle Grades, and then add:

". . . . *Make and hold a shape* with: five parts touching the floor . . . another . . . another . . . four parts touching the floor . . . another . . . another . . . three parts touching the floor . . . another . . . another . . . two parts touching the floor . . . another . . . another . . . one part touching the floor . . . hold it still . . . another . . . another."

Front

Back

Arms

Legs

Shoulder

Review: Using different body parts

When children demonstrate an achievement of the objectives on page 110, go on to Theme 8.

EIGHTH SET OF PROBLEMS/ORGANIZING THEME:
CHANGING RELATIONSHIPS OF BODY PARTS (MEETING AND PARTING)

Content structure (for teachers)	Objectives (for children)

Concept

Movement for environmental control

Major ideas

1 The body is the instrument of movement.
2 Body awareness is essential for skilled movement performance.

Selected facts

1 To achieve greater mastery of the body, children need to be aware of:
different body parts, and
the relationship of one body part to another (as in meeting and parting).
2 To make two body parts meet accurately, children must have a developed kinesthetic sense.

Children need to understand (knowledge)

1 That they can consciously move specific body parts together and apart (meeting and parting) in many different ways. B–M–L
2 That they can move in a wide variety of ways on benches (beams) as well as on the floor. B–M–L

Children need to learn how (skill)

1 To move two body parts together accurately (meeting). B–M–L
2 To move two body parts far apart in many different ways (parting). B–M–L
3 To be aware of the changing relationships of body parts when moving. M–L
4 To cooperate in getting out and putting away apparatus and in organizing themselves into harmonious small working groups. B–M–L
5 To develop more controlled flight: takeoff, actual flight, soft landing on the feet. B–M–L

Children need to become (attitude)

The attitude objectives for this physical education program (see page 52) are broad and cannot be achieved quickly; therefore, they will be the same throughout the entire three years. Please review them occasionally.

Teaching tips for eighth set of problems

1 *Arrange equipment . . . before the physical education period:* As many low benches or low balance beams as you can collect (see page 41 for suggestions). Minimum of 4. Place them around the edges of the room.

2 *Discuss movement vocabulary . . . in the classroom:*
meeting   roll
parting   curl

Introduction

"Today we will work on knowing <u>where</u> the different <u>parts</u> of our <u>bodies</u> are in space and <u>how they move toward</u> each other (<u>meeting</u>) and <u>away</u> from each other (<u>parting</u>)."

Developmental problems and expected outcomes

PROBLEM 48

Beginning Grade	Middle Grade	Last Grade
"On the signal, move quickly into general space. When you hear a <u>drum beat, stop</u> with your <u>back nearest</u> to me." (Repeat, stopping on signal with fronts, then sides nearest to teacher.) ". . . . When you hear a drum beat, stop with one foot nearest to me . . . with two feet nearest to me . . . with one shoulder nearest to me . . . with two heels nearest to me . . . with the back of your head nearest to me." (And so on.)	▶ Repeat all material from Beginning Grade, and then add: **"On the signal, move quickly into general space keeping your front nearest to me all the time."** ". . . . Can you *change levels* as you go, still keeping your front nearest to me? . . . keep *changing directions* . . . forward, backward, sideward, still keeping your front nearest to me all the time . . . how quickly can you change direction?" (Repeat with sides, then backs, nearest to teacher while moving quickly.)	▶ Repeat all material from Beginning and Middle Grades, and then add: **"Keep moving in general space and listen for which part of your body to make important."** ". . . . Make your *shoulders* important . . . move in a large range . . . quickly . . . playfully . . . dance up and down . . . take weight on the move . . . swing the body . . . lift the body into the air . . . make your elbows important . . . your wrists important . . . your fingers important . . . your hips important . . . your knees important . . . your heels important . . . your toes important . . . your head important."

Checklist of quality factors for Problem 48

☐ B: Knowing the names of body parts and body surfaces. Relating body parts accurately to objects in space (teacher).

☐ M: Relating body parts accurately to objects in space while on the move

☐ L: Making body parts visibly important in a variety of ways while on the move

When children demonstrate these factors, go on to Problem 49.

PROBLEM 49

Beginning Grade	Middle Grade	Last Grade

"On the signal, find a self space and see how many different ways you can make your wrist move toward and away from your ankle."

A. ". . . . Wrist and ankle meet and part, meet and part . . . are they really *touching* and then *moving far apart?* . . . how far apart can you move them? . . . a big stretch to move ankle and wrist far apart."

B. (Repeat with shoulder and knee.)

C. (Repeat with ear and knee.)

D. (Repeat with foot and foot, staying in self space).

E. (Repeat entire problem with partners moving in self space, one mirroring the other's movements.)

▶ Repeat section A from Beginning Grade, and then add:

". . . . How many ways can you make your wrist and ankle meet and part when your whole body is at a *low level?* . . . when your wrist and ankle are at a *middle level?* . . . when they meet at *one side* of *your body?* . . . when the inside of your wrist meets the outside of your ankle?"

(And so on.)

▶ Repeat section B of Beginning Grade and then add:

B. ". . . . Both shoulders to both knees . . . one shoulder to the opposite knee."

(And so on.)

▶ Repeat sections C and D of Beginning Grade, and then add:

D. ". . . . How many ways can you make your feet meet and part when both feet are at a low *level?* . . . when one foot stays at a low level? . . . when both feet stay at a middle level while meeting and parting? . . . try taking one foot in a *different direction* each time your feet part . . . forward, side, back."

▶ Follow directions in section E of Beginning Grade.

▶ Repeat sections A and B from Beginning and Middle Grades, and then add:

". . . . Keep moving continuously . . . never stop . . . when you have found one pathway to meet, find a different pathway for parting . . . open and close on different pathways . . . curving pathways . . . straight pathways . . . zigzag pathways . . . meeting and parting at different levels, in different directions, in different ranges . . . moving and thinking all the time."

▶ Repeat section B of Beginning and Middle Grades.

▶ Repeat sections C and D of Beginning and Middle Grades, and then add:

". . . . Keep your feet meeting and parting while doing *different things with the rest of your body:* . . . head on the floor near hairline . . . both hands and one foot on the floor . . . both hands and both feet on the floor (jump feet apart and together) . . . the back of your shoulders on the floor."

▶ Follow directions in section E of Beginning Grade.

Checklist of quality factors for Problem 49

☐ B: Accurate meeting and parting of specific body parts, e.g., shoulder and knee touching accurately then stretching as far apart as possible.

☐ M: Varying level and direction of specific body parts while meeting and parting accurately.

☐ L: Continuous body flow while specific body parts meet and part accurately in different pathways.

When children demonstrate these factors, go on to Problem 50.

PROBLEM 50

Beginning Grade	Middle Grade	Last Grade

A. "On the signal, move into <u>general space</u>, making your <u>legs meet and part in different ways</u>."

(Free exploration. Then) . . . .

". . . . Keep your feet widely apart all the time . . . keep your feet tightly together all the time (jumping variations) . . . feet together . . . feet apart . . . make your legs pass each other and stretch far out for long, long steps . . . make your feet stay close to each other after passing . . . is this easier to do on your *toes* or on your flat feet?"

B. (Explain and demonstrate a method for getting out and putting away balance beams or benches. If they are light enough for small groups of students to move, establish a system by which they will be handled the rest of the year. For example, have children point to the bench closest to them. Check distribution to see that each bench has enough children to handle it safely. *While* they are pointing, give the problem, "Get out your bench, and find different ways to make your feet meet and part as you move along it." It is important that a problem be given before children move the apparatus so there will be no need for the group that finishes first to wait for the others. Random placement of benches or beams is best . . . allowing children to use their spacial understandings in finding the space they will need. Allow children to devise their own systems of lining up and taking turns within their groups. The teacher should act as reference source rather than as demonstrator within the groups. Establish one rule: Only one child on the equipment at a time.)

"On the signal, point to the <u>bench</u> (or beam) closest to you, help <u>bring it out</u> to an open space, and then take turns making your <u>legs meet and part in different ways</u> as you move along it."

". . . . Try all the different things you did on the floor . . . are they possible on the bench (or beam)? . . . legs far apart . . . close together . . . long steps . . . short steps . . . have you found a way to keep your feet tight together all the time as you move along? (jumping) . . . keep thinking about all the different things your legs can do."

▶ Repeat section A from Beginning Grade, and then add:

A. ". . . . Keep *one foot ahead* of the other foot all the time (galloping may result) . . . make your feet meet and part while moving *sideways,* with one foot leading . . . are you stepping sideways? . . . sliding? . . . make different *pathways* on the floor (curving and zigzagging) . . . knowing what your feet are doing all the time."

▶ Repeat section B from Beginning Grade, and then add:

". . . . Have you tried keeping *one foot ahead* of the other all the time? . . . have you tried moving in different *directions?* . . . forward, backward, sideward? . . . what are your feet and legs doing? . . . are they meeting and parting? . . . what different things can you do with your *other body parts* while your feet move along the bench (or beam)?"

▶ Repeat section A from Beginning and Middle Grades, and then add:

". . . . See if you can make your hands meet and part in the same way that your feet are meeting and parting . . . keep exploring to see how many ways you can make your hands meet and part the same as your feet are meeting and parting."

▶ Repeat section B from Beginning and Middle Grades, and then add:

". . . . Try changing your *level* as you move along . . . head from a high level to a medium level and back to a high level . . . change the *range* of your steps . . . see how many big steps it takes to move along the bench . . . how many little steps can you take? . . . can you *lift one foot* far up in front of you before taking another step? . . . far out to the side? . . . keep thinking about making your feet meet and part in different ways . . . arms, too, if you can."

Checklist of quality factors for Problem 50

☐ Demonstrating a variety of ways for legs to meet and part, both on the floor and on apparatus (bench or beam). Suggested minimums:

   B—6 ways, including walking, running, jumping;

   M—10 ways, including one foot leading at all times, as in galloping, side stepping, or sliding;

L—12 ways, including level change and matching arm and leg movements.

☐ Acting cooperatively in small groups to get out the apparatus, to place it so all groups have enough space, and to devise a system by which all children have an equal number of turns on the apparatus.

When children demonstrate these factors, go on to Problem 51.

PROBLEM 51

Beginning Grade	Middle Grade	Last Grade

"On the signal, take turns <u>moving along the bench</u>. When you come to the end, <u>fly off</u> and <u>land on your feet</u>."

(Free exploration. Then . . . .)

". . . . Are you flying high up into the air? . . . push off hard with your feet . . . remember to bend your knees and ankles to get a strong push off . . . how softly are you landing? . . . can you land more softly? . . . how? . . . just squish down—knees and ankles bent—and bounce right back up . . . soft, squishy landings . . . keep trying different ways to use your legs."

▶ Repeat all material from Beginning Grade, and then add:

". . . . Make *one part of your body important* while you are in the air . . . knee, elbow, hand, foot . . . watch the others in your group . . . can you guess which part is important? . . . how far apart can you get your legs while you are in the air? . . . can you keep your legs really together while you are in the air? . . . soft landings."

▶ Repeat all material from Beginning and Middle Grades, and then add:

". . . . How many *different ways* can you *land on your feet*? . . . with feet close together? . . . with feet far apart? . . . with one foot in front of the other? . . . go high in the air and land in many different ways . . . be sure to have a soft, squishy landing . . . can you make your arms do the same thing your feet are doing? . . . far apart . . . close together."

Checklist of quality factors for Problem 51

☐ Demonstrating a variety of ways to move along the apparatus and fly off, landing softly on the feet. Suggested minimums:

    B—3 ways, including increasing height of flight by pushing off strongly and including landing softly;

    M—10 ways, including making single body parts visibly important while in the air;

    L—14 ways, including using different foot positions for landing and matching arm movements to leg movements.

When children demonstrate these factors, go on to Problem 52.

PROBLEM 52

Beginning Grade	Middle Grade	Last Grade
(A free exploration problem.) **"On the signal, see what all you can do on your bench (or beam)."**	▶ Repeat Beginning Grade.	▶ Repeat Beginning Grade.

Review: Changing relationships of body parts

When children demonstrate an achievement of the objectives on page 117, go on to Theme 9.

NINTH SET OF PROBLEMS/ORGANIZING THEME: REVIEW—MOVING THE BODY IN SPACE

Content structure (for teachers)	Objectives (for children)

Concept

Movement for environmental control

Major ideas

1 A child moves to discover and cope with his environment.
2 The body is the instrument of movement.
3 Movement results from nerve and muscle coordination.
4 Space, force, time, and flow are the elements of movement.
5 The dimensions of *space* are directions, levels, planes, and ranges.
6 Body awareness is a critical factor in man's total physical and mental development.

Selected facts

1 Space is the medium of movement.
2 Self space is the immediate area surrounding the body. Its outer boundary is ascertained by stretching as far as possible.
3 General space is the area surrounding self space. Its outer boundary is arbitrarily formed by walls, lines, or any predetermined boundary.
4 The body can move in six named directions: up, down, forward, backward, right side, left side.
5 The body can move in three named levels: high, medium, and low.
6 The body can move in different ranges. Range is the relationship of the body to self space denoting how much self space the body extends into. Range can be large or small, with body parts "near to" or "far from" each other.
7 Shape is the position the body takes in space at any given instant in time. The four main types of body shapes are rounded, straight and narrow, straight and wide, and twisted.
8 The body need not be earthbound. Flight can occur for brief periods of time. There are three phases to flight: takeoff, actual flight, and landing.
9 While traveling, the body inscribes various pathways (straight lines, curved lines, zigzags) on the floor and in the air.
10 Perception of the body includes being aware of different body parts, the relationship of one body part to another, the importance of single body parts in movement, the position of the body and its parts in space, the relationship of the body and its parts to objects in space.

Children need to understand (knowledge)

1 That they can move in a great variety of ways in self space and in general space.
2 That they can move many ways and with control in:
   directions— up and down, forward and backward, to one side, and to the other side;
   levels—high, medium, low;
   ranges—large and small, near to and far from.
3 That they can move into and hold a great variety of shapes: rounded, straight and narrow, straight and wide, and twisted.
4 That they can fly for brief periods of time.
5 That they produce recognizable floor and air pathways (straight, curved, or zigzag) when moving.
6 That they can consciously use specific body parts to lead movement, take the body weight, lift the body into the air, move the body in different directions, levels, and ranges, and swing the body.

Children need to learn how (skill)

1 To move in a great variety of controlled ways in self space and in general space.
2 To respond to starting and stopping signals.
3 To listen and think *while* moving.
4 To move in a variety of controlled ways in all directions, all levels, all ranges.
5 To move into and hold a variety of shapes which are variations of the four basic shapes.
6 To develop controlled flight: strong takeoff, held shape in flight, light and safe landings on the feet.
7 To produce recognizable floor and air patterns.
8 To move specific body parts consciously and purposefully.

Children need to become (attitude)

1 Willing to listen to problems, to think about them, and to seek increasingly more skillful, thoughtful, and original ways of solving them through movement.
2 Willing to carry tasks through to completion.
3 Increasingly self-motivated, self-determined, and self-disciplined so that each child grows in appreciative self-realization.
4 Appreciative of others like and unlike themselves.
5 Willing to help and work with others.
6 Success-oriented in movement, so that they have an increasing appreciation for and enjoyment of movement.

Teaching tips for ninth set of problems

1 *Arrange equipment . . . before the physical education period:*
   One movement chart (on page 125).

All the jumping boxes you have (minimum of 4).
One ball per child (a variety of types—yarn balls, paper balls, bouncing balls, and so on).

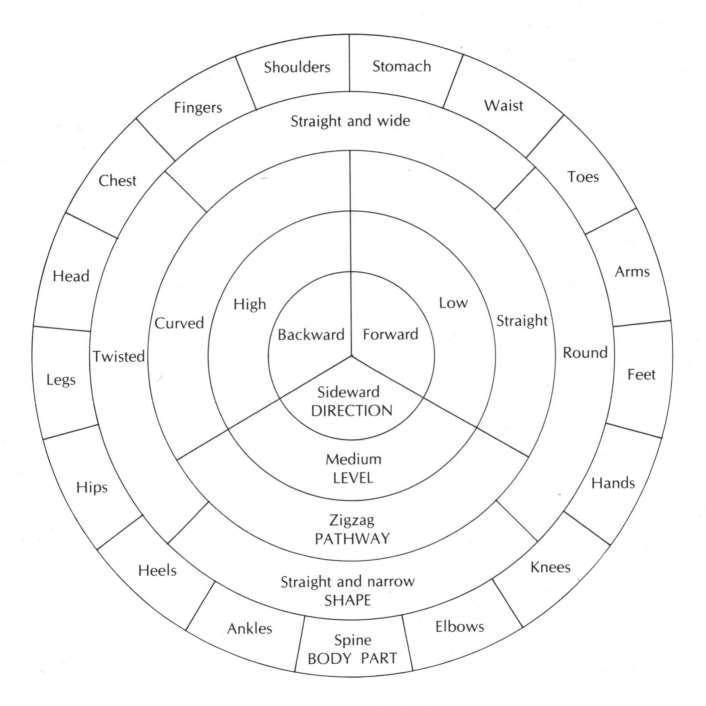

MOVEMENT CHART II

Shoulders

Stomach

Fingers

Waist

Straight and wide

Chest

Toes

Head

Arms

High

Low

Curved

Straight

Backward Forward

Twisted

Round

Legs

Feet

Sideward
DIRECTION

Hips

Medium
LEVEL

Hands

Zigzag
PATHWAY

Heels

Knees

Straight and narrow
SHAPE

Ankles

Elbows

Spine
BODY PART

Introduction

"This week we are going to review all the ways of moving we have discovered, and add rolling as another way to move."

Developmental problems and expected outcomes

PROBLEM 53

Beginning Grade	Middle Grade	Last Grade
A. (Use the movement chart, p. 125. Select one direction in the inner circle for children to move. When all are responding accurately, select one level (next circle). Continue adding one more movement limitation at a time from each circle. Direction, then level, then pathway, then shape, then body part to make important. An example follows.)	▶ Repeat section A from Beginning Grade. Then	▶ Repeat section A from Beginning and Middle Grades. Then . . . .
"How many ways can you move into general space and:"	A. (Use the movement chart again but give direction and level, at the same time. Free exploration. Then add shape and pathway together. Free exploration. Then add body part to make important. Free exploration.)	(Children may devise a movement game using the chart; e.g., an arrow may be added to the chart and spun to give the requirements, or students chosen for unique solutions may call the requirements each time. The opposite approach may be taken—children move freely, then the class watches one child move and analyzes his movements from the chart.)
". . . . Move *forward* into general space . . . at a *medium level* . . . in a *curved pathway* . . . in a *twisted shape* . . . making your *head* important."		
B. (Repeat, using different combinations, one factor from each of the circles. Review all previous lessons in which children demonstrated need for more work. Teachers will be able to observe the areas of weakness readily through use of the chart. If children have difficulty following all sets of movement requirements (all circles), try using only two or three until they respond easily and in a wide variety of movements.)	▶ Repeat section B from Beginning Grade.	▶ Repeat section B from Beginning Grade.

Checklist of quality factors for Problem 53

☐ Demonstrating mastery of a functional movement vocabulary—responding to movement words with appropriate body movement, not by defining movement words verbally.

☐ Thinking and moving simultaneously—continuous movement response with maximum individual participation.

☐ Continuing to try a variety of movement responses within several sets of limitations.

When children demonstrate these factors, go on to Problem 54.

Backward direction

Low level

Zigzag pathway

Straight and narrow shape

Making arms important

PROBLEM 54

Beginning Grade	Middle Grade	Last Grade

A. (Use the movement chart again, p. 125, to define requirements for static shapes to he held still. Use only level, type of shape, and body part to be made important. An example follows.)

"How many ways can you stay in <u>self space</u> and . . . . "

". . . . Make a shape at a low level . . . hold it very still . . . make it a straight and wide shape at the low level . . . make your toes very important in your low, straight, and wide shape."

▶ Repeat section A from Beginning Grade. Then . . . .

A. (Use the movement chart again, but *allow movement* (not static shape) *in self space*. Pathway, when working in self space, refers to the pathway to be described in the air. Stress continuous movement—no held shapes. Omit only the direction circle. An example follows.)

"Staying in your self space, how many ways can you move. . . . "

". . . . At a high level? . . . making a curved pathway? . . . with your body in a rounded shape? . . . making your arms important?"

▶ Repeat section A from Beginning and Middle Grades. Then . . . .

(Use the movement chart again to define requirements for static shapes to be held—level, shape, body part. Then add direction and pathway for *moving away from self space* into another self space where the same shape is to be made and held. An example follows.)

". . . . Make a low, twisted shape in which your elbows are important . . . move backward in a straight line to a new self space . . . then make the same shape and hold it."

B. (Repeat problem, using different combinations from the chart. Review weak areas. Repeat with partners, one mirroring the other's held shapes.)

▶ Follow directions in section B of Beginning Grade.

▶ Follow directions in section B of Beginning Grade.

Checklist of quality factors for Problem 54

☐ Demonstrating mastery of functional movement vocabulary.

☐ B: Holding shapes very still.

☐ M: Continuous movement while fulfilling requirements.

☐ L: Combining held shapes and moving into general space.

☐ Being able to reproduce a held shape.

When children demonstrate these factors, go on to Problem 55.

PROBLEM 55

Beginning Grade	Middle Grade	Last Grade

"On the signal, choose a <u>ball</u> that is near you, find a <u>self space</u>, and <u>explore ways</u> to <u>control</u> the ball."

(After a period of free exploration, use the movement chart, again starting from the inner circle and working outward. Give only one requirement at a time. An example follows.)

".... How many ways can you *control the ball while you are moving* forward, backward, or sideward . . . while you are moving at a low, medium, or high level . . . while you move the ball at a low, medium, or high level . . . while you are moving in a curved or zigzag pathway . . . while you make a shape (self space) that is rounded, straight and narrow, straight and wide, or twisted . . . while you make one body part important . . . feet, heels, fingers."

(Repeat, selecting different requirements from chart.)

▶ Repeat the approach used in Beginning Grade. Then . . . .

(Give two requirements at a time. An example follows.)

".... How many ways can you control the ball while moving the ball at a low level and taking a curved pathway?"

(Repeat using different combinations, selecting one factor from each circle.)

▶ Repeat the approaches used in Beginning and Middle Grades. Then . . . .

(Give three requirements at a time. An example follows.)

".... Try to control the ball with your feet, with your head at a high level and your body in a rounded shape."

(Repeat, using different combinations. Children will discover that some combinations limit movement possibilities. Discuss problems that occur and have children rate the efficiency of different combinations.)

Checklist of quality factors for Problem 55

☐ Demonstrating mastery of a functional movement vocabulary while manipulating (controlling) balls.

☐ B: Controlling balls while moving in different directions, levels, pathways, and body shapes. Controlling balls when the balls are at different levels. Using different body parts to control balls.

☐ M–L: Keeping balls under control while moving in two or more specified ways at the same time.

☐ Realizing the vast variety of ways in which the body can move while manipulating objects.

☐ Beginning to understand why some ways of moving are more efficient than other ways.

When children demonstrate these factors, go on to Problem 56.

PROBLEM 56

Beginning Grade	Middle Grade	Last Grade

A. "On the signal, put the balls away, find a self space, and see how many ways you can roll very softly and smoothly in and near your own space."

".... There are many different ways to roll ... find several very soft, safe ways to roll ... can you make your body very round or curved so that your rolls are softer? ... a ball rolls very softly, doesn't it? ... can you make your body parts nearly as round as a ball? ... no elbows or feet sticking out."

(Expect and accept a wide variety of ability levels. A simple, stretched-out log roll is as correct a solution to the problem as is a full backward roll in good form. At this point, stress soft, rounded rolls and a variety of rolls, not one form or kind.)

B. "Everyone stand up. On the signal, just melt right down to the floor, roll over and stand up. Each time you hear a beat, collapse, roll, and stand up."

▶ Repeat section A from Beginning Grade, and then add:

A. ".... Have you tried rolling in different *directions*? ... forward, backward, sideward? ... have you tried rolling in different *pathways*? ... a straight line across the floor? ... a curved pathway? ... back and forth or in zigzags? ... think about the *range* of your movements ... try keeping all your body parts near to each other ... all curled up in a ball ... think about the *shape* of your body ... is it as rounded as it can be? ... can you roll when your body is straight and narrow? ... twisted? ... why do you roll more easily when you are in a rounded shape?"

▶ Repeat section B from Beginning Grade, and then add:

B. "This time listen for a shape, hold it very still, then on the beat, collapse, roll, and make that shape again."

".... Shape on hands and feet, hold, collapse, roll, and hold the same shape ... shape on hands and knees ... shape with tummies high ... twisted (rounded, straight and narrow, straight and wide) shape at a high (medium, low) level."

(And so on.)

▶ Repeat section A from Beginning and Middle Grades, and then add:

".... How many different *body parts* can you roll over? ... some of you are rolling over one shoulder ... others are rolling over your head backward ... can anyone roll forward without touching your head to the floor at all? ... pay attention to your hands ... what are they doing to help you roll softly? ... do they push against the floor (take your weight) for a short time? ... if they are going to take your weight, should they be palms down? (yes) ... *open* or closed? ... keep thinking about what your body parts are doing."

▶ Repeat section B from Beginning and Middle Grades, and then add:

"This time, run quickly into general space. Whenever you hear a beat, jump high in the air, land on your feet, collapse, roll, and run again. Work for smooth, continuous flow of movement."

Checklist of quality factors for Problem 56

☐ Performing a variety of simple, safe rolls. Suggested minimums:

B—3 ways, including long, stretched-out log rolls and a smooth "stand, collapse, roll, stand";

M—6 ways, including direction, pathway, range, and shape variations. Ability to hold a specified shape,

collapse, roll, and hold the same shape again with some smoothness of movement flow;

L—10 ways, including rolling over different body parts and being aware of hands while rolling. Ability to run, jump, collapse, roll, and run on in a smooth flowing movement pattern.

When children demonstrate these factors, go on to Problem 57.

PROBLEM 57

Beginning Grade	Middle Grade	Last Grade

"Point to the <u>box</u> nearest to you. On the signal, get out that box and take turns getting on and flying off. <u>Land on your feet, collapse, and roll.</u>"

". . . . Make your landings as soft as you can (flexed knees, hips, and ankles) . . . notice that when you land softly you can melt right on down to the floor to do your roll . . . it is important to have enough space for landing and rolling . . . think about just how much space you will need . . . are you flying high and rolling low? . . . very soft rolls."

▶ Repeat all material from Beginning Grade. Then . . . .

(Use the movement chart on page 125 again to vary the flight. Examples follow.)

"Direction . . . Try flying off backward, collapse, and roll.

Level . . . See how high you can fly, then collapse, and roll.

Pathway . . . Can you roll all the way back to where you started in a curved pathway?

Shape . . . Make a straight and narrow shape while you are in flight, collapse, and roll.

Body part . . . Make your legs important while you are in flight, collapse, and roll. (Legs wide apart, close together, and so on. Legs and arms doing the same thing.)"

▶ Repeat all material from Beginning and Middle Grades.

Review moving the body in space.

When children demonstrate an achievement of the objectives on page 124, go on to Unit 3, Theme 10.

UNIT THREE

HOW DO YOU MOVE? (FORCE, BALANCE, WEIGHT TRANSFER)

Set of problems	Dates	Theme	Equipment needed
10		Creating force—weak and strong	One yarn ball per child. One balloon per child. Empty walls (to throw balls against). Middle grade only—one short rope per 4 children.
11		Absorbing force	One ball that bounces per child. As many jumping boxes as you have, minimum of 4.
12		Moving on-balance and off-balance (gravity)	As many low balance beams and benches as you have, minimum of 4. A pathway drawn or taped on the floor. *Optional equipment:* As many mats as you have.
13		Transferring weight (rocking, rolling, sliding)	A variety of apparatus: benches, boxes, beams, inclined boards for sliding, mats if you have them. Improvise!
14		Transferring weight (steplike movements)	One hoop or used bicycle tire per child. As many low balance beams or beam-type pieces of apparatus as you have, minimum of 4.
15		Transferring weight when flight is involved *Review:* Force, balance, weight transfer	One ball per child. A variety of apparatus: boxes, beams, inclined boards for sliding, hanging ropes for swinging, etc. Improvise!

TENTH SET OF PROBLEMS/ORGANIZING THEME: CREATING FORCE—WEAK AND STRONG

Content structure (for teachers)	Objectives (for children)

Concept

Movement for environmental control

Major ideas

1 Space, *force*, time, and flow are the elements of movement.
2 *Force* is produced by muscle tension which may range from firm (strong, powerful feeling) to light (weak, nearly weightless feeling).

Selected facts

1 The body can produce varying amounts of force; the dimensions of force range from weak to strong.
2 For efficient use of the body, one produces just enough force to do the task at hand successfully but not more force than is needed.
3 Changing muscular tensions in the body can be felt (kinesthetic sense).
4 When muscles are tensed, the body is active regardless of whether it is moving or holding a shape.
5 Gathering tension to produce force is a process of gripping in the whole or in parts of the body.
6 Releasing tension to reduce force is a process of relaxation which leads to heaviness and eventually to complete lack of body control (collapse).
7 More force can be generated by strong, well-exercised muscles than by weak, unused muscles.

Children need to understand (knowledge)

1 That they can create force by tensing muscles (gripping in the whole body or in parts of the body). B–M–L
2 That they can consciously vary the amount of force produced by their muscles. B–M–L
3 That they can control the amount of force produced to fit the task at hand. B–M–L
4 That they can increase their muscular strength through use, which in turn allows them to produce more force. B–M–L
5 That two ways to move more forcefully are to use more body parts and to increase the range of the movement. M–L

Children need to learn how (skill)

1 To move forcefully in a wide variety of ways, using the whole body or selected parts. B–M–L
2 To develop quicker, more forceful running starts. B–M–L
3 To increase the force of a swing by using more body parts and by increasing the range of the movement. B–M–L
4 To throw balls more forcefully by using the whole body, by causing the motion to flow toward the target, and by increasing the range of the movement. M–L
5 To feel the difference between strong and weak muscle tension. B–M–L

Children need to become (attitude)

1 Willing to listen to problems, to think about them, and to seek increasingly more skillful, thoughtful, and original ways of solving them through movement.
2 Willing to carry tasks through to completion.
3 Increasingly self-motivated, self-determined, and self-disciplined so that each child grows in appreciative self-realization.
4 Appreciative of others like and unlike themselves.
5 Willing to help and work with others.
6 Success-oriented in movement, so that they have an increasing appreciation for and enjoyment of movement.

Teaching tips for tenth set of problems

1 *Arrange equipment . . . before the physical education period:*

One yarn ball (or substitute soft ball) per child.
One balloon per child.
Empty walls (for throwing the balls against the walls).
Middle grade only—one short rope for 4 children.
Optional equipment: one "slinky" or other springlike toy.

2 *Discuss movement vocabulary . . . in the classroom:*

Force	Muscles
strong, weak	tensed, relaxed
light, heavy	gripped, loose
gentle, hard	hard, soft

Speed	Movements
take off quickly	push, thrust
"speed out"	swing, throw underhand
slow down	follow through

Introduction

"How strong are you? Are you very strong . . . very forceful? What makes you strong and forceful?"
(Discuss. Muscles make the body move. The stronger the muscles are, the more forcefully the body can move. The way to make muscles stronger is to use them more often.)

"Do you think your muscles always move your body very forcefully? Let's find out.
First, can you all <u>find and touch a muscle</u> in your arm? Now <u>freeze</u>—grip with all your muscles as tightly and strongly as you can. Do you feel very strong now? Touch that muscle again. Is it <u>hard</u> and squeezing together and gripping?"

"Now <u>relax</u>, be very limp. Touch that muscle again. Does it feel the same way?"

(No . . . soft, loose, relaxed, no squeezing or gripping.)

"Try it again. <u>Freeze</u>. Now <u>relax part way</u> . . . let go a little more, a little more, and now <u>relax</u> completely. What have we found out? We can <u>control the amount of force we make</u>. We can tell our muscles to make a lot of force or just a little force. We can tell our muscles to make a lot of force to throw a ball very hard. Or we can tell our muscles, "I need just a little force to pick up a feather." Try that. <u>Throw a pretend ball very hard</u> several times . . . now throw it only <u>half as hard</u>, or half as far—gentle, easy throws. Now with very, very little force <u>pick up a pretend feather and toss it gently</u>. Do you feel the difference in your muscles? You can control the amount of force you make, can't you?"

Quick start

Developmental problems and expected outcomes

PROBLEM 58

Beginning Grade	Middle Grade	Last Grade

"On the signal, move into general space using very strong, forceful movements."

(Stop for a moment's rest whenever children seem to be waning in strength of movement.)

". . . . How many ways can you move very strongly? . . . at different *levels* . . . high . . . low . . . middle . . . in different *directions* . . . how forcefully can you move backward? . . . really grip those muscles and push hard off the floor to move forcefully backward . . . sideward . . . how many *body parts* can you use to fly? . . . can you really push hard off the floor with your legs and lift strongly with your arms to get high in the air? . . . see if you can *move strongly* and make *a lot of noise* with your feet on the floor . . . now see if you can *move strongly* and not make any noise . . . very strong and very quiet . . . try making *big, slow, quiet moves* that are very strong . . . now big, *fast,* quiet moves that are very strong."

"Getting a quick start to run very fast is one time when you need to use a lot of force. Your leg muscles need to be very strong to 'speed out' fast. Let's see how strong your leg muscles are. When you hear one beat, start to run as quickly and forcefully as you can—really 'speed out.' When you hear two beats, stop as fast as you can without falling down."

(Start and stop several times.)

". . . . You have to *watch your spacing* carefully when you are running fast, so you won't collide with others . . . can you point your body toward an empty space before 'speeding out'?"

▶ Repeat all material from Beginning Grade, and then add:

"Try putting your feet different ways before 'speeding out' powerfully."

". . . . Try it with feet together."

(Start . . . stop.)

". . . . Feet apart and parallel . . . called a side stride position."

(Start and stop several times with different widths of side stride—feet only a few inches apart . . . feet wide apart.)

". . . . One foot forward and one foot back . . . called a forward stride position."

(Start and stop several times with different widths of stride. Discuss the foot position which works best for getting a fast start. Most children will get quicker starts in a forward stride position, toes pointing straight ahead, with feet no farther apart than their shoulders are wide.)

"This time, try changing your level when you are in your powerful 'speeding out' position."

". . . . High level, knees not bent at all."

(Start . . . stop)

". . . . Medium level, knees bent greatly, body upright . . . medium level, knees bent slightly, body leaning forward."

(Most children will get quicker starts in the last position above.)

▶ Repeat all material from Beginning and Middle Grades, and then add:

"This time, explore the size (range) of steps you can take to get started."

". . . . Start and stop on your own . . . do *short, hard, driving steps* help you to take off fast? (yes) . . . keep on practicing 'speeding out' and stopping without any signals . . . find the best way for *you* to be very strong and quick . . . think about starting position, level, pushing hard against the floor, taking short powerful steps."

Checklist of quality factors for Problem 58

☐ Moving forcefully in a wide variety of ways—realizing that they can move strongly and quietly at the same time and that they can move strongly and slowly at the same time.

☐ Moving forcefully to produce quick running starts.

☐ B–M–L: Using space well; no collisions. Consciously thrusting feet hard against the floor for quicker takeoffs.

☐ M–L: Developing an efficient starting stance. For most children, a forward stride position, feet about shoulder width apart, toes pointing forward, knees, ankles, and hips slightly bent, lowering the body level, and body leaning forward with most of the weight on the front foot.

☐ L: Taking powerful, short, hard, driving steps to accelerate quickly.

When children demonstrate these factors, go on to Problem 59.

PROBLEM 59

Beginning Grade	Middle Grade	Last Grade

"On the signal, <u>move very lightly</u>, very gently, into <u>general space</u>."

". . . . Move just as lightly as possible . . . very little force . . . can you almost float through the air? . . . use only enough force to keep you moving . . . very gently . . . feel how relaxed your muscles are . . . your body is almost like a bubble floating away . . . soft . . . smooth . . . bending . . . and turning . . . your legs and arms and torso are nearly weightless, like an astronaut walking in space . . . move very gently at high levels and low levels . . . in different *directions* . . . in *different ranges* . . . big and small movements . . . very relaxed . . . feet high and low . . . are you still controlling the amount of force you need? (yes)"

▶ Repeat all material from Beginning Grade, and then add:

"On the signal, <u>start moving very lightly</u> into <u>general space</u> at a high level, then listen for changes."

". . . . low and strong . . . high and strong . . . backward and gently, lightly . . . sideways and strong . . . slow and strong . . . fast and strong . . . slow and weak . . . faster and weak."

(And so on. Allow enough time between calls for thinking and responding fully. Combine three or more element requirements when children are responding well to two.)

▶ Repeat all material from Beginning and Middle Grades, and then add:

". . . . See if you can *gradually change* the amount of *force* you are using. Get in a good *starting position for running fast* then *listen:* 'speed out' . . . run as fast as you can . . . slow down a little . . . slower . . . very slowly . . . now just a little faster . . . a little faster yet . . . very fast . . . very slowly . . . very fast."

(Check to see whether short, driving steps were taken to accelerate speed. Then continue.)

Checklist of quality factors for Problem 59

☐ Moving in a wide variety of ways with very little force:

B—using different parts of the body weakly while moving,

M—controlling force produced to alternate between strong and weak,

L—being conscious of more and less amounts of force produced to accelerate and decelerate.

When children demonstrate these factors, go on to Problem 60.

PROBLEM 60

Beginning Grade	Middle Grade	Last Grade

(A "slinky" spring toy may be used for the following demonstration, or the teacher may simply use the biceps on the inside of his arm to show the same thing. Have children find a *self space* and *sit down* during the demonstration.)

"Your muscles act very much like a spring toy. They can be very relaxed and loose like this . . . or they can be very tight and gripping like this . . . .
    "When you are in your freeze position, are your muscles tight and gripping, or are they loose and relaxed? Do you think it is possible to be loose and relaxed in half your body and tight and gripping in the other half? Try it."

(Top and bottom, right and left sides, arms and legs, and so on.)

"On the signal, stay in your own self space and see if you can do some of the things with your muscles that this spring does."

". . . . *Low level shape,* tight muscles, hold . . . *relax* until you have loose muscles in the *same shape* . . . *high level shape,* tight muscles, hold . . . *relax* until you have loose muscles in the *same shape* . . . *middle level shape,* tight muscles hold . . . gradually *relax* until you have loose muscles in the *same shape.*"

(And so on, using rounded, straight and narrow, straight and wide, twisted shapes, etc. Check to see whether arms, legs, necks, backs, and faces are really relaxed . . . very limp, although holding the same shape . . . or really tight and gripping . . . no wavering of body parts.)

▶ Repeat all material from Beginning Grade, and then add:

"On the signal, make a very strong shape that you like and hold it. Then listen."

". . . . Very *slowly* let your muscles *relax,* and finally become so weak that you *melt right down* to the floor (complete collapse)."

(Repeat several times.)

". . . . Make another *strong shape, hold* it, and listen: *slowly relax* that shape and let it *flow into another shape* . . . make the new shape very firm and strong . . . relax, flow to a new shape . . . hold."

(Repeat several times.)

▶ Repeat all material from the Beginning and Middle Grades, and then add:

"Make a small, tight shape in your self space, hold it very still, and listen."

". . . . *Thrust one body part out, away* from the center of you so *strongly* that it takes you to a different level or shape . . . now *pull that body part back in very softly* and gently . . . back to the same small, tight shape."

(Repeat several times, with different body parts being thrust out strongly and pulled in gently, then reverse the action . . . soft gentle movement out from the center and strong action back in.)

Checklist of quality factors for Problem 60

☐ Understanding and feeling the gripping action in muscles that produces force.

☐ Demonstrating the ability to control the amount of muscle tension in the body, from strong to weak.

☐ M–L: Producing flowing movements which may be stopped and held firmly, then continued.

☐ L: Changing muscular tensions in individual body parts.

When children demonstrate these factors, go on to Problem 61.

PROBLEM 61

Beginning Grade	Middle Grade	Last Grade

"On the signal, stay in your <u>self space</u> and try <u>swinging</u> just <u>one arm forward and back at your side</u> while you listen."

". . . . Add the other arm and keep on swinging . . . add your head to the swing, too . . . does your whole body want to get in on the swing? . . . can your knees help out? . . . knees bending at the bottom of the swing? . . . can you make the swing more forceful by using more body parts? (yes) . . . some of you are swinging so hard you are lifting your whole body off the floor . . . try stepping forward and backward (rocking steps) along with your swing . . . does that make it more powerful? (yes)."

▶ Repeat all material from Beginning Grade, and then add:

". . . . Change the direction of your *swing* so it goes *from side to side* . . . try little swings and big swings . . . which is more forceful? . . . can more force be produced by making the range of your movement larger? (yes) . . . some of you are swinging so hard that you are making a whole circle . . . does stepping from side to side make the swinging more powerful? . . . why?"

▶ Repeat all material from Beginning and Middle Grades, and then add:

". . . . Try *swinging one leg* in different directions . . . can you swing it just from the knee down? . . . and then from the hip down? . . . can you get your whole body in on the swing? . . . what is the most powerful way you can swing that leg? (large range, whole body action) . . . use your other leg now."

Checklist of quality factors for Problem 61

☐ Beginning to develop a smooth body swing, using the whole body.

☐ B–M–L: Understanding that more force can be produced when more body parts are added to the

action, especially stepping (rocking weight from foot to foot) in line with the swing.

☐ M–L: Understanding that more force can be produced by making the range (size) of movement larger.

When children demonstrate these factors, go on to Problem 62.

PROBLEM 62

Beginning Grade	Middle Grade	Last Grade

"On the signal, get a yarn ball, find a self space facing an empty wall, and try different ways to throw the ball as forcefully as you can against the wall."

". . . . Throw as hard as you can and as straight as you can . . . can you make the ball go farther if you *step out toward the wall* when you throw? . . . as you did in the swing? . . . is that using more body parts for more force? (yes) . . . hold the ball in one hand now and don't throw it . . . try *swinging that arm back and forth* . . . *step back and forth*, too, to make your swing more powerful . . . if right-handed, step back with right foot on back swing and forward on left foot on forward swing . . . now try throwing the ball hard as you step forward."

(Practice. Work for smooth swings . . . legs and arms working together.)

▶ Repeat material from Beginning Grade, but stress hand and whole arm follow-through, pointing to the target. This will require frequent practice. Repeat the problem at least once a week for a month. Work toward smooth, powerful throws . . . stepping out on the opposite foot and controlling the path of the ball so it travels in a straight line to the wall. The ball need not be caught on the rebound.

▶ Repeat directions given for Middle Grade.

Checklist of quality factors for Problem 62

☐ Exploring a variety of ways to throw a ball forcefully.

☐ Increasing the force and accuracy of an underhand throw by:

    B—stepping toward the target with the opposite foot when throwing (right-hand throw, step out on left foot) . . . using more body parts to increase the force produced;

M–L—following through with the throwing hand and arm pointing toward the target to control the path of the ball . . . this motion increases the range of the movement, thus producing more force.

When children demonstrate these factors, go on to Problem 63.

PROBLEM 63

Beginning Grade	Middle Grade	Last Grade

"You have been throwing the balls very hard . . . very forcefully so far. On the signal, <u>put the ball away, get a balloon</u>, and see what you can do with it very softly in your self space."

". . . . *Control* the balloon by using only the force you need to keep it in the air in your space . . . can you feel how little force it takes to keep the balloon in control? . . . very light, soft, taps . . . now give the balloon a *very forceful hit* . . . how high can you make it go? . . . can you feel the difference in your muscles between gentle and strong hits?"

▶ Repeat all material from Beginning Grade, and then add:

"On the signal, <u>get a partner, put one balloon away</u>, and staying in a small space, see how gently you can <u>tap the balloon back and forth</u>."

". . . . Can you stay in your own space? . . . see how long you can keep the balloon in the air . . . tapping it very softly will help . . . gradually back away from your partner and keep the balloon going . . . does this take a bit more force?"

▶ Repeat all material from Beginning and Middle Grades, and then add:

"Listen for signals, then make up your <u>own game</u>. First, you and your partner find two more people close to you."

(Start . . . then stop when children are in fours.)

"Now decide who will put <u>one balloon away</u> and get <u>one rope</u>."

(Start . . . then stop when each group of four has *one balloon and one rope*.)

"Now the four of you <u>make up a game</u>, with two holding the rope and two sending the balloon back and forth over the rope."

(Start. After a few minutes, rope holders and players change places, and the game continues.)

Checklist of quality factors for Problem 63

☐ Applying very light force in controlling a balloon.

☐ Feeling the difference between light tension and strong tension in muscles.

☐ M: Quickly choosing partners and deciding who will put one balloon away. Cooperating with a partner

to keep the balloon in the air and to keep it in the partners' self space.

☐ L: Beginning to be self-sufficient in órganizing and creating a game harmoniously (introduction to net type of activity).

When children demonstrate these factors, go on to Problem 64.

PROBLEM 64

Beginning Grade	Middle Grade	Last Grade
"On the signal, put all the equipment away, find a self space and make an unusual, strong, big shape."	▶ Repeat all material from Beginning Grade.	▶ Repeat all material from Beginning Grade.

"... Do you feel strong all over? ... are your muscles gripping hard? ... now, *very slowly* let those muscles *relax* ... more relaxed ... more relaxed ... beginning to collapse ... and melt right down to the floor."

Review: Creating varying degrees of force

When children demonstrate an achievement of the objectives on page 133, go on to Theme 11.

ELEVENTH SET OF PROBLEMS/ORGANIZING THEME: ABSORBING FORCE

Content structure (for teachers)	Objectives (for children)

Concept

Movement for environmental control

Major ideas

1 Space, force, time, and flow are the elements of movement.
2 The force created by the body's own momentum and by other moving objects can be absorbed through use of the joints acting as shock absorbers.
3 The force to be absorbed may be in a horizontal plane (such as running or catching), a vertical plane (such as landing from a vertical jump or catching a vertical toss), or both (such as landing after a running long jump).

Selected facts

1 Absorbing force gradually may be accomplished in at least four ways:
increasing the distance over which the force is absorbed,
increasing the time over which the force is absorbed,
increasing the area over which the force is absorbed (ball glove vs. hand),
increasing the number of shock-absorbing joints used (whole body vs. one arm).
2 The more gradual the absorption of force, the less likely is the danger of injury from the force.

Children need to understand (knowledge)

1 That they can absorb force (slow down and stop momentum of their own body or of objects in motion) more safely by absorbing the force gradually.   B–M–L
2 That force can be absorbed more gradually by increasing the distance over which it is absorbed, increasing the time over which it can be absorbed, using as many joints as possible to absorb the force.   M–L

Children need to learn how (skill)

1 To catch and safely absorb the force of balls thrown by themselves or by classmates.   B–M–L
2 To absorb more efficiently the force created by their own momentum both horizontally (such as quick stops after running) and vertically such as soft, "squishy" landings after flight).   B–M–L

Children need to become (attitude)

The attitude objectives for this physical education program (page 52) are broad and cannot be achieved quickly; therefore, they will be the same throughout the entire three years. Please review them occasionally.

Teaching tips for eleventh set of problems

1 *Arrange equipment . . . before the physical education period:*
One ball that bounces per child.
As many jumping boxes as you have (minimum of 4).

2 *Discuss movement vocabulary . . . in the classroom:*

force	"squishy landings"
absorb force	forward stride position
"give"	

Introduction

"Last week we worked on creating force—moving very forcefully: running fast, jumping high, throwing hard. Sometimes we want to stop the force we've made: to quit running, to land softly after jumping high, to catch and hold a ball that was thrown hard."

"Absorbing force is like putting on the brakes in your car or bicycle. What happens if you stop too quickly? What we need to learn is to slow down (absorb force) gradually enough to be safe—not too jarring—and yet quickly enough to stop in a hurry."

Developmental problems and expected outcomes

PROBLEM 65

Beginning Grade	Middle Grade	Last Grade

"First we will try to stop after running. On the signal, speed out and run as fast as you can. Listen for a stopping signal and see how quickly you can stop without falling down."

(Start . . . then stop, many times. Check to see that good running starts are made each time.)

". . . . Can you feel the way your legs "give" to stop quickly? . . . your knees, ankles, and hips bend . . . so what happens to your *level*? . . . see what happens when you bend a little to stop quickly . . . notice, too, that you *lean backward* a little to stop quickly . . . can you see that you are *absorbing* your forward *force*? . . . that you are taking it inside of you *gradually*? . . . there is no reason to fall down when stopping."

▶ Repeat all material from Beginning Grade, and then add the following.

Continue to give starting and stopping signals frequently.

". . . . What kind of *foot position* is best for stopping quickly? . . . try out several . . . feet parallel and close together . . . far apart . . . forward stride position with feet far from each other . . . near to each other . . . about shoulder width apart . . . which foot position helps you stay on your feet instead of falling? . . . most of you have found a *forward stride position* very much like your starting position . . . be sure your *toes are pointing straight ahead* . . . why? . . . don't strain your ankle or knee by twisting."

▶ Repeat all material from Beginning and Middle Grades, and then add:

". . . What happens to the size (range) of your steps as you come to a quick stop? . . . try big steps and little steps . . . have you found that *short, choppy, 'giving' steps* really slow you down in a hurry? . . . no signals now, just practice quick starts and stops by yourself . . . see how much of your body you can use to produce force and to absorb force."

Checklist of quality factors for Problem 65

☐ Stopping quickly and safely on the feet . . . absorbing the forward force produced when running by:

B—lowering the body level (more joints) and by leaning slightly backward;

M—stopping with feet in a forward stride position, at least shoulder width apart (from toe of rear foot

to heel of forward foot), toes pointing straight ahead . . . flexing knees, ankles, and hips enough to absorb the forward momentum gradually and make a smooth, nonjolting stop,

L—shortening steps just prior to stopping . . . being aware of using the whole body to absorb force.

When children demonstrate these factors, go on to Problem 66.

PROBLEM 66

Beginning Grade	Middle Grade	Last Grade

"You discovered last week that putting more body parts into a movement makes the movement more forceful. Is it also true that putting more body parts into a movement makes it easier to absorb force?

"On the signal, get a ball, find a self space and bounce the ball straight down as forcefully as you can. See how high you can make the ball bounce, then catch it as it comes down. How many body parts can you use to absorb the force of the ball as you catch it?"

". . . . Give with your whole body as you catch the ball . . . 'squish' down a little . . . are you 'giving' with your knees? . . . with your chest? . . . with your stomach? . . . are you *pulling the ball* in to your body so you are 'giving' with your arms, too? . . . *reach high* for the ball, and then let your whole body help catch it . . . show me your most forceful bounce and your most 'squishy' catch."

(Have several student demonstrations. What makes the ball go up so high and straight? What makes the catch so soft and accurate? Practice again after discussion.)

▶ Repeat all material from Beginning Grade, and then add:

". . . . Instead of bouncing the ball, *toss it high* into the air and *catch it* as it comes down . . . how do you get the ball to go straight up? . . . let your *whole body be very 'squishy'* to absorb the downward force of the ball . . . *reach high* for the ball and let it and your body travel down until the force is absorbed . . . try to let the *ball in your hands flow all the way to the floor and right back up* for a new toss . . . see if you can find a rhythm of your own for tossing and catching . . . for example: up . . . wait . . . wait . . . catch-down and up." (Have student demonstrations, followed by discussion and then more practice.)

▶ Repeat all material from Beginning and Middle Grades. Then add:

". . . . This time, toss the ball up so you have to *run a few steps to catch it* . . . not so high at first . . . control the ball . . . when you *catch it*, let it *flow down and back up into the next toss* . . . some of you might try letting the flow take you into a roll on the floor . . . toss . . . catch-down-roll and up-toss . . . can you feel how the force is gradually absorbed? . . . using more body parts, more distance, more time?"

(Have student demonstrations, followed by discussion and then more practice.)

Checklist of quality factors for Problem 66

☐ Using arms, torso, and legs together to absorb the downward force of a falling ball. Suggested minimums:

   B—catching three out of four high bounces in self space,

   M—catching three out of four high tosses in self space,

   L—catching three out of four high tosses while moving in general space.

☐ Beginning to understand that using more body parts, more distance, and more time to absorb force makes

the absorption safer and easier. An exaggeration of the amount of "give" needed for receiving light objects is acceptable behavior at this point. Producing the amount of "give" appropriate to different forces is a longer-term goal.

☐ M–L: Making the movement more flowing: coordinating catching and giving, tossing and producing force without a break in the movement flow.

When children demonstrate these factors, go on to Problem 67.

PROBLEM 67

Beginning Grade	Middle Grade	Last Grade

"On the signal, get a partner, put one ball away, and bounce the other ball forcefully to each other."

".... Stay in your own space if you can ... try to send the ball right into your partner's hands ... are you still *reaching out for the ball and 'giving'* with it to catch it? ... try letting the ball flow right into your stomach or right by your side ... hold it firmly with your *fingers* ... how *smoothly* can you *catch and throw*? ... catch and throw ... to bounce it forcefully, does it help to *step out toward your partner*? ... does it help to let your *hands point to the floor* where you want the ball to bounce after you let go of the ball? ... catch and throw very smoothly."

▶ Repeat all material from Beginning Grade, and then add:

".... *Explore different ways* to pass the ball back and forth in self space without letting the ball touch the floor ... try *high tosses* ... and tosses that go *straight across* to your partner ... do you notice the difference in the way you absorb the force? ... if the ball is coming down, what direction do you let it flow in your hands? (down) ... if the ball is coming straight across at you, what direction do you let it flow in your hands? (into the body or straight past the side of the body) ... how *smoothly* can you absorb that force and go right on to throw the ball back? ... mix up high tosses and straight across tosses ... underhand and overhand ... find different, good ways to send the ball smoothly to your partner."

▶ Repeat all material from Beginning Grade, and then add:

".... *Slowly move into general space* while you are playing catch ... use any kind of throw ... bounce ... straight ... or high level toss ... be sure the ball is in control ... think about *follow through* with your whole body toward your partner so he can catch the ball ... think about *'giving' smoothly* with your body to absorb the force of a throw ... what do you notice about where to aim the ball when your partner is moving? ... can you aim it right where he is or do you have to *aim in front of him*? ... why?"

Checklist of quality factors for Problem 67

☐ B: Catching 3 out of 4 bounce passes in self space. Stepping out toward partner to generate more force in the pass. Reaching out for the ball and giving with the whole body to receive the pass.

☐ M: Catching 3 out of 4 passes in self space. Changing the direction of the "give" from downward to horizontal depending on the path of the ball.

☐ L: Catching 3 out of 4 passes while moving in general space. Beginning to "lead the receiver" ... aim the pass slightly ahead of the receiver so he will be there when the pass arrives.

When children demonstrate these factors, go on to Problem 68.

PROBLEM 68

Beginning Grade	Middle Grade	Last Grade

"On the signal, put the balls away, find a self space, and see how many different ways you can jump up and land softly. Notice what your knees do to absorb the force of your jump."

". . . . If you don't bend your knees, you land with a jolt, don't you? . . . can you make your *whole body* into a shock absorber? . . . very quiet, soft, 'squishy' landings after high jumps . . . can you *let your body 'give' all the way down to the floor in a collapse?* . . . a very forceful jump high up and a very *quiet* landing and collapse . . . how smooth can you make this whole motion? . . . try not to stop between the landing and the collapsing to the floor . . . keep trying different ways to jump, land, and collapse."

▶ Repeat all material in Beginning Grade, and then add:

". . . . Add a roll after your collapse . . . *jump, land, collapse, and roll* out to your feet . . . think of as many ways to do this as you can . . . different ways to jump . . . different ways to land and collapse . . . different ways to roll out and onto your feet . . . how *strong* is your *take-off*? . . . how *soft* is your *landing*? . . . can you absorb the force of your landing more gradually by rolling? . . . why? (more distance, more time, more area, whole body)."

▶ Repeat all material from Beginning and Middle Grades, and then add:

"Move into general space now . . . run, jump, land softly, collapse, roll to your feet and run on . . . what direction should you roll?"

(Free exploration, then . . . .)

". . . . Listen for signals . . . get ready to start quickly . . . start quickly . . . run fast . . . slow down . . . run fast and jump, collapse, and roll . . . run backward . . . change direction quickly . . . move sideways . . . move forward slowly . . . jump high, collapse, and roll . . . run slowly . . . get ready to stop quickly . . . stop, now!

(And so on.)

Option

This may be developed into a game, rewarding those who respond most quickly by allowing them to call movement requirements. The movement chart (page 125) may be used again, with flight, collapse, and roll added.

Checklist of quality factors for Problem 68

☐ B: Landing quietly and smoothly and "giving" to the floor in a collapse when jumping in self space. Realizing that the body must absorb its own force upon landing and that bending knees, ankles, and hips helps to absorb the force more gradually.

☐ M: Absorbing the force of the falling body gradually by smoothly collapsing and rolling in self space (using a large area to receive the force).

☐ L: Collapsing and rolling in the same direction as the force, when moving in general space.

When children demonstrate these factors, go on to Problem 69.

PROBLEM 69

Beginning Grade	Middle Grade	Last Grade

"Point to the box nearest you. On the signal, bring out that box and take turns flying off the box in different ways. When you land on your feet, collapse and roll."

". . . . See if you can absorb the force of your flight very softly . . . be sure to 'give' with all parts of your body . . . strong, high flights . . . can you do different things with your body while you are in the air? . . . make a lot of force to get up in the air, and absorb the force gradually, softly, and safely when you come down . . . how rounded can you be when you roll? . . . how 'squishy' are you when you land, collapse, and roll?"

▶ Repeat all material from Beginning Grade, and then add:

"On the signal, arrange the boxes in a big circle. When you are finished, sit down in the pathway between the boxes."

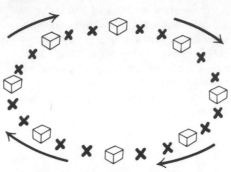

"On the signal, move around the equipment circuit, watching your spacing as you go . . . when you come to a box, fly onto it (if low enough), fly off in different ways, land softly, collapse, and roll . . . move to the next box in a very strong way."

". . . . how *high* can you fly? . . . how many *shapes* can you make in the air? . . . how *softly* can you land and roll out? . . . how much *force* can you create? . . . how? . . . how much *force* can you *absorb*? . . . how? . . . how many different ways can you move strongly from one box to the next? (vary level, direction, range, shape, and so on) . . . how *well spaced out* can you stay? . . . no waiting in line . . . could you do two or more rolls between boxes? . . . can you make your whole movement pattern around the room *smooth* and *flowing*?"

▶ Repeat all material from Beginning and Middle Grades, and then add:

"On the signal, sit down in the middle of the circle."

(Have *individual students demonstrate* one circuit around the room. After each, have the *class analyze the movement:* strength of takeoff . . . softness and safeness of land, collapse, and roll . . . difference of shapes made in the air . . . smooth, flowing quality of entire movement pattern, and so on.

After analyses, have children practice again to take advantage of what they have learned from the demonstrations.)

Review: Creating and absorbing force

When children demonstrate an achievement of the objectives on page 142, go on to Theme 12.

TWELFTH SET OF PROBLEMS/ORGANIZING THEME: MOVING ON-BALANCE AND OFF-BALANCE (GRAVITY)

Content structure (for teachers)	Objectives (for children)

Concept

Movement for environmental control

Major ideas

1 Gravity is a force pulling downward toward the center of the earth.
2 The force of gravity limits movement as it pulls the weight of the body downward toward the center of the earth.
3 Gravity pulls on all parts of the body in such a way that a single force exists through the weight center of the body which is called the body's center of gravity.

Selected facts

1 The center of gravity of a human being is in the region of the hips when the human being is standing.
2 Any movement of a body part will cause the center of gravity to shift in the direction of the movement.
3 When a person moves in an on-balance way, the center of gravity falls inside the base of support.
4 When a person moves in an off-balance way (flying or falling), the center of gravity falls outside the base of support.
5 The larger the base of support, the more stable the body position.

Children need to understand (knowledge)

1 That gravity is pulling downward on their bodies constantly.   B–M–L
2 That to maintain balance, their body weight must be over the base of support (e.g., feet, hands and feet).   B–M–L
3 That the larger the base of support, the easier it is to be on-balance.   B–M–L

Children need to learn how (skill)

1 To move in a variety of ways on-balance.   B–M–L
2 To develop balance on smaller and smaller bases of support.   B–M–L
3 To achieve balance in a wide variety of positions, moving and motionless.   B–M–L
4 To begin to put more weight on the arms to achieve an on-balance position.   B–M–L

Children need to become (attitude)

The attitude objectives for this physical education program (page 52) are broad and cannot be achieved quickly; therefore, they will be the same throughout the entire three years. Please review them occasionally.

Teaching tips for twelfth set of problems

1 *Arrange equipment . . . before the physical education period:* As many benches and low balance beams as you have (minimum of 4).
A pathway drawn on the floor with chalk, tape, or white shoe polish.

Optional equipment: as many mats as you have (minimum of 4).

2 *Discuss movement vocabulary . . . in the classroom:*

balance	gravity
on-balance	base of support—
off-balance	wide, narrow,
stable (stability)	big, little

Introduction

"This week we are going to work on balance—moving on-balance and going off-balance. What happens if you move on-balance? (Your muscles hold you upright and you don't fall down.) What happens if you move off-balance? (You fall or fly and fall.) What is it that makes you fall when you are off-balance? Why can't you just move in any position like an astronaut does in space? (Gravity, a force pulling downward toward the center of the earth.) On the signal, hold your arms over your head. Now relax your arm muscles as much as you can—just let go. What made your arms fall down to your sides? (Gravity.) Think about holding a ball out in front of you and then just letting go of it. Why wouldn't it stay right there in space where you put it? (Gravity.)"

"We know that our muscles are strong enough to hold us up to walk even with gravity pulling down on us all the time. But are our muscles able to hold us up in any position? Try it. On the signal make a balanced shape and hold it. On what are you balanced? (Feet, shoulders, hips, knees?) That is called your base of support—that is what supports your weight—those are the parts that touch the floor and hold your weight. Are you on-balance now? (Yes.) How big is your base of support? Can you make it bigger? Are you still on-balance? You are if your weight is over your base of support. Can you make your base of support much smaller? Can you still be on-balance over that little base of support? Is it easier or harder to be on-balance with a little base of support? (Harder.) Try it again."

(Repeat several times.)

". . . . Make a new shape and hold it very still . . . are you on-balance or off-balance? . . . what is your base of support? . . . how big is it? . . . try making the base bigger . . . now smaller . . . try leaning your shape until you go off-balance . . . from a big base . . . from a little base . . . what makes you fall or change your base of support when you lean too far? (Gravity—the body weight is no longer over the base of support, so gravity pulls it down.) . . . try leaning too far again."

(Repeat several times.)

". . . . See how many different shapes you can make with four body parts on the floor . . . make the biggest base you can . . . relax . . . how small a base can you make on four parts? . . . relax . . . how big a base can you make on three parts? . . . is it smaller than with four parts? (Yes.) . . . is it more stable (more on-balance)? (No.) . . . how small a base can you make on these three parts? . . . is it more stable than your big base? (No.) . . . how big a base can you make on two parts? . . . how many different ways can you balance on one part? . . . why is this harder than balancing on four parts? (Smaller base—harder to keep the weight over the base.)"

Moving on-balance

Moving off-balance
(flight or falling)

Base of support

Developmental problems and expected outcomes

PROBLEM 70

Beginning Grade	Middle Grade	Last Grade

"You all know that we walk on-balance and on just two feet, which is a small base. On the signal, see how many ways you can move into general space, taking some of the weight on your hands as you go."

". . . . What is your *base of support?* . . . how big is it? . . . how stable is it? . . . if someone bumped into you, would you be more stable, more balanced than if you were walking on two feet? . . . why? (bigger base) . . . try moving *quickly*, then more *slowly* . . . try changing the *range* of your movement . . . very long steps . . . very short steps . . . can you change *direction* and *level* very quickly, still staying on-balance?"

▶ Repeat all material from Beginning Grade, and then add:

"Keep moving into general space and see how many body parts you can use as part of your base of support."

". . . . Have you taken some of your weight on your shoulders? . . . hips? . . . toes? . . . chest? . . . spine? . . . elbows? . . . fingers? . . . whole legs? . . . head? . . . heels?"

(And so on. Give freeze signal frequently; then have children identify their bases of support in that shape. Discuss why that shape can be held— why it is on-balance.)

▶ Repeat all material from Beginning and Middle Grades, and then add:

"Find a way to move on hands and feet that is very balanced and stable, and then listen."

". . . . On all fours . . . change level . . . change direction . . . change range . . . change the amount of force . . . change the way the feet and hands are meeting and parting . . . change pathway . . . change shape."

(And so on.)

". . . . On your own, look at the *starting position* that you use for running fast . . . is it balanced? . . . is it stable? . . . where is your body weight? . . . speed out and stop quickly . . . look at your stopping position . . . is it balanced? . . . is it stable? . . . where is your body weight? . . . how big is your base of support?"

Checklist of quality factors for Problem 70

☐ Identifying the base of support while moving in a wide variety of ways:

  B—including changes in speed, range, direction, and level while taking some of the weight on the hands;

  M—including awareness of a wide variety of body parts which can be used as the base of support;

  L—maintaining balance while moving on hands and feet in a wide variety of ways;

  L—relating the balance ideas to starting and stopping positions.

☐ Increasing stability by enlarging the base of support.

☐ Taking some body weight on hands and arms.

When children demonstrate these factors, go on to Problem 71.

PROBLEM 71

Beginning Grade	Middle Grade	Last Grade

"So far we have been trying to be on-balance. Let's work now on going off-balance safely and rolling out to the feet. On the signal, make some kind of balanced shape; then listen for signals."

". . . . Very carefully, *lean that shape until you go off-balance* . . . curl your body, make it very round, and *roll out* . . . soft safe rolls right out until you are standing on your feet . . . now *balance on two hands and a knee* . . . *lean and roll out to your feet* . . . now balance on one hand and one foot . . . lean, roll out, recover . . . balance with one leg at a high level . . . lean, roll out, recover . . . balance with a big base of support . . . lean, roll out, recover . . . balance with a narrower base of support . . . lean, roll out, recover."

(And so on.)

▶ Repeat all material from Beginning Grade, and then add:

". . . . See how many *different balances* you can make on *three parts* . . . *hold* each balance very still until you count to five . . . then *roll out to a new balance on three parts* . . . a different balance on three parts each time with a soft roll in between . . . can you make your roll flow smoothly into the new balance? . . . see how many *different balances* you can make on *two parts* with a *soft roll in between* . . . have you used different body parts? . . . shoulders and arms, for example? . . . make balanced shapes at different levels . . . have you tried making different kinds of shapes while balanced on two parts? . . . rounded? . . . twisted? . . . be sure to tuck all body parts in when rolling."

▶ Repeat all material from Beginning and Middle Grades, and then add:

". . . . This time, make a *balanced shape, hold it,* then see if you can *roll out and recover in exactly the same shape* . . . try it on your own."

(Free exploration. Then . . . .)

". . . . How many *different balances* can you make on *just one body part*? . . . be sure that you hold your balance very still before going on to a new one . . . why is this harder? (smaller base of support) . . . find your most stable balanced position on one body part; then listen: twist your position until you go off-balance, roll, recover into the same balance . . . stretch it until you go off-balance, roll, recover . . . bend it until you go off-balance, roll, recover."

Balance

Lean

Roll out

Balance

Checklist of quality factors for Problem 71

☐ Developing confidence in going off-balance.

☐ Using a soft, tucked roll to absorb the force of the fall and to position the body for a recovery of balance.

☐ Beginning to roll out of an off-balanced situation without thinking about it.

☐ Gaining skill in recovering balance quickly and safely.

☐ Developing ability to balance on many different bases of support:

   B—on specified body parts with broader and narrower bases;

   M—on three body parts and on two body parts;

   L—on one body part, being able to duplicate a balance exactly (balance . . . roll . . . *same* balance).

When children demonstrate these factors, go on to Problem 72.

PROBLEM 72

Beginning Grade	Middle Grade	Last Grade

"On the signal, find a self space and try to keep your hands on the floor in one spot while you move your feet around in different ways."

". . . . Can you find ways to take some of your weight on your hands while your feet are moving around? . . . are your hands part of your base of support? . . . how many places can you take your feet? . . . into different levels? . . . have you tried different ways of jumping or hopping your feet around as well as running them around your hands? . . . how many different ways can your feet meet and part? . . . have you tried to have your stomach up toward the ceiling part of the time? . . . can you keep moving s-m-o-o-t-h-l-y all the time? . . . how strong can you make your arms so that gravity won't pull you down? . . . how many ways can you move if your base of support is very big? . . . hands far apart, and at least one foot far from your hands? . . . how many ways can you move if your base of support is very small? . . . hands close together and at least one foot close to your hands? . . . find a way to move in which you are very stable, very much on-balance."

▶ Repeat all material from Beginning Grade, and then add the following.

Option

Use mats if you wish. Allow children who are confident without them to work on the floor.

"Now, keep both hands on the floor and see how many ways you can get one or two feet higher than your head."

". . . . When both feet are off the ground, are you balanced on your hands for just a second? (not unless the body weight is over the hands) . . . explore different ways of getting your hips up high while your hands remain on the floor, taking some or all of your weight . . . try changing the width of your hand placement on the floor again . . . find a way in which you feel most stable, most on-balance . . . have you found several ways to balance in which you can hold very still with at least one foot at a high level? . . . have you tried moving from one balance to another very s-m-o-o-t-h-l-y?"

(Expect and allow great variation in the students' abilities to maintain balance even momentarily on the hands. If children are not pushed to go beyond their abilities, they will explore safely and without fear.)

▶ Repeat all material from the Beginning and Middle Grades, and then add the following. Again, mats may be used.

"This time, put your head and both hands on the floor. See how many ways you can move your feet around this base."

". . . . Have you tried getting one or both feet into a high level? . . . what can you do to get one or both feet as high as possible? . . . look carefully at your hands and head on the floor . . . what kind of base do they make? . . . think about this . . . would your head and hands make a better base for balancing if they were lined up in a straight row like this:

X   O   X

. . . or would they make a better base for balancing if they were placed in a triangle like this:

O

X   X

. . . why would the triangle be better? (larger area in the middle for the weight to be over) . . . find a good triangle position for your head and hands and see if you can get most of your weight over them . . . are your hips and spine up over the triangle? . . . some of you have one foot really stretched high over your triangle . . . has anyone been able to balance for a short time with both feet off the ground? . . . how many different ways can you balance for a short time with both feet off the ground? . . . how many different ways can you balance your legs over your base? . . . if you should go off-balance, what is a soft, safe way to recover your balance? (curl up, roll out to a new balance)."

(Again, much variation in ability will be evident. Praise the child who finally gets one toe over the head as much as the child who does a headstand easily.)

Checklist of quality factors for Problem 72

☐ B: Taking more body weight on the hands and arms while moving on balance.

☐ M: Beginning to achieve controlled balance with the hands as the most important part of the base of support. Getting the hips and one or two feet over the base of support (lead up to a handstand).

☐ L: Beginning to achieve controlled balance with the head and hands as the most important part of the base of support. Feeling the weight placement over the triangle made by head and hands on the floor. Getting the hips and one or two feet over the base of support (lead up to a headstand).

☐ Using soft, curled rolls to recover balance quickly and safely.

When children demonstrate these factors, go on to Problem 73.

PROBLEM 73

Beginning Grade	Middle Grade	Last Grade

"Point to the balance beam or bench nearest to you. On the signal, bring out the beam or bench to an open space and take turns finding very on-balanced ways to move across it."

". . . . Have you tried moving on all fours? . . . on three body parts? . . . on two body parts? . . . can anyone move across without using the feet? . . . is your base of support very wide? (no, only as wide as the bench or beam) . . . *stop in the middle of the bench or beam and make a strong balanced shape* . . . try a different balance each time you cross . . . can you *hold your balanced shape very still while you count to five?* . . . have you tried low balances and high balances? . . . twisted balances and rounded balances? . . . if you should topple off the bench or beam, what could you do to absorb the force of the fall? (land on feet, collapse, then roll out and recover balance)."

▶ Repeat all material from Beginning Grade, and then add:

"Take turns making a balanced shape at the end of the bench or beam before you get on; then get on and make the same balanced shape on the bench . . . get off at the other end and make the same balanced shape at the finish."

". . . . Balance—get on—balance—get off—balance . . . work on finding a new shape for the sequence while you are waiting in line . . . how *smoothly* can you do the *whole sequence?* . . . think about different ways to center your weight over your base of support."

▶ Repeat all material from Beginning and Middle Grades. In addition:

(Have *demonstrations* by students who produce sequences in which the *three shapes are very similar*, and who are beginning to produce smooth, flowing movements to tie the sequence together. *Discuss* the good points of each demonstration—how still each shape was held, why it was possible for the shape to be held very still, how big the base was, how many body parts made up the base, etc. After each demonstration, have all the students try variations of the same sequence. Several students can then verbalize what the variation is, e.g., level, range, rounded rather than twisted, etc.)

Checklist of quality factors for Problem 73

☐ Gaining confidence and control when moving and balancing off the ground (on bench or beam). Suggested minimums:

   B—Trying a wide variety of ways to move across the apparatus, including using different body parts and changing levels. Holding a wide variety of shapes still when balancing on apparatus.

   M—Being able to repeat the same balanced shape on the floor and on the bench. Producing a flowing movement sequence.

   L—Analyzing and verbalizing the similarity between two held shapes and the base of support for them. Reproducing balances made by others and producing specific variations of them, indicating an understanding of the movement elements being varied.

☐ Always landing on the feet first (then rolling, if necessary) when dismounting.

When children demonstrate these factors, go on to Problem 74.

PROBLEM 74

Beginning Grade	Middle Grade	Last Grade

(A chalk, tape, or white shoe polish pathway is drawn on the floor. Existing lines in a gymnasium can be used, although they are not as challenging as drawn lines because the width of line does not vary.)

"On the signal, put the benches and beams away and find a self space on the pathway marked on the floor. See how many balanced shapes you can make in your self space on the pathway."

".... Now start *moving* into *general space* very slowly, *staying on the pathway* ... see if you can stay right on it ... pretend it is up high and you don't want to fall off ... if you meet someone on the pathway find a way to pass him so neither of you must step off the path ... can you change *levels* as you go? ... *directions?* ... *range?* ... where the path is very narrow, see how small you can make your base of support ... see how stable and balanced you can be on your small base of support."

▶ Repeat all material from Beginning Grade, and then add:

".... See if all of you can *move in the same direction on the pathway* now ... all flowing along in the same direction ... can you *space* yourselves *out* so there is no crowding or bumping ... now listen to the *drum beat*—as it goes *faster,* you go faster ... as it goes *slower,* you go slower ... try moving on *different body parts:* on your whole body (sliding) ... on all fours ... different ways ... on three parts ... different ways ... on two parts ... different ways ... on one foot ... different ways to use your body while you are hopping on one foot."

(And so on.)

▶ Repeat all material from Beginning and Middle Grades, and then add:

".... Put four of the *benches or beams* on the pathway ... continue moving along the pathway, but fly off the benches or beams *when you come to* them ... make soft, squishy landings *on the pathway,* then freeze for a second so you don't fall off ... watch the spacing ... *listen:* move at a _____ level ... move with your _____ leading (front, back, side) ... move very forcefully ... move very lightly ... freeze in a twisted shape ... lean until you go off-balance, roll and recover back on the pathway ... pick up speed gradually ... slow down gradually ... make a high shape with one body part touching the floor ... relax."

(And so on.)

Review: Moving on-balance and off-balance

When children demonstrate an achievement of the objectives on page 150, go on to Theme 13.

THIRTEENTH SET OF PROBLEMS/ORGANIZING THEME: TRANSFERRING WEIGHT (ROCKING, ROLLING, SLIDING)

Content structure (for teachers)	Objectives (for children)

Concept

Movement for environmental control

Major ideas

1 Locomotion is achieved by transferring the body weight from one body part to another.
2 Body weight can be transferred in four different ways:

rocking and rolling sliding	(weight transfers to adjacent body parts),
steplike actions	(weight transfers to nonadjacent body parts),
flight	(weight transfers into the air).

Selected facts

1 Rocking is achieved by moving the weight of the body gradually along the body, using the parts *naturally next* (anatomically adjacent) to each other (e.g., rocking forward and backward with each part of the spine taking the weight in turn).
2 Rolling is achieved by moving the weight of the body gradually along the body, using body parts *naturally next to each other* as in rocking *and* by bringing next to each other parts of the body which are not naturally adjacent (e.g., feet next to shoulders in a forward or backward roll).
3 In rocking or rolling, the body should be in a rounded, curved position wherever it touches the floor. The head is an extension of the spine and should be included in the curve. The angular parts (arms, legs) should be brought within the curved shape of the body.
4 Sliding is achieved by moving while the body weight remains in constant contact with a surface (floor, board) on the same body part (hips, front, side, or thigh). The body slides better when streamlined and when the weight is taken on a small area (less friction).

Children need to understand (knowledge)

1	That movement from place to place is dependent on weight transference.	B–M–L
2	That they can transfer their body weight to body parts that are naturally next to each other (rocking).	B–M–L
3	That they can transfer their body weight to body parts brought next to each other.	B–M–L
4	That safe rocking and rolling require a rounded surface next to the floor and all body parts touching the floor brought into a compact curved shape.	B–M–L
5	That after gaining momentum, they can move on the floor on one body part (sliding).	B–M–L

Children need to learn how (skill)

1	To rock, roll, and slide safely by controlling the transfer of body weight to parts that are next to each other.	B–M–L
2	To *feel* the transference of weight to adjacent body parts.	M–L

Children need to become (attitude)

The attitude objectives for this physical education program (page 52) are broad and cannot be achieved quickly; therefore, they will be the same throughout the entire three years. Please review them occasionally.

Teaching tips for thirteenth set of problems

1 *Arrange equipment . . . before the physical education period:* A variety of apparatus on which children can balance, move across, slide, rock, and roll. Suggestions: benches, 2 or 3 boxes pushed together, low flat beams, inclined boards hooked onto boxes or stools. If you have mats, scatter them about general space prior to the lesson for children who prefer rocking and rolling on them.

2 *Discuss movement vocabulary . . . in the classroom:*

transfer weight	sliding
shift weight	body parts that grow
move weight	next to each other
rocking	body parts that are brought
rolling	next to each other

Introduction

"Last week, we discovered that if we lean too far . . . what happens? (Go off-balance.) Why? (Weight is not over the base of support.) We also found that we can shift our weight from one body part to another. Try this: put all your weight on one foot . . . now shift all your weight to the other foot . . . now shift your weight to both feet . . . now shift your weight to your hands and feet . . . now shift your weight to your seat and your feet. Where is most of your weight? (On your seat)."

"In the next few weeks, we are going to find many ways to shift or transfer weight. Any time you move, you are shifting or transferring your weight. And there are four main ways to shift weight: (1) rocking and rolling, (2) sliding, (3) taking steps, and (4) flying."

"This week we will work on rocking, rolling, and sliding. When we rock or roll or slide, we shift our weight to body parts that are next to each other. See if you can feel the transfer of weight during these problems."

Rocking and rolling

Rolling

Stepping

Flight

Developmental problems and expected outcomes

PROBLEM 75

Beginning Grade	Middle Grade	Last Grade

"On the signal, see how many different ways you can find to rock your weight back and forth on body parts that are next to each other."

(Free exploration. Encourage rocking from *different positions*—sitting, lying on front, lying on back. Ask, "Where is your weight?")

". . . Now try shifting your weight *up and down your spine* . . . *lying on your back* . . . can you do a bigger rock when you are all stretched out or when you are *curled*? . . . is every part of your spine touching the floor during the rock? . . . how many different places can you put your feet and hands while you are rocking? . . . now see how many ways you can *rock on your tummy* . . . can you make your rocking smooth with no stops? . . . how many places can you put your hands while you are rocking? (near the chest on the floor to push off, behind the back, holding the ankles, and so on) . . . does this take a lot of force? (yes) . . . which is easier, rocking on your front or on your back? . . . why? (because the body can be more rounded by curling than it can be by arching) . . . try to feel your weight moving up and down your front."

▶ Repeat all material from Beginning Grade, and then add:

". . . How many *different ways* can you *rock on your back*? . . . change *direction* (side to side, forward and back) . . . change *speed* (slowly and quickly) . . . change *range* (small and large) . . . think about your *feet* while you are rocking . . . can you touch your toes over your head on the floor and then rock back? . . . how can your *hands* help? . . . can any of you rock hard enough to *rock up to your feet*? . . . work on rocking hard enough to shift all your weight onto your feet."

▶ Repeat all material from Beginning and Middle Grades, and then add:

"On the signal, choose a partner close to you and decide who will be leader first . . . the leader will rock in different ways and the follower will try to match the leader's movements."

(Free exploration. Encourage leaders to restrict their movements to the limits of the followers' abilities. Also encourage the students to "teach each other" to keep body parts close together in a curled position to rock more easily and, if they are ready, to help transfer the body weight from the spine to the feet. *Reverse leader-follower roles.*)

Checklist of quality factors for Problem 75

☐ Rocking in a wide variety of ways while being aware of the transfer of weight from one body part to another body part that grows next to it (up and down the spine, up and down the front, from one hip to the other, and so on).

☐ Controlling weight transfer while rocking, so that the rock is smooth rather than jerky.

☐ M: Rocking in different directions, speeds, ranges. Rocking with enough force to transfer weight to the feet.

☐ L: Matching a partner's movements.

When children demonstrate these factors, go on to Problem 76.

PROBLEM 76

Beginning Grade	Middle Grade	Last Grade

"So far you have been shifting your weight from one body part to another body part that grows next to it. Do you think that you can <u>put body parts next to each other that don't grow next to each other?</u> Try putting your feet next to your hands, and shifting your weight back and forth."

". . . . Curl up in a tight, little ball with your chin tucked down to your chest. Try shifting your weight from your hands to your feet . . . if you start to lose your balance, just roll out and recover . . . stop."

"To change a rock into a roll, you have to keep the movement going in the same direction."

Choose a student to demonstrate.

1   Rock side to side on the front in a stretched out position; then keep the movement going in one direction, resulting in a log roll.
2   Rock side to side on the back in a stretched position; then rock with enough force to keep the movement going in one direction, resulting in a log roll.
3   Rock forward and back on the spine, with the body in a curled position. When body weight is on the shoulders, drop feet over the head onto the floor, push lightly against the floor with hands placed behind the shoulders, and keep the movement going in the same direction, resulting in a backward roll.
4   Squat down in a curled position with hands on the floor just in front of feet, chin tucked to chest. Transfer weight slowly from feet to hands (raising hips) to back of shoulders (not head) and roll out, resulting in a forward roll.

"On the signal, practice <u>changing a rock into a roll.</u>"

". . . . How smoothly can you roll from one body part to another? . . . how *rounded* can you be? . . . can you roll in different *directions?* . . . can you roll when you are *curled up* and when you are *stretched out* long and narrow? . . . can any of you *finish your roll on your feet,* then do another roll? . . . remember to roll as smoothly and softly as you can . . . try to keep your arms and legs tucked into your rolling shape . . . if they poke out of the shape, your roll will not be so smooth and soft."

▶ Repeat all material from Beginning Grade, and then add:

". . . . When you are rolling forward or backward, *pay attention to your hands* . . . do you shift your weight onto your hands? (yes) . . . how far apart should your hands be? (about shoulder width apart) . . . be sure your *hands are open with fingers straight* . . . why? (bigger base of support) . . . also *pay attention to your head* . . . can you make your head *a part of the curve of your spine?* . . . if you are doing a forward roll, can you tuck your head down so far that your *weight is never on your head?* . . . shift your weight from your hands to your shoulders."

▶ Repeat all material from Beginning and Middle Grades, and then add:

". . . . Try starting on your *feet,* doing *two rolls,* and finishing on your *feet* . . . practice until you can do this sequence very smoothly—no stops or jerks . . . now see how many *different pathways* you can take while doing your sequence: stand, two rolls, stand . . . have you tried going back and forth with your sequence? . . . or making a curved pathway? . . . or a zigzag pathway?"

See illustrations on next page

Checklist of quality factors for Problem 76

☐ Gaining enough momentum in a rock so that it becomes a roll; understanding that a rock that keeps going in the same direction becomes a roll.

☐ Rolling in a wide variety of ways—stretched, curled, sideways, forward, backward, over the shoulders.

   B: Smooth, soft rolls on rounded body parts, with arms and legs tucked into the shape.

   M: Conscious use of widespread open hands pressing against the floor to take the body weight

momentarily during a roll. Consciously including the head in the curve of the spine, thus not using the head for weight-bearing in a forward roll.

L: Creating sequences of movement in which a starting position, two rolls in specific pathways, and a finishing position are recognizable and performed in a smooth flow.

When children demonstrate these factors, go on to Problem 77.

PROBLEM 77

Beginning Grade	Middle Grade	Last Grade

(Use this problem only if you have a smooth floor.)

"Sliding is another way to move on parts that are next to each other, and sometimes you can move on just one part. On the signal, see how many ways you can slide."

". . . . How many body parts can be used for sliding? . . . how far can you go in your slide?"

▶ Repeat all material from Beginning Grade, and then add:

". . . . Most of you are running and then sliding . . . can you think of *other ways to start your slide?* . . . standing? . . . sitting? . . . lying down?"

▶ Repeat all material from Beginning and Middle Grades, and then add:

". . . . See how long you can *keep moving just by rocking, rolling, and sliding* . . . keep going . . . smoothly."

Checklist of quality factors for Problem 77

☐ Sliding in a wide variety of ways.

☐ Gaining momentum for a slide in a wide variety of ways: running, pushing, pulling.

When children demonstrate these factors, go on to Problem 78.

PROBLEM 78

(This problem is designed for children to explore rocking, rolling, and sliding off the floor, on apparatus. Use whatever apparatus you have, with no more than six children at one piece of apparatus. The following is an example of organization that could be used at all three grade levels.)

"On the signal, get out the equipment and explore ways of moving on it."

(When all equipment is in place and all children are organized into harmonious working groups, then give problems to each group. Examples follow.)

A's: Find different ways to *mount, rock* on the boxes, *dismount,* and *roll.*

B's: Find different ways to *mount, roll* on the bench, *dismount,* and *roll.*

C's: Find different ways to *mount, slide, dismount,* and *roll.*

". . . . Use your space wisely . . . wait until the equipment is empty before getting on . . . land on your feet first, then "give" and roll to absorb the force . . . if you have the space, practice rocking, rolling, and sliding while you are waiting your turn on the equipment . . . think about shifting your weight smoothly."

(After a period of exploration, rotate A's to B position, B's to C position, C's to A position. Rotate again after another period of exploration, thus giving each child the opportunity to work on all three pieces of apparatus and on all three skills.)

A. Rocking — Two boxes secured together

B. Rolling — Wide benches

C. Sliding — Stool or box with an inclined board attached

Checklist of quality factors for Problem 78

☐ Exploring many ways of rocking, rolling, and sliding on apparatus; gaining confidence in moving off the ground.

☐ Moving onto the apparatus after the preceding person has dismounted.

When children demonstrate these factors, go on to Problem 79.

PROBLEM 79

Beginning Grade	Middle Grade	Last Grade

"On the signal, put the equipment away, find a self space, and practice curling and stretching."

". . . . How many different ways can you stretch? . . . how many different ways can you curl? . . . and how tightly can you curl? . . . where is your weight when you are stretched? . . . and when you are curled? . . . what is your base of support? . . . put a rock between the curl and stretch: *curl . . . rock . . . stretch . . . rock* . . . can you feel how you are shifting your weight? . . . now put a roll between your curl and stretch: *curl . . . roll . . . stretch . . . roll.*"

▶ Repeat all material from Beginning Grade, and then add:

"Make up a short sequence of your own in which you curl, stretch, rock, and roll . . . be sure it has a start and a finish . . . practice until you can do it the same way every time."

(Have the class evaluate individual children's demonstrations. Were the stretches fully extended? Were the curls tight and compact? Were the rolls soft and smooth? Was the sequence flowing?)

▶ Repeat all material from Beginning and Middle Grades, and then add:

"Find a partner close to you and decide who will be leader first. Leader, teach your sequence to your partner."

". . . . Can you do your sequence side by side at the same time? . . . reverse roles . . . follower, teach your sequence to the leader."

Review: Transfer of weight (rock, roll, slide)

When children demonstrate an achievement of the objectives on page 158, go on to Theme 14.

FOURTEENTH SET OF PROBLEMS/ORGANIZING THEME: TRANSFERRING WEIGHT (STEPLIKE MOVEMENTS)

Content structure (for teachers)	Objectives (for children)

Concept

Movement for environmental control

Major idea

1 Body weight may be transferred in four different ways:
   steplike actions,
   flight,
   rocking and rolling,
   sliding.

Selected facts

1 Many nonadjacent parts of the body can receive weight in turn—usually the parts receiving weight are flat or flattened, e.g., hands, feet, forearms, seat, lower leg.
2 When weight is transferred from one body part to another which is comparatively far away, a great deal of body adjustment and control are required. More energy and control are required to transfer weight onto body parts which are comparatively far apart.
3 Twisting occurs when one or more body parts are fixed in one spot, and other body parts rotate to face a different direction, e.g., shoulders when hips are fixed, hips when shoulders are fixed, one end of the spine when the other end is fixed.
4 Twisting is a fundamental skill; twisted is a basic shape.

Children need to understand (knowledge)

1 That they can travel (transfer weight) in steplike ways on flattened parts other than just the feet (hands, forearms, seat, lower leg). B–M–L
2 That transferring weight over comparatively long distances requires more effort and control than transferring weight over short distances. M–L
3 That in taking weight on arms, the most stable base for hand placement is approximately shoulder width apart. B–M–L
4 That they can twist their bodies in many ways by fixing one or more body parts and rotating others around the fixed parts. B–M–L

Children need to learn how (skill)

1 To transfer weight using steplike actions in a wide variety of ways (foot to foot, hands to feet, hands to knees and lower legs). B–M–L
2 To twist shoulders, hips, and spine in a wide variety of ways. B–M–L
3 To take weight on hands briefly. B–M–L
4 To place hands (base of support) approximately shoulder width apart, keeping elbows straight for better balance. M–L

Children need to become (attitude)

The attitude objectives for this physical education program (page 52) are broad and cannot be accomplished quickly; therefore, they will be the same throughout the entire three years. Please review them occasionally.

Teaching tips for fourteenth set of problems

1 *Arrange equipment . . . before the physical education period:*
As many low balance beams or beamlike pieces of apparatus as you have (minimum of 4).
One hoop or used bicycle tire per child.

2 *Discuss movement vocabulary . . . in the classroom:*

transfer weight
steps (not just on feet) on different body parts

balance
"put hands on floor shoulder width apart"

Introduction

"Last week we discovered that we can shift our weight by rocking and rolling. What other way do we usually shift weight? (Steplike movements, e.g., walking, crawling on hands and knees.) This week, we will work on finding out how many different ways we can move by stepping. And we will do some twisting, too."

Developmental problems and expected outcomes

PROBLEM 80

Beginning Grade	Middle Grade	Last Grade

"On the signal, move into general space, shifting your weight from two hands to two feet."

". . . . Can you *feel your weight shift* from your hands to your feet? . . . how many different ways can you step from hands to feet to hands to feet? . . . can you go *faster?* . . . then *slower?* . . . can you change the range of your steps? . . . big ones and small ones? . . . which is easier to do—big steps or little steps? (little steps) . . . why? (weight does not have to be transferred so far off-balance) . . . try keeping your feet *close together* . . . then very *far apart* . . . try keeping your hands close together, then very far apart . . . explore until you find the easiest way to move on your hands . . . have you found that it is *easier to balance on your hands* when they are about *shoulder width* apart? . . . your balance is more stable when your hands are about shoulder width apart."

▶ Repeat all material from Beginning Grade, and then add:

". . . . Now take away one of your hands . . . move by *shifting* your *weight* from *two feet to one hand* . . . really get your weight on that one hand while you are stepping . . . if you are all spread out in a big range, is it harder to take steps? . . . *the longer the steps, the more control and energy you need. . .* see now how many ways you can move into general space by *shifting* your *weight* from *one foot to two hands* . . . can you put all your weight on that one foot before putting your hands down again? . . . how many different things can you do with your other foot? . . . the foot that is not taking your weight . . . can you get it into a high level? . . . can you stretch it and curl it?"

▶ Repeat all material from Beginning and Middle Grades, and then add:

". . . . So far you have taken steps on your hands and feet only . . . now see how many other parts of your body can be used for stepping . . . try to stay off your hands and feet as much as you can . . . have you taken your weight on your seat? . . . or your forearms? . . . on the side of your legs?"

(And so on. Have demonstrations by children who have found ways to keep moving in general space with steplike movements.)

Checklist of quality factors for Problem 80

☐ Traveling in general space with steplike movements by transferring weight in a variety of ways.

  B: Transferring weight from feet to hands consecutively. Beginning to place hands about shoulder width apart for bearing weight on the hands efficiently.

  M: Transferring weight (stepping) on three body parts (two hands and one foot, one hand and two feet). Beginning to understand that the longer the distance between weight-bearing parts, the more energy and control are needed.

  L: Traveling with steplike movements on other flattened body parts (seat, forearms, legs, and so on).

☐ Feeling the transfer of weight; conscious awareness of where the body weight is being supported.

When children demonstrate these factors, go on to Problem 81.

PROBLEM 81

Beginning Grade	Middle Grade	Last Grade

"On the signal, find a self space, put your hands down on the floor about shoulder width apart, and keep them there. Now, how many different things can you do with your feet?"

". . . . Can you take them for a *walk* around your body? . . . can you jump them together so they land in a new place each time? . . . make your arms as straight and strong as you can . . . why? (base of support) . . . can you get first one foot, then the other foot, high in the air? . . . can you make one foot pass the other foot in the air? . . . have you tried fluttering your feet in the air? . . . what is the safest thing to do if you should topple off-balance? . . . right, collapse and roll out."

▶ Repeat all material from Beginning Grade, and then add:

"Make a sequence in which you move both feet together four times and then move on just one foot four times."

". . . . Remember to keep your hands on the floor about shoulder width apart all the time . . . practice until you can do your sequence exactly the same way every time . . . be sure your sequence has a beginning and an ending."

(After sequences are completed, have half the class demonstrate for the other half, and vice versa.)

▶ Repeat all material from Beginning and Middle Grades, and then add:

". . . . This time, put *some* of your *weight* on your *head,* too . . . remember the *triangle* you made with your head and hands last week?

". . . . now, how many ways can you move in this position? . . . see if you can get one leg completely extended . . . long and straight, clear to the tips of your toes."

Checklist of quality factors for Problem 81

☐ Placing hands shoulder width apart on the floor to make a stable base for taking weight on the hands.

☐ Doing a wide variety of steplike movements with the rest of the body while some weight is being taken by the hands.

☐ Beginning to achieve control of the body in an inverted position.

☐ Collapsing and rolling out softly and safely when off-balance.

When children demonstrate these factors, go on to Problem 82.

PROBLEM 82

Beginning Grade	Middle Grade	Last Grade

"Let's find out how much your body can twist. On the signal, lie flat on your back on the floor. Keep your shoulders on the floor and see how far over you can twist with your legs before your legs pull your shoulders over into a roll."

"... Twist your legs over ... keep twisting ... keep twisting ... then roll out."

(Free exploration.)

"... Can you twist to one side, to the other side, back to the first side, then roll? ... *twist, twist, twist, and roll* ... keep it going smoothly."

▶ Repeat all material from Beginning Grade, and then add:

"... *Widen your base of support* when you are lying on your back ... how much floor space can you cover when lying on your back? ... now try to twist into a roll, keeping your shoulders on the floor until last ... again, it takes *more energy* and *control* to *move over long distances* than over short distances ... work on twist, twist, twist before rolling."

(Repeat with twisting shoulders first, hips rolling over last.)

▶ Repeat all material from Beginning and Middle Grades, and then add:

"... Try taking your *weight on* the *knees and one hand* ... can you *twist* your head and your shoulder *through the "hole" made by your arm and the floor*? ... can you twist so far through, that you *roll out softly* over your shoulder? ... what other ways can you twist when you are on your hands and knees? ... can you feel how the twisting can pull you until you are off-balance and must shift your weight?"

(Repeat, substituting hands and feet for hands and knees.)

Checklist of quality factors for Problem 82

☐ Twisting the body in a variety of ways.
☐ Twisting to the point where the body is off-balance, then rolling out.

☐ L: Beginning to feel the *lead* made by the head as it twists through the hole made by the arm and the floor. The whole body will follow the lead made by the head.

When children demonstrate these factors, go on to Problem 83.

PROBLEM 83

Beginning Grade	Middle Grade	Last Grade

"On the signal, get a <u>hoop</u> (or tire) and explore ways of <u>twisting</u> and bending while you hold the hoop."

(Free exploration of new equipment.)

". . . . How smoothly can you keep the movement going in your self space? . . . see how far you can twist and take the hoop to different levels . . . try twisting all the way up high and untwisting all the way down low . . . can anyone stretch and curl and roll while holding the hoop? . . . is there anything you can do with a foot and two hands holding the hoop?"

(Repeat with partners, one mirroring the other's movements. Then reverse leader-follower roles.)

▶ Repeat all material from Beginning Grade, and then add:

"Put <u>one edge</u> of the <u>hoop</u> down on the floor and explore ways to <u>step in and out, through, around,</u> and <u>over the hoop."</u>

". . . . Shift your weight onto different body parts as you go—seat, knees, legs, head, forearms . . . keep moving."

▶ Repeat all material from Beginning and Middle Grades, and then add:

"Find a <u>partner</u> close to you, put <u>one</u> of the <u>hoops away,</u> and see how many ways the two of you can <u>move in and out, through, around,</u> and <u>over the hoop."</u>

". . . . You may want to put the hoop on the floor, or take turns holding it, or both hold it and move with it at the same time."

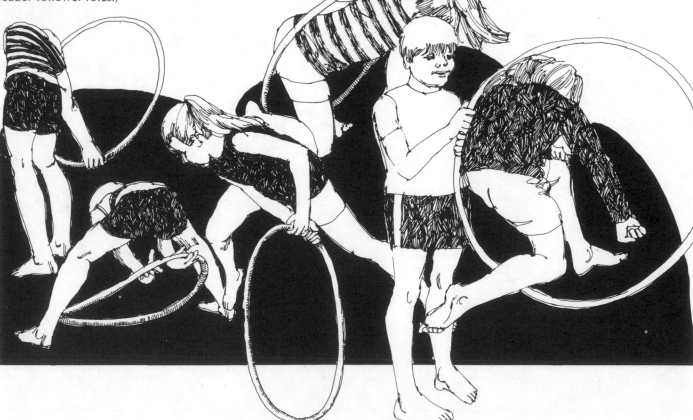

Checklist of quality factors for Problem 83

☐ Manipulating the body in a wide variety of ways while using a hoop.

   B: Twisting, bending, curling, stretching, rolling.

M: Using steplike movements.
L: Coordinating movements with a partner.

☐ Moving smoothly and continuously in self space.

When children demonstrate these factors, go on to Problem 84.

PROBLEM 84

Beginning Grade	Middle Grade	Last Grade

"On the signal, put your hoops away, find a self space, and make a bridgelike shape that you can hold."

". . . . Hold the bridge very still . . . every time you hear a beat, transfer your weight to a different stable bridge." (Give a drumbeat when all children are still.)

▶ Repeat all material from Beginning Grade, and then add:

"Find a partner close to you and together make a bridgelike shape and hold it very still . . . then listen for the beat . . . whenever you hear it, shift weight to a new bridge."

". . . . What is your base of support? . . . are you on-balance or off-balance?"

▶ Repeat all material from Beginning and Middle Grades, and then add:

"Now one of you make a very big bridge . . . the other person move under your partner's big bridge without touching him."

(Reverse roles.)

Checklist of quality factors for Problem 84

☐ Making and holding still a wide variety of large base balances (bridgelike shapes).

☐ M–L: Coordinating movements with a partner.

When children demonstrate these factors, go on to Problem 85.

PROBLEM 85

Beginning Grade	Middle Grade	Last Grade

"Point to the <u>beam</u> (or beamlike apparatus) closest to you. On the signal, bring it out and take turns seeing <u>how many ways you can move across it, using steplike actions."</u>

". . . . Some of you are stepping just with your feet . . . others are stepping on hands and feet or hands and knees . . . see how many different body parts you can use to step across the equipment . . . are you landing softly? . . . letting your knees "give" as you come off the beam?"

▶ Repeat all material from Beginning Grade, and then add:

". . . . This time, *move in different bridgelike shapes on, over, and around your equipment* . . . can you keep moving all the time? . . . if it is not your turn to be *on* the beam, move around the beam and around each other in bridgelike shapes . . . change level . . . direction . . . range (big and little steps)."

▶ Repeat all material from Beginning and Middle Grades, and then add:

"On the signal, move the equipment until it is in one big circle, and then space yourselves out on the circle:

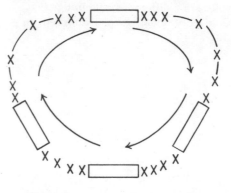

"Using only steplike actions, move around the circuit of equipment. Then listen:"

(These calls apply to all the children all the time, both when they are moving on the floor between the equipment and when they are moving on the equipment.)

". . . . Move forward . . . move backward . . . move sideways . . . move at a higher level . . . move at a lower level . . . twist as you go . . . make a rounded shape as you go . . . take very large steps . . . take very small steps . . . stop and make a strong, twisted shape . . . roll out of the twist and go on."

(And so on.)

Review: Transfer of weight (stepping)

When children demonstrate an understanding of the objectives on page 167, go on to Theme 15.

FIFTEENTH SET OF PROBLEMS/ORGANIZING THEMES: TRANSFERRING WEIGHT (FLIGHT) AND REVIEW—FORCE, BALANCE, WEIGHT TRANSFER

Content structure (for teachers)	Objectives (for children)

Concept

Movement for environmental control

Review of major ideas in Unit Three

1 Space, *force*, time, and flow are the elements of movement.
2 *Force* is *produced* by muscle tension, ranging from strong to weak.
3 The *force* created by the body's own momentum or by other moving objects may be more *gradually absorbed* by increasing the distance, time, and area over which it is absorbed and by using more of the body's shock-absorbing joints.
4 The force of *gravity* limits movement as it pulls the weight of the body downward toward the center of the earth. When a person moves in an *on-balanced* way, his center of gravity falls inside his base of support. When a person moves in an *off-balanced* way (flying or falling), his center of gravity falls outside the base of support.
5 Locomotion is achieved by *transferring* body *weight* from one body part to another by rocking, rolling, sliding, stepping, or *flying*.

Selected new facts

1 For efficient flight, the body weight should be over the point of the takeoff (one foot, two feet, hands and feet, etc.) so that the strength of the legs (arms, etc.) can be fully used to lift the body into the air.
2 Greater force is needed to achieve flight than to transfer weight when flight is not involved.
3 Greater force is also needed to absorb the force of the falling body after flight than is needed to recover balance when weight is transferred by rocking, rolling, sliding, or stepping.
4 Skillful use of the body requires awareness of body parts and their relationship to the whole body—where each part is, how it is being used, and how to control the movement of each part.

Children need to understand (knowledge)

Review objectives for Themes 10, 11, 12, 13, and 14.

1 That controlled flight—takeoff, actual flight, and landing—requires more force than do other forms of weight transference. B–M–L
2 That the body weight should be over the point of takeoff for efficient and forceful flight. M–L
3 How they can produce and absorb force. B–M–L
4 How they can move on-balance and off-balance. B–M–L
5 How they can transfer weight by rocking, rolling, and sliding on adjacent body parts, by stepping on nonadjacent body parts, and by taking off forcefully and landing softly when flight is involved. B–M–L

Children need to learn how (skill)

1 To fly forcefully in a wide variety of controlled ways off the floor and off equipment. B–M–L
2 To land on feet, and then collapse and roll as a means of absorbing the force of landing after flight. B–M–L
3 To gain greater muscular control of the production and absorption of force. B–M–L
4 To achieve greater control of balanced shapes. B–M–L
5 To be consciously aware of weight transference. B–M–L

Children need to become (attitude)

1 Willing to listen to problems, to think about them, and to seek increasingly more skillful, thoughtful, and original ways of solving them through movement.
2 Willing to carry tasks through to completion.
3 Increasingly self-motivated, self-determined, and self-disciplined so that each child grows in appreciative self-realization.
4 Appreciative of others like and unlike themselves.
5 Willing to help and work with others.
6 Success-oriented in movement, so that they have an increasing appreciation for and enjoyment of movement.

Teaching tips for fifteenth set of problems

1 *Arrange equipment . . . before the physical education period:*
One ball per child (yarn or paper ball preferred).
A variety of apparatus: boxes, low double beams (or two chalked paths), inclined boards for sliding, hanging ropes for swinging, etc. Use as many pieces as you can.
2 *Discuss movement vocabulary . . . review in the classroom:*

force
strong, weak
light, heavy
gentle, hard
producing force

absorbing force
"giving"
"squishy landings"

muscles
tensed, relaxed
gripped, loose
hard, soft

balance
gravity
on-balance
off-balance
base of support

transferring weight
rocking, rolling
sliding
steplike movements
flight

movements
stretch
curl
twist
throw underhand
throw overhand

Introduction

"This week we are going to review how we move: the ways we can produce force, the ways we can absorb force, the ways we can move on-balance and off-balance, and the ways we transfer weight to move. Do you know how you transfer your weight when you fly? Is it by rocking, or rolling, or stepping? No. You gather your weight over your base of support, and then forcefully push against the floor to transfer your weight up into the air. Once your weight is up in the air, why doesn't it stay up there? (Gravity.)

Developmental problems and expected outcomes

PROBLEM 86

Beginning Grade	Middle Grade	Last Grade

"On the signal, run quickly into general space, taking off forcefully and flying in different ways as you go."

". . . . How can you fly *higher* or farther? . . . are you bending your *knees, ankles, and hips* before you *take off*? . . . that helps you gather all your parts over your base so you can explode up into the air . . . and what can you do to make your landings softer and "squishier"? . . . let your *whole body give, by bending your knees and ankles and hips again* . . . are your *arms* adding to the force of your flight? . . . can you get them pulling in the direction of your flight? . . . think now of all that your *knees and feet* can do while you are in the air . . . can you get one knee close to your chest? . . . can you get both knees close to your chest? . . . how high in the air can you get your feet? . . . in front of you . . . behind you . . . out to the sides?"

▶ Repeat all material from Beginning Grade, and then add:

"Do you remember that two ways to produce more force are to use more body parts and to increase the range of the movement? On the signal, see which is more forceful—flight in a curled position or flight in a stretched position."

". . . . Now try these flights as they are called: from a big base of support (feet far from each other) . . . from a small base of support (feet close together) . . . from one foot to the other (leaping) . . . find the most powerful way you can to take off, then twist while you are in the air . . . spin around in the air . . . do something different with your elbows . . . knees . . . head . . . spine."

(And so on.)

▶ Repeat all material from Beginning and Middle Grades, and then add:

"On the signal, find a partner near you and take turns flying over each other . . . no touching . . . what different ways can you find to fly over your partner?"

". . . . *Add a roll* after you fly over your partner . . . can you land and roll into a new shape for your partner to fly over very smoothly? . . . make the movements of both of you seem very flowing . . . no stopping . . . continuous flow of movement."

Checklist of quality factors for Problem 86

☐ Transferring weight into the air (flight) more forcefully by:
  a) flexing knees, ankles, and hips before take-off;
  b) gathering body parts over the takeoff point, then thrusting the weight strongly against the floor to propel the body into the air;
  c) using the whole body in the upward stretch (increasing the range of the movement).

☐ Absorbing the force of the landing by bending knees, ankles, and hips.

☐ Consciously varying the shape of the body in flight (knowing where body parts are and controlling movements of them).

  B: Awareness of arms, knees, and feet while in flight.

  M: Awareness of head and spine while in flight.

  L: Awareness of spacial relationships while in flight; coordinating movements with a partner (one down and rolling, one up and jumping over the other) so that no collisions occur.

When children demonstrate these factors, go on to Problem 87.

(In the following sequence of problems, stop frequently to ask children to verbally relate their understanding about producing and absorbing force and about balance to their understanding about throwing and catching balls.)

PROBLEM 87

"On the signal, get a yarn ball, find a self space facing an empty wall, and try different ways to throw the ball as forcefully as you can against the wall."

This is a repeat of Problem 62. Give individual help to children who are having difficulty in:

1. stepping toward the target with the foot opposite the throwing arm,
2. using the whole body to increase the force produced,
3. releasing the ball at the point at which it will travel in nearly a straight line to the target,
4. following through with the throwing hand and arm pointing toward the target to control the path of the ball and to increase the range of the movement, which also produces more force,
5. discovering that both overhand and underhand styles of throwing can be very forceful.

PROBLEM 88

"On the signal, find a self space and practice very forceful tosses of the balls straight up into the air as high as you can make them go, and catch them on the way down."

This is a repeat of Problem 14. Stress control—tossing the ball only as high as it can be controlled and caught. Give individual help to children who are having difficulty in:

1. making the ball go straight up into the air (try looking up first just before tossing the ball),
2. following through with the throwing hand(s) and arm(s) straight up in the air (the target),
3. keeping eyes on the ball as it comes down,
4. moving to stand right under the ball as it comes down, if necessary,
5. pulling the ball into the body so it doesn't slip through the hands,
6. self-discipline—limiting tosses to height that can be controlled (caught) in self space.

PROBLEM 89

"On the signal, move carefully into general space while tossing and catching the ball yourself. See how far you can go without dropping the ball."

This is a repeat of Problem 15. When children are controlling the ball well, call changes in direction, height of toss, pathway, etc. *Add a collapse and roll* after each catch.

PROBLEM 90

"On the signal, find a partner near you, put one ball away, find a self space, and find out how far apart you can stand to pass the ball back and forth without dropping it."

This is a repeat of Problem 16. Encourage underhand and overhand styles of throwing, stepping out on the opposite foot toward the partner, aiming for the middle level of the partner, following through, "giving" when catching the ball. When children are controlling the ball well, have them move carefully into *general space* while passing the ball back and forth. *Add a collapse and roll* after catching the ball if children are ready for it.

PROBLEM 91

Beginning Grade	Middle Grade	Last Grade

"On the signal, put the balls away, find a self space, and make a strong shape with a small base of support. Hold it until everyone is ready."

". . . . Now, let's see how many ways you can *transfer* your *weight* from that shape to another shape . . . can you *rock* that shape back and forth? . . . can you *roll* out of that shape into another one? . . . can you *slide* out of that shape into another one? . . . can you *step* out of that shape into another one? . . . can you *fly* out of that shape into another one? . . . make sure your shapes are very stable and not shaky."

(Repeat several times from different shapes—large base of support, balance on three parts, and so on.)

▶ Repeat all material from Beginning Grade, and then add:

"Moving into general space now, transfer your weight by rolling . . . keep going until you hear a new call:

". . . . transfer weight by *stepping* . . . keep going . . . transfer weight by *sliding* . . . keep going . . . transfer weight by *rocking* . . . keep going . . . transfer weight by *stepping* . . . keep going . . . try different ways of *flying* with a *stretch* in the air . . . combine *stepping* and *twisting* . . . combine flying and curling."

(And so on.)

▶ Repeat all material from Beginning and Middle Grades, and then add:

"Make up a sequence in which you transfer weight in three different ways . . . practice it until you can do it the same way every time and it is smooth and flowing."

(Have demonstrations. Let the rest of the class analyze the sequence: what three ways of transferring weight were used? were they tied together smoothly? did the sequence have a recognizable beginning and ending?)

Checklist of quality factors for Problem 91

☐ Demonstrating mastery of a functional movement vocabulary—responding to movement words with appropriate body movement, not by defining movement words verbally.

☐ Thinking and moving simultaneously—continuous movement response with maximum individual participation.

When children demonstrate these factors, go on to Problem 92.

PROBLEM 92

(This problem is designed for review of weight transfer and balance principles off the floor, on apparatus. Use whatever apparatus you have, with no more than six children at one piece of apparatus. The following is an example of organization that could be used at all three grade levels.)

"On the signal, <u>get out the equipment</u> and explore ways of <u>transferring your weight and balancing on it</u>."

(When all equipment is in place and all children are organized into harmonious working groups, then give specific problems to each group. Examples follow.)

A's: Different ways to step your weight onto the equipment.
Different ways to make stable balances on the equipment.
Different ways to fly off the equipment—stress forceful flight.
Different ways to "give", to roll out—stress soft absorption of force.
And so on.

B's: Different ways to transfer your weight from one beam to another.
Different body parts to lead the weight transfer.
Different levels at which to move from one to the other.
Different amounts of force to be used in transferring weight.
And so on.

C's: On ropes—Different ways to fly onto and off the rope.
Different ways to swing on the rope.
Different shapes to hold while on the rope.
And so on.

On horse or bench—same as A.

(Rotate groups frequently until each child has had the opportunity to work on all pieces of apparatus.)

Also see illustrations on the next page.

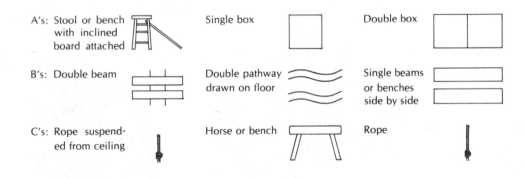

A's: Stool or bench with inclined board attached   Single box   Double box

B's: Double beam   Double pathway drawn on floor   Single beams or benches side by side

C's: Rope suspended from ceiling   Horse or bench   Rope

Review: Force, balance, weight transfer

When children demonstrate an achievement of the objectives on page 175, go on to Theme 16, Unit 4.

UNIT FOUR

HOW CAN YOU MOVE BETTER? (TIME, FLOW)

Set of problems	Dates	Theme	Equipment needed
16		Moving at different speeds	One ball per child. One very long rope (or several ropes tied together) to be suspended horizontally across the room. Magic stretch ropes may be used.
17		Moving in response to different rhythms (pulse beats)	*For the teacher:* rhythm instruments, records, or piano for establishing slow, moderate, and fast pulse beats. *Beginning grade children:* none. *Middle grade children:* one short rope per child. *Last grade children:* one ball and one short rope per child.
18		Moving in bound or free flow and creating movement sequences	One short rope per child. As many jumping boxes as you have. Four to eight empty boxes or wastepaper baskets. Four to eight targets taped or drawn on walls. Four to eight Indian pins or small obstacles such as books.
19		Moving in response to different rhythms (phrases) and creating movement sequences	*For the teacher:* a variety of musical accompaniment with easily recognizable phrases: records, songs, poems, or piano. The nursery rhyme "Humpty Dumpty" is used as an example in the lesson. *For the children:* one ball that bounces per child.
20		Creating movement sequences as a review of basic movement	One bouncing ball per child. As many boxes, beams, and benches as you have.

SIXTEENTH SET OF PROBLEMS/ORGANIZING THEME: MOVING AT DIFFERENT SPEEDS

Content structure (for teachers)	Objectives (for children)

Concept

Movement for environmental control

Major ideas

1 *Time,* space, force, and flow are the elements of movement.
2 Time, as a movement element, is measured by speed of movement, ranging from quick to slow.
3 Movements in an ordered structure in time are called rhythmic movements.

Selected facts

1 Whenever movement occurs, a degree of speed is present.
2 Within most movements, changes in speed occur which result in acceleration, deceleration, or development of a rhythm.
3 Gradual deceleration is more difficult for young children to achieve than is rapid deceleration. Gradual deceleration, however, is one way to absorb force more safely and on-balance.
4 Quick acceleration, especially of an explosive quality, is one way to create greater force, both in moving the body and in moving objects.

Children need to understand (knowledge)

1 That all movement is performed in time and is measured by speed.   B–M–L
2 That speeds of movements vary from very slow to very fast.   B–M–L
3 That one way to vary a movement is to change the amount of time it takes to do the movement.   B–M–L
4 That gradual deceleration is one way to absorb force more safely and on-balance.   B–M–L

Children need to learn how (skill)

1 To vary the speed of movements.   B–M–L
2 To accelerate and decelerate slowly and quickly.   B–M–L
3 To develop the perception necessary for moving at a speed appropriate to the task.   M–L
4 To control consciously the speed at which the body moves.   B–M–L

Children need to become (attitude)

1 Willing to listen to problems, to think about them, and to seek increasingly more skillful, thoughtful, and original ways of solving them through movement.
2 Willing to carry tasks through to completion.
3 Increasingly self-motivated, self-determined, and self-disciplined so that each child grows in appreciative self-realization.
4 Appreciative of others like and unlike themselves.
5 Willing to help and work with others.
6 Success-oriented in movement, so that they have an increasing appreciation for and enjoyment of movement.

Teaching tips for sixteenth set of problems

1 *Arrange equipment . . . before physical education period:*
One ball that bounces per child.
One very long rope (or several ropes tied together), to be suspended horizontally across the room.

2 *Discuss movement vocabulary . . . in the classroom:*
time
speed

fast, quick	speed up (accelerate)
slow	slow down (decelerate)

Introduction

"For the next few weeks, we are going to work on <u>time</u>. What do you think of when you hear the word <u>time</u>? Do you think about having a good time? Or about what time it is? We <u>are</u> going to think about time when we are moving. Every movement you do takes time. We measure the time a movement takes by speed and by rhythm. This week we will work on moving at different speeds. Speed goes all the way from very slow to very fast."

". . . . Try this: on the signal, staying in your own *self space,* see how *slowly* you can *move* your *whole body* . . . now see how *quickly* you can *move* your *whole body* in *self space* . . . now *follow the sound of the drum beats* (or hand claps) . . . when they go faster, you move faster in self space . . . when they slow down, you move more slowly."

(Practice acceleration, deceleration, and even beats at different tempos.)

Explosive starts

Balanced stops

Gradual acceleration

Developmental problems and expected outcomes

PROBLEM 93

Beginning Grade	Middle Grade	Last Grade

"On the signal, run into general space, changing speeds as you run."

". . . . Running very fast, then running very slowly . . . how much time does it take you to run across the room when you are moving very fast? . . . and how much time does it take you to move across the room when you are moving very slowly? . . . can you *speed up and slow down very gradually?* . . . listen for calls: run very fast . . . slow down . . . speed up . . . run very slowly . . . speed up just a little . . . a little faster yet . . . as fast as you can go . . . now slow down a bit . . . a little more . . . a little slower . . . and come to a balanced stop."

See illustrations on previous page.

▶ Repeat all material from Beginning Grade, and then add:

"Do you remember when we worked on a good starting position for running very fast? On the signal, show me a good starting position."

(Check for: forward stride position . . . feet about shoulder width apart . . . toes pointing forward . . . knees, ankles, hips slightly bent, lowering the body level . . . body leaning forward with most of the weight on the front foot.)

"Now, on the signal, get the quickest running start you can."

". . . . Keep running very fast into general space, never touching anyone . . . now *very gradually slow down* . . . slower . . . slower . . . and stop."

(Check stopping position: forward stride position . . . feet at least shoulder width apart . . . toes pointing straight ahead . . . knees, ankles, and hips flexed enough to absorb the forward momentum smoothly. Repeat several times, stressing explosive starts, gradual decelerations, and smooth stops.)

See illustrations on previous page.

▶ Repeat all material from Beginning and Middle Grades, and then add:

"Listen to the speed of the drumbeat now, and run into general space, following the speed of the drumbeat."

(You, as teacher and rhythm setter, will need to watch the children carefully to find the tempos to which most children can move. *Accelerate and decelerate slowly.* Children this age find gradual deceleration particularly difficult.)

". . . . Still following the drumbeats, use *different ways to move*, not just running . . . some of you are hopping, skipping, jumping . . . others are moving on all fours . . . some of you are changing levels and directions . . . has anyone tried rocking or rolling, curling, stretching, or twisting as you go?"

See illustrations on previous page.

Checklist of quality factors for Problem 93

☐ Demonstrating the ability to change speed of movement abruptly, from very fast to very slow while running.

☐ Demonstrating the ability to change speed of movement gradually, slow acceleration and slow deceleration.

☐ M–L: Using an efficient forward stride position for starting and stopping.

☐ L: Duplicating an imposed speed of beat while running in general space. Finding a variety of movements to fit an imposed speed.

When children demonstrate these factors, go on to Problem 94.

PROBLEM 94

Beginning Grade	Middle Grade	Last Grade

"Do you know what slow motion looks like? Try moving in <u>slow motion</u>, taking <u>long, slow, controlled steps.</u>"

". . . . Imagine that you are in a slow motion movie . . . this takes a lot of *control* to stay *on-balance*, doesn't it? . . . the longer the step, the more control and energy you need . . . can you make your arms move in slow motion as well as your feet? . . . what other body parts can you move in slow motion as you go?"

(Repeat, with partners facing each other, one mirroring the other's movements.)

▶ Repeat all material from Beginning Grade, and then add:

". . . . Try moving in *slow motion* while on your: hands and knees . . . hands and feet (tummy up) . . . hands and feet (tummy down) . . . twisting and stepping . . . rocking and rolling . . . sliding . . . making a bridge . . . moving around someone else . . . moving under someone else's bridge."

▶ Repeat all material from Beginning and Middle Grades, and then add:

"Work now on taking the <u>longest</u>, <u>slowest steps</u> you can . . . whenever you hear a <u>drumbeat</u>, drop into a <u>balanced</u> <u>shape</u> with a <u>wide base.</u>"

(Explore. Then add the following.)

". . . . Balance on four parts . . . middle level . . . low level . . . balance on three parts . . . high . . . middle . . . low . . . balance on two parts."

(And so on.)

Checklist of quality factors for Problem 94

☐ Moving very slowly in a wide variety of ways.

☐ Controlling body tension so that balance is maintained while taking long, slow, controlled steps.

☐ L: Dropping into a balanced, held shape with a wide base on signal.

When children demonstrate these factors, go on to Problem 95.

PROBLEM 95

Beginning Grade	Middle Grade	Last Grade

"On the signal, find a self space, and make a low balanced shape. Keep one hand free to tap on the floor in the same time that I am tapping on the drum. Then listen for changes."

". . . . Make a *different* low balanced shape, and free *one foot* to tap on the floor . . . make a *different* low balanced shape and free one body part to move in the *air* on the drumbeat . . . can you move it with force and still keep your balance? . . . how *high* in the air can you get *one foot* to keep the beat?"

(And so on. Use different even tempos in each position. Do not accelerate and decelerate.)

▶ Repeat all material from Beginning Grade, and then add:

". . . . Take *four slow beats* to do a *curl* and *four slow beats* to do a *stretch.*"

(Repeat several times to get variety in movement and to improve slow, smooth flow of movement.)

". . . . Take *four slow beats* to do a *roll.*"

(Repeat, changing tempo.)

". . . . Take *four slow beats* to do a *collapse, roll,* and *recover* onto the feet."

(Repeat, changing tempo. Have children suggest movements to try in four slow beats.)

▶ Repeat all material from Beginning and Middle Grades, and then add:

"Try chanting this:
Slow-two-three-four,
Fast-2-3-4-5-6-7-8,
Slow-two-three-four,
Fast-2-3-4-5-6-7-8.

"On the signal, take about five minutes to make up a sequence of movement to fit the chant . . . practice it until you can do it the same way every time. Then we will look at it."

(Demonstration and evaluation: Did the movements fit the time requirements? Could the sequence be repeated nearly the same way? Did the sequence have a recognizable beginning and ending? Were the movements smooth and flowing from the fast part to the slow part? Were the movements performed well? Example: a *full stretch* achieved during the four slow counts.)

Checklist of quality factors for Problem 95

☐ Duplicating an imposed speed of beat in movement:

    B—by tapping the floor or in the air with different body parts while holding a balanced shape;

    M—by executing a *full* stretch (curl, roll, etc.) in a prescribed amount of time and by taking the full amount of time to perform the movement;

    L—by creating an individual movement sequence to fit an imposed rhythmic structure, including fast and slow movements.

When children demonstrate these factors, go on to Problem 96.

PROBLEM 96

Beginning Grade	Middle Grade	Last Grade

"On the signal, get a <u>ball</u>, find a <u>self space</u> and try to stay in or near it. Then <u>bounce</u> the ball as <u>quickly</u> as you can with control."

". . . . Remember to control that ball so you don't have to move from your spot . . . can you bounce the ball more quickly when you bounce it *high* or *low*? . . . what can you do to keep the ball at a lower level? . . . should you hit the ball hard or *push it down gently*? . . . what happens if you hit the ball too hard? (loss of control; it rebounds too high to be bounced rapidly) . . . can you *spread out your fingers* so they touch more of the ball to send it in the direction you want it to go . . . can any of you bounce the ball all around the spot where you are standing? . . . now try *tossing and catching* the ball as quickly as you can in your own self space . . . soft, low, quick tosses . . . what are some of the things we have learned about control? *direction*—toss straight up . . . *follow through*—hands follow the ball in the direction you want it to go (up) . . . *"reaching"*—up or out to catch the ball . . . *"giving"*—pulling the ball into the body to absorb the force when catching . . . using only the amount of force that can be *controlled* . . . using the *whole body* . . . toss the ball *higher and higher* . . . how high can you get it to go and still control it? . . . notice that *the more force you use, the longer the ball is in the air* . . . it takes more time to toss and catch a ball at a high level than at a low level . . . do you have to move your arms faster to get the ball up high? (yes—increased speed of movement produces more force)."

▶ Repeat all material from Beginning Grade. Then . . . .

(Repeat the Beginning Grade, with children *moving into general space* while bouncing and tossing the ball, instead of staying in self space. Try:

Quick starts (check foot position),
Quick stops (check foot position),
Gradual acceleration (of the feet, not the ball),
Gradual deceleration,
Moving near to and away from another person,
Taking different *pathways*.

Repeat, moving the ball with the feet instead of bouncing or tossing. Work on control: keeping the ball close to the feet while accelerating and decelerating.)

▶ Repeat all material from Beginning and Middle Grades, and then add:

"Find a <u>self space</u> to stay in now, and think about the amount of time you have with nothing to do when you have tossed the ball straight up very high. See how many <u>movements you can do</u> while the ball is in the air."

". . . . Try to do your movements quickly enough so you can catch the ball on the way down or after the first bounce . . . keep trying different moves: different levels . . . different ranges . . . different shapes . . . can you put your weight on your hands for a second? . . . have you tried curling or stretching, rocking or rolling?"

Checklist of quality factors for Problem 96

☐ Controlling ball handling at different speeds:

   B—in self space (bouncing, tossing, and catching),

   M—in general space (dribbling with hands and feet, tossing, and catching),

   L—tossing accurately and forcefully enough to do a variety of movements while the ball is in the air.

☐ Beginning to grasp the relationship between speed of movement and force produced.

When children demonstrate these factors, go on to Problem 97.

PROBLEM 97

Beginning Grade	Middle Grade	Last Grade

(Attach a *long rope* horizontally across the middle of the room about 5 feet above the floor. If this cannot be arranged, have children hold shorter ropes for each other.)

"On the signal, experiment with standing close to the rope and <u>throwing your ball over the rope</u>. <u>Move quickly under the rope to catch it</u> when it comes down on the other side."

"... Remember, if you throw it too far you won't be able to catch it ... *run quickly, keeping your eyes on the ball* ... catching it after one bounce is good ... some of you can catch it before it bounces at all ... think about how much time you need to run under the rope and how much force you need to get the ball high in the air."

▶ Repeat all material from Beginning Grade, and then add:

"On the signal, get a <u>partner</u> near you, <u>put one of the balls away</u>, and <u>toss and catch over the rope</u> with control."

"... Try different ways to get the ball over the rope and into your partner's hands ... very high, two-handed tosses ... an overhand throw ... what works best for you?"

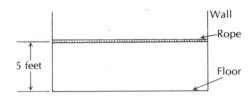

▶ Repeat all material from Beginning and Middle Grades, and then add:

"On the signal, put the rope away, get in <u>groups of four</u>, put one ball away, and <u>make up a keep-away game</u>. You and your partner toss the ball back and forth .. the other couple try to get the ball away so they can toss and catch it. One rule—<u>no touching</u> each other."

Review: Moving at different speeds

When children demonstrate an achievement of the objectives on page 182, go on to Theme 17.

SEVENTEENTH SET OF PROBLEMS/ORGANIZING THEME: MOVING IN RESPONSE TO DIFFERENT RHYTHMS (PULSE BEATS)

Content structure (for teachers)	Objectives (for children)

Concept

Movement for environmental control

Major ideas

1 *Time,* space, force, and flow are the elements of movement.
2 Movements in an ordered structure in time are called rhythmic movements.
3 A pulse beat is the underlying beat of a rhythmic structure which defines a series of *even time intervals.*

Selected facts

1 Moving in response to pulse beats is done by synchronizing the climax of the movement exactly with the beat, e.g., "keeping time" by clapping, tapping, walking, running, bouncing a ball, or shifting weight exactly in time with the beat.
2 Freedom to move in many ways to a pulse beat accompaniment will assist children in accurate rhythmic response. A sense of rhythm can be improved by practice and concentration, but the freer the experiences are from criticism and hard drill, the sooner the child will feel the security and order of the rhythm.

Children need to understand (knowledge)

1 That pulse beats are an even measurement of time, just as inches are an even measurement of distance.   B–M–L
2 That the even speed of pulse beats can be slow, fast, moderate, or anywhere in between, but once the tempo (speed) of pulse beats is established, it continues the same.   B–M–L

Children need to learn how (skill)

1 To move in a variety of ways while responding to pulse beats in slow, moderate, and fast tempos.   B–M–L
2 To develop their rhythmic skills through practice in listening to a set pulse beat accompaniment, identifying and creating even pulse beats, and ordering movement to a set pulse beat.   B–M–L

Children need to become (attitude)

The attitude objectives stated for this physical education program (page 52) are broad and cannot be achieved quickly; therefore, they will be the same throughout the entire three years. Please review them occasionally.

Teaching tips for seventeenth set of problems

1 *Arrange equipment . . . before physical education period:*
For the teacher—one or more rhythm instruments, records with even pulse beats at slow, moderate, and fast tempos, or use of a piano.
Beginning grade—none.
Middle grade—one short rope per child.
Last grade—one ball per child.

2 *Discuss movement vocabulary . . . in the classroom:*

rhythm	pulse beat
tempo	slow
pulse	moderate
phrase	fast

Introduction

"Last time, we learned that moving in time is measured by <u>speed</u> and by <u>rhythm</u>. With what do we measure distance? (Yard stick, ruler, <u>inches</u>.) An inch is an even measurement of distance. What would be an even <u>measurement of time</u>? (Seconds, minutes, hours, days, etc.)

"Your body has a time keeper that you can feel beating out even amounts of time. What is it? (Heart.) See if you can feel your heart making your <u>pulse beat</u>. (Put thumb and forefinger on each side of your Adam's apple and slide them up your throat just a little.) When you <u>feel the pulse beat</u> in your throat, use your other hand to <u>tap that beat on the floor</u>."

". . . . Is it even? (Yes.) . . . Fast or slow? (Slow.)"

"Now, on the signal get up and <u>jump up and down</u> as forcefully and as fast as possible."

(At least *one minute.*)

". . . . Now, feel your pulse beat again . . . tap it on the floor . . . is it still even? (Yes.) . . . is it still slow? (No, much faster.) . . . is it still a pulse beat even though it is not going at the same speed? (Yes—a pulse beat is an even measurement of time, regardless of speed or tempo.)"

Developmental problems and expected outcomes

PROBLEM 98

Beginning Grade	Middle Grade	Last Grade

"Now let's see how many ways you can move with a moderate (medium) pulse beat."

(One way to establish the tempo of a moderate beat if you are not using a record is to have the children walk in general space. Beat the time in which an average child's heels hit the floor.)

A. *Self space—sitting down* . . .
"Try different hand and arm responses . . . try different foot and leg responses . . . try different upper body responses . . . make up your *own responses.*"

B. *Standing* . . .
"Walking in place, use knees (arms) in different ways . . . walking in general space, change direction (forward, backward, sideward) . . . change range (big steps and little steps) . . . change shape (move in rounded, twisted, straight and narrow, straight and wide shapes) . . . change pathways (zigzag and curved pathways) . . . make up your *own response.*"

▶ Repeat Beginning Grade through step A. Then add step A below:

A. ". . . . Move your hands and arms in different directions on each beat . . . put your head (toe) at a different level on each beat . . . twist your body in different ways on each beat . . . swing different body parts on the beat . . . make up your *own responses.*"

▶ Repeat step B from Beginning Grade, and then add:

B. ". . . . Bouncing in place, different ways . . . jumping on two feet in general space, change direction . . . range . . . shape . . . pathway . . . force (lightly, forcefully) . . . use of arms (for distance, for height)."

▶ Repeat Beginning and Middle Grades through step A, and then add:

". . . . Use an elbow (head, shoulder) lead as you move on the beat . . . have different parts of your body meet and part on the beat . . . curl and stretch in different ways on the beat . . . make up your *own responses.*"

▶ Repeat step B from Beginning and Middle Grades, and then add:

"Get a ball, and see how many ways you can keep the beat with the ball."

(Free exploration, then . . . .)

". . . . Bounce in self space . . . bounce in general space . . . toss and catch in self space . . . toss and catch in general space . . . move around someone else while bouncing or tossing . . . put the balls away, and find a self space."

Checklist of quality factors for Problem 98

☐ Moving in a wide variety of ways to a moderate pulse beat.

☐ Review—demonstrating a functional movement vocabulary:

direction	body lead
level	stretch
range	curl

self space	bounce
general space	toss
shape	hop
pathway	jump
meeting and parting	

☐ Creating new movement responses which fit the beat.

When children demonstrate these factors, go on to Problem 99.

PROBLEM 99

Beginning Grade	Middle Grade	Last Grade

A. **"Make a low balanced shape in self space. Hold it very still and listen for ways to tap out the slow beat."**

(Teacher continues to tap the beat and then gives these calls:)

". . . . One whole arm . . . stay in a low, balanced shape . . . one whole leg . . . sway your upper body . . . push and pull (softly, then forcefully) . . . twist and straighten . . . make up your *own response.*"

(Repeat from different starting positions: on four parts . . . on three parts . . . with head on floor . . . and so on. Repeat with a partner, one mirroring the other's movements.)

B. **"Moving into general space on the beat, try different ways to move."**

". . . . Different ways at a low level . . . different ways at a high level . . . use large movements . . . use small movements . . . make up your *own response.*"

▶ Repeat material from Beginning Grade through step A, and then add:

A. **"Make a medium-level, balanced shape in self space. Hold it still and listen for ways to tap out the beat while staying in your shape."**

(Ask different children to suggest different body parts with which to tap the beat on the floor or in the air.)

▶ Repeat step B from Beginning Grade, and then add:

B. **"Moving into general space on the beat, transfer your weight by stepping on different body parts, not just the feet."**

C. **"Get a rope, find a self space, and see how many ways you can move across the rope on the beat (flat on the floor and turning the rope)."**

▶ Repeat step A from Beginning and Middle Grades, and then add:

A. **"Make a high-level, balanced shape in self space. Use different body parts to respond to the beat while holding the balance as still as possible."**

". . . . Try other high level shapes . . . with one toe at a high level, how many ways can you keep the beat? . . . make up your *own response* to the beat."

▶ Repeat step B from Beginning Grade and steps B and C from Middle Grade. Then add:

B. **"Make up a sequence of three different ways to move in general space on the slow pulse beat."**

(Demonstration . . . evaluation.)

C. **"Get a partner and one ball for the two of you. Explore to find different ways of passing the ball back and forth rhythmically."**

". . . . How far apart can you stand? . . . how much force do you have to use? . . . can you change the pathway of the ball and still stay with the slow beat? . . . try a curved pathway . . . straight pathway . . . bounce pathway . . . make up a sequence of three different ways to pass the ball on the beat, and practice it until you can do it the same way every time."

(Demonstration . . . evaluation.)

Checklist of quality factors for Problem 99

☐ Moving in a wide variety of ways to a slow pulse beat.

☐ Realizing that pulse beats are an even measurement of time but that they may be accomplished at different tempos.

When children demonstrate these factors, go on to Problem 100.

PROBLEM 100

Beginning Grade	Middle Grade	Last Grade

"This time, let's find out how many ways you can move to a fast pulse beat."

(One way to establish the tempo of a fast pulse beat is to have the children run in general space. Beat the times when the average child's feet hit the floor.)

A. Self space . . . free exploration.

B. General space . . . free exploration.

C. Move on different body parts . . . hands and feet . . . hands and knees . . . seat and feet . . . others.

▶ Repeat all material from Beginning Grade, and then add:

"Get a rope and see how many ways you can move over and around your rope to the fast beat."

▶ Repeat all material from Beginning and Middle Grades, and then add:

"Find a partner close to you. You and your partner put your ropes together on the floor in an interesting fun pattern, and make up a game of moving over and around the ropes on the beat."

(Examples: follow the leader or hopscotch-type games may evolve.)

Checklist of quality factors for Problem 100

☐ Moving to a fast beat in a variety of unstructured ways in self and general space.

☐ M–L: Quick foot movement over a rope, i.e., jumping, hopping, using hands to take some of the weight, etc.

L: Creative and harmonious rhythmic play over a rope in twos.

When children demonstrate these factors, go on to Problem 101.

PROBLEM 101

Beginning Grade	Middle Grade	Last Grade

Game: My Beat

"Make your own accompaniment and set your own pulse beat. You may use your mouth to make clicks or pops or whatever, or you may clap a hand on your body."

(Rhythm instruments may be used if you have them.)

"Once you have an even pulse beat started, then move in self space to your own beat."

(Free exploration, then . . . .)

"Move into general space on your own beat."

(Free exploration, then . . . .)

"Change the tempo of your beat and see how many ways you can move."

▶ Repeat all material from Beginning Grade, and then add:

"Find a partner close to you. Together, make your own accompaniment and set your own pulse beat."

". . . . Now what can the two of you do to your own pulse beat? . . . in *self space* first . . . then in *general space.*"

▶ Repeat all material from Beginning and Middle Grades. Then play the following game.

Game: Moving Beats

1   Divide children into three groups: those who will move on moderate speed beats . . . those who will move on slow speed beats . . . those who will move on fast speed beats.

2   Have each group in turn explore moving in self space to its own tempo of beats. (Teacher accompaniment.)

3   Have children scatter so the groups are not together.

4   The teacher then beats the drum in *patterns of slow, moderate, and fast beats* without pausing in between. Each child *responds only to his own tempo of beat.* When his beat is not being tapped out, he freezes in place

5   When the children are successful at hearing and moving only on their own tempo in self space, then play the game again, moving into *general space.*

Review: Moving in response to different rhythms (pulse beats)

When children demonstrate an achievement of the objectives on page 190, go on to Theme 18.

EIGHTEENTH SET OF PROBLEMS/ORGANIZING THEME:
MOVING IN BOUND OR FREE FLOW AND CREATING MOVEMENT SEQUENCES

Content structure (for teachers)	Objectives (for children)

Concept

Movement for environmental control

Major ideas

1 The elements of movement are *flow*, space, time, and force.
2 The dimensions of flow are *bound* and *free*.
3 Flow is the element which binds together a variety of actions so smoothly that the separate phases of preparation for action, action, and recovery from action are indistinguishable from each other.

Selected facts

1 In *bound flow,* the body fights against a continuity of movement. The feeling of moving with bound flow is that of careful restraint, in which the body can be stopped at any moment on-balance.
2 In *free flow,* the body indulges in a continuity of movement. The feeling of moving with free flow is that of ongoing smoothness and fluidity.
3 Practically, free flow allows ongoing movement.
4 Practically, bound flow allows stopping or changing control at any moment. It enables one to bring his movement to a stillness on smaller and smaller bases of support. When stillness or balance is achieved, the center of gravity is over the base of support.

Children need to understand (knowledge)

1 That *flow* is one of the four elements of movement. Time, space, and force are the other three elements of movement. B–M–L
2 That *bound* and *free* are the two types of flow. B–M–L
3 That *free flow* is ongoing movement in which actions follow each other so smoothly that one action arises as a natural outcome of the previous action. B–M–L
4 That *bound flow* is careful, controlled movement which can be stopped on-balance at any moment. B–M–L

Children need to learn how (skill)

1 To move with free flow in a variety of ways; to make one movement lead naturally and smoothly into another movement. B–M–L
2 To move with bound flow in a variety of ways; to be able to bring movement to a stillness at will, on-balance, with the center of gravity over the base of support. B–M–L
3 To feel the difference between bound and free flow: bound feeling careful and restrained, free feeling ongoing and smooth. B–M–L
4 To observe and evaluate the flow of movement. M–L

Children need to become (attitude)

The attitude objectives stated for this physical education program (page 52) are broad and cannot be achieved quickly; therefore, they will be the same throughout the entire three years. Please review them occasionally.

Teaching tips for eighteenth set of problems

1 *Arrange equipment . . . before the physical education period:*
One short rope per child.
As many jumping boxes as you have, minimum of 4. Scatter them in random fashion before the lesson begins. (They can remain on the floor until the last problem.)
One yarn ball (soft ball) per child.
Four to eight empty boxes or wastepaper baskets.
Four to eight targets taped or drawn on walls (make them hip- to top-of-head-height and two feet wide).
Four to eight Indian pins or small obstacles such as books.
2 *Discuss movement vocabulary . . . in the classroom:*
flow
bound flow: careful, restrained, able to be stopped on-balance.
free flow: on-going, smooth, continuous, natural.

Introduction

(Jumping boxes scattered randomly before beginning.)

"On the signal, do a relaxed, smooth swing with your whole body."

". . . . Keep it going . . . let it flow freely . . . let it take you anywhere . . . let your whole body get in on it . . . doesn't it feel good?"

"Now, on the signal, do a very careful swing, but keep stopping and starting it."

". . . . Make it so controlled that you can *stop it anywhere* . . . down low . . . up high . . . in the middle . . . and *hold your balance* very still at that spot . . . then, *continue* your swing and stop it again . . . how does it feel? . . . more jerky? . . . Yet it feels good, too, to know that you can control your body so well that you can stop on-balance at any time."

"What is the difference in feeling? We're talking about flow in movement. All movement flows, but different movements flow in different ways. Sometimes there is free flow in movement, and it feels as if it will go on forever—smoothly, never stopping, as when you were swinging freely. Try it again.

"At other times, there is bound flow in movement, and it feels very careful and controlled. You can tell your body to stop at any time, and it will stop on-balance—no falling or quivering. Try your bound flow swing again, and stop on-balance whenever you hear a beat."

Bound flow

Free flow

Developmental problems and expected outcomes

PROBLEM 102

Beginning Grade	Middle Grade	Last Grade

"On the signal, move into general space with free flowing movements. If you come to a box, try to flow up onto it and off without ever stopping."

". . . . Keep on moving . . . never stopping . . . feel how freely and continuously you are going . . . let one movement lead into another . . . use your space so well that you flow around each other and into all parts of the room . . . here are some ideas: run . . . fly . . . jump . . . hop . . . rock . . . roll . . . crawl . . . find as many ways to go over the boxes as possible . . . change level . . . change range . . . change direction . . . change speed . . . change force of movement . . . keep going continuously and smoothly . . . accelerate . . . decelerate."

▶ Repeat all material from Beginning Grade, and then add:

". . . . *Bounce along using two feet together* now . . . free flow . . . never stopping . . . make your arms and whole bodies flow freely, too . . . can you bounce along and *put a roll in very smoothly as you go?* . . . bounce, roll, recover, and bounce on . . . try using a *hop on one foot* instead of a bounce on two feet . . . *add a smooth roll* every once in a while . . . still going over the boxes whenever you come to an empty one . . . what *different ways can you use your free leg* as you go? (swinging or held still, in front, at the sides, or in back, knee bent or straight) . . . keep going continuously and smoothly."

▶ Repeat all material from Beginning and Middle Grades, and then add:

". . . . Try *chanting*: *bounce-bounce-bounce-bounce-hold-two-three-four* . . . now see how many *different ways you can move to this chant* . . . keep repeating it and going very smoothly and freely . . . can you feel the free-bound-free-bound flow? . . . On the hold, try high balances on one foot . . . you have to use a lot of control to hold the balance still for four counts . . . then let it flow right into four smooth bounces."

Checklist of quality factors for Problem 102

☐ Moving in a variety of ways with free flow . . . on-going, continuous, relaxed, natural movement in general space . . . avoiding collisions . . . going over empty boxes when they are in the pathway . . . changing the other elements of movement while maintaining free flow. (*Children usually take great delight in this freedom, and it should be encouraged.*)

☐ M–L: Maintaining free flow while restricting movements to hopping and jumping; achieving smoothness in inserting rolls in the movement flow.

☐ L: Alternating free flow and bound flow in a rhythmic pattern . . . free fluency during bounces . . . controlled stillness during balances . . . being able to move on self-determined pulse beats.

When children demonstrate these factors, go on to Problem 103.

PROBLEM 103

Beginning Grade	Middle Grade	Last Grade

"This time, we will work on bound flow. On the signal find a <u>self space</u>, and make a <u>low balanced shape on three body parts.</u> Hold it very still and listen."

". . . . Slowly shift your weight to different body parts."

(Stop. Check stillness.)

". . . . Again, *shift* your weight so carefully to other body parts that you can stop on balance at any time." (Stop. *Check stillness.* If still, the weight or center of gravity is over the base of support.)

". . . . This time, *keep on shifting* your weight very carefully . . . stop and *hold whenever you hear a beat.*"

(Repeat several times, stressing the careful feeling of bound flow.)

▶ Repeat all material from Beginning Grade, and then add:

". . . . Move into general space, now, with the same careful, controlled feeling . . . transfer your weight carefully by stepping on different body parts and by rocking, rolling, and sliding . . . see if you can *stop on-balance* at any point . . . can you stop your roll at any point and hold it very still? (only when the weight is over a stable base) . . . how many different ways can you move with bound flow and stop yourself on-balance?"

▶ Repeat all material from Beginning and Middle Grades, and then add:

". . . . Staying in self space now, move one or two feet into a high level in as many ways as you can, using careful bound flow . . . lift one or two legs very carefully, so you can stop at any time . . . try it with your head on the floor . . . and try it with your head off the floor . . . practice one way until you can do it the same way over and over."

(Demonstration . . . evaluation. Those who are ready may do headstands, handstands, or balances on the back of the shoulders, neck, and upper arms—inverted bicycle position. An equally correct response, from the child who is not as skilled, would be a balance with two hands and one foot on the floor with the other foot extended overhead. Bound flow should be demonstrated in getting into and out of the held balance with one or two feet at a high level.)

Checklist of quality factors for Problem 103

☐ Feeling the movement sensation of bound flow . . . carefulness, withholding of free flow, being able to stop on-balance at any moment.

☐ Being able to hold a balanced position absolutely still for a few seconds:

B—in a low balanced position,

M—while transferring weight by stepping and rolling,

L—in an inverted balance position.

When children demonstrate these factors, go on to Problem 104.

PROBLEM 104

Beginning Grade	Middle Grade	Last Grade

"On the signal, get a short rope, and put it on the floor in an open self space. See how smoothly you can start at one end, jump from side to side to the other end, turn around, and come back. Free flow throughout, even when turning."

". . . . How can you make the whole sequence smoother and more free flowing? . . . make your turn a part of the whole flow of movement . . . vary the level of jumps—high, low . . . distance of jumps—long, short . . . force of jumps—strong, weak . . . body shape during jumps . . . speed of jumps— quick, slow . . . direction of jumps— backward, sideward."

(Repeat with hops, moving on four body parts, and moving on three body parts.)

". . . . Now, find a way to move down the rope and turn with *free flow*, then come back and turn with *bound flow* . . . very free and easy one way, very controlled and careful the other way . . . can you feel the difference? . . . can you see the difference in others?"

▶ Repeat all material from Beginning Grade, and then add:

"Leave your ropes on the floor and go to the nearest box. Make up an interesting sequence of four jumps on the floor approaching the box, get on smoothly, do a controlled balance on the box, get off smoothly, and do four jumps away from the box."

". . . . Show us that you have a beginning and end to your sequence . . . use the time while others are on your box to practice your sequence on the floor . . . *free flow toward and up onto the box, bound flow to balance, then free flow down off and away from the box* . . . can you feel the difference between the free and bound flow? . . . can you see it in others?"

(Demonstration . . . evaluation.)

▶ Repeat all material from Beginning and Middle Grades, and then add:

"Pick up your own rope, bring it back to your box, and all of you at that box make a pathway with your ropes to and away from your box. Then, take turns moving in a very smooth, free flow of movement down the pathway, over the box, and out the pathway."

". . . . See if you all can keep moving all the time without any crowding or waiting . . . just smooth continuous flow of movement . . . rolls, weight on hands, many different ways to move . . . no stopping."

See illustrations on next page.

Checklist of quality factors for Problem 104

☐ Developing smooth flowing sequences of movement in which transitions such as turns, getting on and off boxes, rolls, etc., blend into the free flow of the movement.

☐ Demonstrating knowledge of the difference between free and bound flow; alternating between them.

When children demonstrate these factors, go on to Problem 105.

PROBLEM 105

"On the signal, put the equipment away (boxes to one side of the room, ropes in the boxes), and find a <u>self space</u> <u>facing me</u>. Now, let's see if you can make the same kind of smooth flowing movements when working with balls as you have been doing on the floor. The sequence will be: <u>bend down</u> . . . <u>pick up a "pretend" ball</u> in front of you . . . <u>throw it to me</u> . . . <u>follow through</u> . . . <u>finish on balance</u>."

(Repeat several times . . . stress *smooth flow, following through* with the throwing hand smoothly down and across the body, and *finishing on-balance*. Point out that *taking a step* when throwing adds to the free flow of the whole body movement. Also point out that balance is better when the foot taking the step is on the opposite side of the body from the throwing hand, i.e., *right hand, left foot*. Work on *finishing in an on-balance position*—weight on two feet. Then have children help you set up a practice arrangement such as the one below. This arrangement is suitable for all three grade levels.)

"On the signal, get a yarn ball and go to one of the four working areas.

A's: Work on *smooth flow and accuracy* in throwing balls overhand and underhand *into the wall targets*. (Accelerate speed when ready.)

B's: Work on *smooth flow and accuracy* in throwing balls into the boxes. (Accelerate speed when ready.)

C's: Work on *smooth flow in pushing (dribbling) balls with your feet* around the obstacles. Control the ball by tapping it softly. Keep the ball close to you.

D's: Work on *smooth flow* in throwing a ball *over the rope*, and catching it yourself on the other side.

(Rotate, until each child has had the opportunity to work at each area. Repeat several times in the coming weeks.)

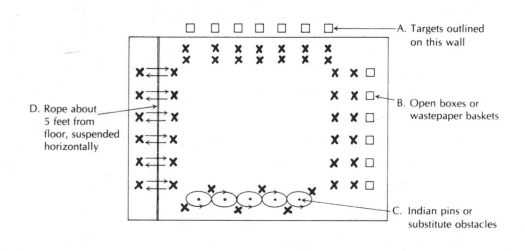

Review: Moving in bound and free flow and creating movement sequences.

When children demonstrate an achievement of the objectives on page 197, go on to Theme 19.

NINETEENTH SET OF PROBLEMS/ORGANIZING THEMES: MOVING IN RESPONSE TO PHRASES AND CREATING MOVEMENT SEQUENCES

Content structure (for teachers)	Objectives (for children)

Concept

Movement for environmental control.

Major ideas

1 The elements of movement are *flow*, *time*, space, and force.
2 A movement sequence is:
a series of movements, one following the other smoothly, with an observable beginning and end,
a logical whole,
a movement phrase,
a series of actions in which preparation, action, and recovery are linked smoothly,
a series of movements which can be repeated the same way again and again.

Selected facts

1 A sequence is to movement what a phrase is to music.
2 A musical phrase is part of a longer piece of music which is at least two measures long, forms a continuous sequence of music, and has a recognizable beginning and end.
3 A movement sequence is always rhythmic, and may be combined with a musical phrase into a dance form.

Children need to understand (knowledge)

1 That a movement sequence is a combination of actions smoothly linked together. B–M–L
2 That a movement sequence has an observable beginning and end. B–M–L
3 That preparation, action, and recovery need to be linked smoothly together in a sequence. M–L
4 That linking actions are called transitions. L
5 That a musical phrase is a sequence of music which has a recognizable beginning and end and is part of a longer musical piece. B–M–L

Children need to learn how (skill)

1 To create smooth, flowing movement sequences. B–M–L
2 To develop movement memory, so that a sequence may be repeated over and over while being refined. B–M–L
3 To link preparation, action, and recovery so smoothly in a sequence that the separate phases are indistinguishable from each other. M–L
4 To recognize and respond in a wide variety of movements to musical phrases. B–M–L

Children need to become (attitude)

The attitude objectives stated for this physical education program (page 52) are broad and cannot be achieved quickly; therefore, they will be the same throughout the entire three years. Please review them occasionally.

Teaching tips for nineteenth set of problems

1 *Arrange equipment . . . before the physical education period:* One ball that bounces per child. *For the teacher:* Accompaniment for response to musical phrases is needed—records, songs, piano, or poems. A variety is preferred.

2 *Discuss movement vocabulary . . . in the classroom:*

movement sequence
beginning, ending
preparation, action, recovery
transition (linking action)
musical phrase

Introduction

(Children sitting on the floor.)

"Today we will work on smooth-flowing movement sequences. But first let's try an experiment. Very quickly, stand up, turn around, and make a low balance.

(Start, stop.)

"Sit down. We could call this a <u>movement sequence</u>. It has a <u>beginning</u> and an <u>ending</u>. What was the beginning position? (Sitting down.) What was the ending position? (A low balance.)

". . . . Try the sequence again . . . stand up, turn around, and make a low balance . . . how smoothly did you do your sequence? . . . if you were sitting on your feet, could you get up and do the sequence quickly and smoothly? . . . try it . . . sit down . . . why did it take longer this time? (Feet were not ready to take the weight.)

"Now, get your feet and <u>bodies ready for the sequence</u> . . . stand . . . turn . . . low balance . . . was it smoother and quicker this time? . . . why? . . . Try it one more time.

"This time make the whole sequence as <u>smooth and flowing</u> as possible. Good. What made the sequence smoother the last time than the first time?

1	Having your body ready (preparation),		Now try the parts:
2	for moving (action), and	1	Get ready . . . hold.
3	finishing on-balance (recovery).	2	Stand up . . . hold.
		3	Turn around . . . hold.
		4	Make a low balance . . . hold.

". . . . Would you call this a smooth flowing sequence? (No.) . . . What was missing? (Free flow—*transitions to link the movements smoothly together.*) . . . Work on this sequence until it flows as smoothly as possible . . . what kinds of transitions could you use? (Example: a step forward after the turn to get into the low balance.) . . . repeat the sequence twice . . . did you do it the *same way both times?* . . . did it have a beginning and an ending? . . . did it have smooth flow? . . . then it has become a real sequence . . . was it just like the first one you did today? . . . what has our experiment shown us? (Through practice and awareness of the parts of a sequence, the sequence will become smoother and more natural.)"

Preparation

Observable beginning

Smooth flowing action

Transitions

Observable ending

Developmental problems and expected outcomes

PROBLEM 106

Beginning Grade	Middle Grade	Last Grade

"On the signal, work on a sequence of: stand . . . collapse and roll . . . walk out (2 to 6 steps) . . . stand (hold)."

". . . . Hold your beginning and ending very still so we can see them . . . how smooth flowing can you make your sequence? . . . after you have tried different kinds of rolls and different ways to walk out, decide on one way to do your sequence, and then practice it so you can do it the same way every time."

Variations
1 "Same sequence, but jump out instead of walk out.
2 "Double the length of the sequence by adding a turn at the end and repeating the sequence back to the starting position (recovery becomes preparation).
3 "Use your arms in an unusual way to show the beginning and ending of your sequence.
4 "Change one part of your sequence so it looks completely different from every one else's sequence."

▶ Repeat all material from Beginning Grade, and then add:

"Work on a new sequence: stand . . . high balance (hold) . . . collapse, and roll to a low balance (hold) . . . collapse and roll to a high balance (hold)."

". . . . Experiment with different balances and different rolls until you find your favorite way to do the sequence . . . then practice it until you can do it the same way every time . . . how can you make your balances steadier (larger base, more force used to achieve stillness) . . . are your *transitions* from action to stillness to action as smooth as you can make them?"

Variations:
1 "Change the speed of your sequence . . . try it slowly then quickly.
2 "Change direction in the middle of your sequence, e.g.,

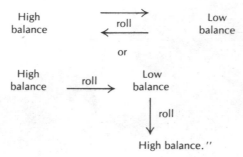

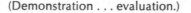

(Demonstration . . . evaluation.)

▶ Repeat all material from Beginning and Middle Grades, and then add:

"Make up a completely new sequence. Put in it the things you like to do best, but keep it short."

". . . . Practice your sequence until you can do it the same way every time . . . pay attention to your *transitions* . . . are you moving *smoothly from preparation to action to recovery?* . . . can you link your movements together in a more flowing way? . . . do you feel good doing your sequence? . . . do you like the sequence you have made?"

(Demonstration . . . evaluation.)

Checklist of quality factors for Problem 106

☐ Demonstrating awareness of the requirements of a movement sequence: observable beginning and ending . . . smooth flowing movement within . . . ability to repeat it in the same way . . . and in the last grade, unobtrusive transitions from preparation to action to recovery.

☐ Refining a movement sequence through practice.

☐ L: Creating completely original movement sequences without teacher direction.

When children demonstrate these factors, go on to Problem 107.

PROBLEM 107

Beginning Grade	Middle Grade	Last Grade

"On the signal, get a ball, find a self space, and make a sequence with the ball, staying in self space. Include at least one bounce and one toss. Make up your own beginning and ending."

(If children have difficulty in thinking of movements to include, suggest one sequence for all to try before they make up their own. Example:
stand . . . 4 bounces in place . . . turn around . . . 4 tosses in place . . . turn around . . . stand. Encourage originality in making sequences, e.g., holding the ball with the feet, or spinning around on the seat with the ball held high overhead with the hands. Demonstration . . . evaluation.)

▶ Repeat all material from Beginning Grade, and then add:

"This time, make a sequence with the ball while moving in general space. Again, include at least one bounce and one toss."

". . . . You will really have to control the ball so you can do your sequence the same way over and over again."
(Give as much individual help as possible while children are working on their sequences. Suggest level, direction, range, pathway, or speed changes to those who can benefit from them. Demonstration . . . evaluation.)

▶ Repeat all material from Beginning and Middle Grades, and then add:

"On the signal, find a partner close to you, put one of the balls away, and make a sequence with your partner that includes at least one bounce pass and one straight pass."

". . . . Make up your own beginning and ending and be sure you hold the beginning and ending long enough for us to see them."

(Allow at least five minutes for creating and practicing sequences in *self space*. Then *repeat* the problem with children moving in *general space*. Demonstration . . . evaluation.)

Checklist of quality factors for Problem 107

☐ Beginning to develop movement memory in ball handling . . . being able to develop a movement pattern, refine it, and practice it until it can be repeated without much conscious awareness of the parts.

☐ L: Cooperating with a partner in a jointly creative effort.

When children demonstrate these factors, go on to Problem 108.

PROBLEMS 108 TO 124†

Beginning Grade	Middle Grade	Last Grade

Beginning Grade

"On the signal, put the balls away, find a self space, and sit down."

(Use this or other poems, musical records or songs with easily recognizable phrases, or play an instrument for accompaniment.)

1 **"Listen to this poem and see if you can feel the pulse beat."**

Humpty Dumpty sat on a wall./
Humpty Dumpty had a great fall./
All the king's horses and all the king's men/*
Couldn't put Humpty together again./

2 **"Say it with me and tap the beat on the floor."**

3 **"We have been working on movement sequences which are short series of moves put smoothly together. There are short parts in this poem which go smoothly together and which have a beginning and an ending that we can feel. Listen to the poem again and see if you can feel the parts that go together. Each part is called a phrase."**

4 **"Listen to each phrase now. I will stop at the end of each phrase. Can you tell where I am going to stop?"**

5 **"This time, tap the beats on the first phrase; then sit quietly on the second phrase."**

6 **"Use your arms to respond to pulse beats on the first phrase; use your legs to respond on the second phrase."**

7 **"Use your whole body on the first phrase; hold a balance very still on the second phrase."**

8 **"Alternate moving into general space and holding still in self space on successive phrases."**

9 **"Alternate stretching on one phrase and curling on the next phrase."**

10 **"Alternate moving at a high level and moving at a low level."**

11 **"Change direction whenever a new phrase begins."**

Middle Grade

▶ Repeat all material from Beginning Grade, and then add:

12 **"Moving into general space, change range of movement whenever a new phrase begins (large, small)."**

13 **"Alternate flight and rolling."**

14 **"Alternate swinging and holding a high balance."**

15 **"Make up your own sequence to the accompaniment. Practice it until you can do it the same way every time."**

Last Grade

▶ Repeat all material from Beginning and Middle Grades, and then add:

16 **"Find a partner near you. One of you move to the first phrase, the other to the second phrase."**

17 **"Together make up a sequence that you can both do at the same time. Be sure we can see a change each time there is a new phrase."**

See illustrations on next page.

---

*   Younger children tend to identify shorter and more regular (i.e., 4 beats in each) phrases than do adults. Thus, most of your children will feel that a phrase ends at "king's men". Adults and some of your children will feel that the last two lines are one phrase. For the purposes of this lesson, either choice is correct.

†   Each of the problems in the series numbered 108–124 is a major problem and should be developed as such. Encourage children to discover subproblems related to each of the major problems that could be passed to the entire class. For example, on the ninth problem of the series, which calls for stretching and curling on alternate phrases, the children could come up with additional movement requirements such as: . . . in self space only . . . while moving in general space . . . with only half of the body . . . with a twist on the stretch . . . with a twist on the curl . . . and so on. This series of problems (except for one and three, which call for covert listening skills) is an evaluative tool for finding out the number of movement variables children can pull out of memory storage and apply in different tasks. Can they devise their own movement chart such as the one in the next (last) set of problems?

Humpty Dumpty sat on a wall.

Humpty Dumpty had a great fall.

Checklist of quality factors for Problems 108 to 124

☐ Ability to recognize rhythmic phrases within a longer piece of music or a poem:
    listening for structure,
    identifying phrases,
    moving in response to phrases,
    alternating movements on alternate phrases.

☐ L: cooperatively creating movement sequences with a partner to a rhythmic accompaniment, showing change of rhythmic phrase by changing movement response.

Review: Moving in response to different rhythms (phrases) and creating movement sequences

When children demonstrate an achievement of the objectives on page 204, go on to Theme 20.

MOVEMENT CHART III: HOW DO I MOVE?

MY BODY MOVES IN SPACE, IN TIME, WITH FORCE, AND WITH FLOW

My body . . .   **moves . . . .**   **in space . . .**

Body parts

1 Head
2 Neck
3 Shoulders
4 Chest
5 Waist
6 Stomach
7 Hips
8 Legs
9 Arms
10 Back
11 Spine
12 Upper arm
13 Elbow
14 Lower arm
15 Wrist
16 Fingers
17 Thumb
18 Hands
19 Toes
20 Feet
21 Heels
22 Ankles
23 Shins
24 Knees
25 Thighs

Body surfaces

26 Front
27 Back
28 Sides

Body shapes

29 Curved
30 Straight and narrow
31 Straight and wide
32 Twisted

Body relationships: body part to body part

33 Near to each other (curled)
34 Far from each other (stretched)
35 Rotated with one part fixed (twisted)

Relationship of body parts to objects: on, off, over, around, across, under, near to, far from

36 Walls, floor
37 Boxes, benches, beams

Manipulating

38 Balls— bouncing, catching, tossing, pushing
39 Ropes, hoops, etc.

Relationship of one person to another or others

40 Near to
41 Far from
42 Meeting
43 Parting
44 Facing
45 Side by side
46 Shadowing
47 Mirroring
48 Leading
49 Following

By transfer of weight

50 Steplike actions
51 Rocking
52 Rolling
53 Sliding
54 Flight

By balancing (active stillness)

55 Balancing weight on different body parts
56 Balancing on different numbers of parts (4, 3, 2, 1)

Divisions of space

57 Self space
58 General space

Dimensions of space

59 Directions
60 Forward
61 Backward
62 To one side
63 To the other side
64 Up
65 Down
66 Levels
67 High
68 Medium
69 Low
70 Ranges
71 Large
72 Medium
73 Small
74 Planes
75 Pathways (floor or air)
76 Straight
77 Curved
78 Zigzag

in time . . .

79 Speed
   80 Slow
   81 Medium
   82 Fast
   83 Accelerat-
      ing
   84 Decelerat-
      ing
85 Rhythm
   86 To pulse
      beats
   87 To phrases
      and
      rhythmic
      patterns

with force . . .

Degrees of force

88 Strong
89 Medium
90 Weak

Qualities of force

91 Sudden, explosive
92 Sustained, smooth

Creating force

93 Quick starts
94 Sustained powerful movements
95 Held balances

Absorbing force

96 Sudden stops on-balance
97 Gradual absorption ("give")

with flow.

Dimensions of flow

98 Free flow
99 Bound flow
100 Movement sequences

Smooth series of move-ments

Beginning and ending

Preparation, action, and recovery smoothly linked

Transitions

TWENTIETH SET OF PROBLEMS/ORGANIZING THEME: CREATING MOVEMENT SEQUENCES AS A REVIEW OF BASIC MOVEMENT

Content structure (for teachers)

Concept

Movement for environmental control

Major ideas

1 A child moves to discover and to cope with his environment.
2 The body is the instrument of movement and can be used in a vast variety of ways.
3 Time, space, force, and flow are the elements of movement.

Selected facts

1 Review Unit 1. Where can you move?
2 Review Unit 2. What can you move?
3 Review Unit 3. How do you move?
4 Review Unit 4. How can you move better?

Teaching tips for twentieth set of problems

1 *Arrange equipment . . . before the physical education period:*
One bouncing ball per child.
As many boxes, beams, and benches as you have.

Introduction

"Today you will create your own movement sequences."

(Use Movement Chart III for selecting movement variables to be incorporated into a movement sequence. Allow children a minimum of 10 minutes to develop and practice each sequence. Then select two or three children to demonstrate their sequences twice. Have the class evaluate each sequence demonstrated.)

PROBLEM 125

Beginning Grade	Middle Grade	Last Grade

"Create a <u>sequence</u>, moving into general space."

(Rather than have all children work on the same sequence problem, divide the class into small groups. Each group can then work on a sequence which includes but is not limited to requirements such as the following examples. Chart numbers refer to Movement Chart III, on pages 212–213.)

▶ Repeat material from Beginning Grade. Then add the following.

(Sequences with partners. If you have the time, give a different sequence problem to each couple. Have class analyze the demonstrations, looking for the themes in each sequence. Examples follow.)

▶ Repeat material from Beginning and Middle Grades. Then add the following.

(Individual sequences. Have children choose their own themes for sequences from the chart. Examples follow.)

Beginning Grade

	Chart #	Theme
1	50	Steplike actions . . . on
	18, 20	Hands and feet . . . with
	93, 96	Quick starts, sudden stops
2	19	Toes
	67	High level
	60–61	Forward, backward
3	52	Rolling
	80	Slow speed
	77	Curved pathway
4	54	Flight
	30	Straight and narrow body shape
	88	Strong force
5	69	Low level
	55	Taking weight on different body parts
6	33, 34	Curling and stretching
	80	Slowly
	50	Steplike actions

(And so on. Continue to select any two to five elements from Movement Chart III for additional themes.)

Middle Grade

	Chart #	Theme
1	42	Meeting and parting
	32	Twisted body shape
	71	Large range
2	45	Side by side
	54	Flight
	97	"Give"—gradual absorption of force
3	7, 21	Move on hips, heels
	62, 63	Sideways
	44	Facing each other
4	50	Steplike actions
	56	Balance together on four body parts
	52	Roll
5	44	Facing each other
	62, 63	Move sideways
	67, 68, 69	Changing level
6	42, 43	Meeting and parting
	33, 34	Curling and stretching
	60, 61	Forward and backward

(And so on.)

Last Grade

	Chart #	Choice of theme
1	1–25	Choose one body part to make important
	88–90	Choose a degree of force
	98–99	Choose free or bound flow
2	29–32	Choose one body shape
	50–54	Choose one way of transferring weight
	60–65	Choose two directions
3	76–78	Choose one pathway
	67–69	Choose two levels
	1–25	Choose two body parts to make important
4	80–84	Choose two speeds
	93	Quick start
	96	Sudden stop on-balance
5	60–65	Change of direction
	82	Fast
	67–69	Choose two levels
6	29–32	Choose two shapes
	50–54	Choose one way to transfer weight
	80–84	Choose one speed

(And so on.)

PROBLEM 126

Beginning Grade	Middle Grade	Last Grade

"Create a sequence staying in or near self space."

(Examples are given below. Chart numbers refer to Movement Chart III, on pages 212–213.)

▶ Repeat material from Beginning Grade, and then add:

▶ Repeat material from Beginning and Middle Grades, and then add:

Beginning Grade

	Chart #	Theme
1	56	Balance on four parts, hold, three parts, hold, two parts, hold.
2	55	Balances on
	3, 1, 20	Shoulders, head, feet
	52	Rolls
3	53	Slides
	56	Balances on three parts
	67	One part at high level
4	51	Rocks
	55	Balances
	52	Rolls
	55	Balances

(And so on.)

Middle Grade

	Chart #	Theme
1	55	Balances, taking some weight on
	18	Hands
	55	Balances, taking some weight on
	1	Head
2	56	Balances on three parts
	67	High level
	52	Rolls
3	80	Slow speed
	50	Steplike actions
	1–25	Different body parts
	96	Sudden stops on balance
4	30	Straight and narrow body shapes
	55	Balancing weight on different body parts

(And so on.)

Last Grade

	Chart #	Theme
1	55	Balance for
	86	Four pulse beats
	50	Steplike actions for
	86	Four pulse beats
	55	Balance for
	86	Four pulse beats
2	55	Balance
	80, 52	Slow roll
	55	Balance
	82, 51	Fast rock
3	52	Rolls
	60–65	Choose three directions
	55, 6	Balance, stomach nearest ceiling
4	33, 55	Curled balance
	34, 55	Stretched balance
	35, 55	Twisted balance

(And so on.)

PROBLEM 127

Beginning Grade	Middle Grade	Last Grade

"Create a short <u>sequence with balls</u>, in <u>self or general space</u>."

(Examples follow. Chart numbers refer to Movement Chart III, on pages 212–213.)

	Chart #	Theme
1	38	Bouncing
	68	Medium level
	60, 61	Forward and backward
2	38	Tossing and catching
	67	High level
	77	Curved pathway
3	38	Pushing
	69, 20	Low level, feet
	77	Curved pathway
4	38	Bouncing and tossing
	59	Changing direction
	82	Quickly (sharp turns)

(And so on.)

▶ Repeat material from Beginning Grade, and then add:

"With a <u>partner and one ball</u>, make up your own sequence of <u>six</u> unusual or very good ways to <u>pass the ball</u> back and forth, staying in your own self space."

▶ Repeat material from Beginning and Middle Grades, and then add:

"With a <u>partner and one ball</u>, make up your own sequence of <u>eight passes</u> while moving in general space. Practice until you can do your sequence the same way every time."

PROBLEMS 128 TO 200

Beginning Grade

(Have children bring out all the boxes, beams, and benches you have. Arrange in random fashion. Allow free exploration of the basic sequence in small groups at each piece of equipment while you *give each child an individual variation for his sequence.* Chart numbers refer to Movement Chart III, on pages 212–213.)

Sequence for all children

**"Balance on floor.
Get on the box, beam, or benches.
Move across.
Get off.
Balance on floor."**

Child's name	Chart #	Variation of sequence for individual child
————	1, 2	Make head or neck important
————	3, 4	Make shoulders or chest important
————	5, 6	Get waist and stomach higher than the head
————	7, 8	Get hips or legs higher than the head
————	9	Take some weight on arms whenever possible
————	10	Keep back nearest to floor whenever possible
————	11	Twist spine whenever you can
————	12, 13	Take weight on upper arms and elbows whenever you can
————	14, 15	Take weight on lower arms and wrists at some time

Child's name	Chart #	Variation of sequence for individual child
————	16, 17, 18	Take weight on fingers and thumbs or hands at some time
————	19, 20, 21	Have feet at high level (together or one at a time). Point toes
————	22, 23	Take weight on ankles and shins
————	24, 25	Take weight on knees and thighs
————	26	Keep the front of your body near to the floor and to the box or beam
————	27	Keep the back of your body near to the floor and to the box or beam
————	28	Keep one side of your body near to the floor and to the box or beam
————	29	Make a curved body shape as often as you can
————	30	Make a straight and narrow body shape as often as you can
————	31	Make a straight and wide body shape as often as you can
————	32	Make a twisted body shape as often as you can
————	33, 34	Curl and stretch as you go
————	35	Twist as you go

Child's name	Chart #	Variation of sequence for individual child
————	50	Use steplike actions
————	51	Use rocking action whenever you can
————	52	Roll whenever you can
————	53	Slide whenever you can
————	54	Fly off the box (beam or bench)
————	61	Move backward all the time
————	62, 63	Move sideways all the time
————	64, 65	Move up and down as you go
————	67	Move at a high level whenever you can
————	68	Move at a medium level whenever you can
————	69	Move at a low level whenever you can
————	71	Make all your movements as big as you can
————	73	Use small movements throughout

(Demonstration . . . evaluation.)

Middle Grade

▶ Repeat material from Beginning Grade, and then add:

Sequence for all children

"Balance on floor.
Mount.
Balance on equipment.
Dismount.
Balance on floor."

Child's name	Chart #	Variation of sequence for individual child	Child's name	Chart #	Variation of sequence for individual child	Child's name	Chart #	Variation of sequence for individual child
	77	Curved pathway approaching equipment		66	Change level as you go		33	Curl during flight
	78	Zigzag pathway approaching equipment		70	Change range of movement as you go		34	Stretch during flight
	82	Move slowly and fast (show change of speed)		20	Use feet as seldom as possible		35	Twist during flight
	83	Accelerate throughout: start slowly, gain speed		52	Roll as much as possible		87	Timing of sequence: Four beats to balance / Four beats to mount / Four beats to balance / Four beats to dismount / Four beats to balance
	84	Decelerate throughout: start fast, slow down		33	Keep body curled throughout			
	86	Hold each balance for eight pulse beats		34	Keep body as stretched as possible throughout		33	Keep hands and feet near to each other throughout
	88	Use very strong movements throughout		35	Twist body strongly in different ways as you go		20	Keep two feet together throughout
	90	Use very light, weak movements throughout		55	Balance on three body parts each time		1–25	Move on three body parts throughout
	91	Show sudden explosive movements whenever you can		56, 1	Make head take part of the weight on each balance		18–20	Move on two hands and one foot throughout
	92, 98	Show smooth flow throughout —don't hold the balances		55, 20	Feet off the floor or box on each balance		18–20	Move on two feet and one hand throughout
	59	Change direction as you go		55, 35	Make each balance as twisted as you can		97	Do a gradual collapse and roll out of each balance
				55, 19	Balance with toes at high level (one foot or two feet)		55	Use a very wide base of support for balances
				54	Fly off the box with a turn in the air (land the same way every time)		55	Use a small base of support for balances
							56	Balance on only one body part each time

(Demonstration . . . evaluation.)

PROBLEMS 128 TO 200 continued

Last Grade

▶ Repeat material from Beginning and Middle Grades, and then add:

"Make up a movement sequence that takes you over the box. Use the movements that make you feel good and that you do well. Be able to tell us how you moved."

1 "What body parts did you use?
2 "How did you transfer your weight?
3 "In what dimensions of space did you move? . . . directions . . . levels . . . ranges . . . pathways?
4 "In what dimensions of time did you move? . . . slow, medium, fast . . . accelerating, decelerating . . . to pulse beats or phrases?
5 "With what degrees of force did you move . . . strong, medium, weak . . . explosive or sustained?
6 "Where did you use bound flow and where did you use free flow?"

(Demonstration . . . evaluation.)

When children have begun to understand the basic concept of movement for environmental control . . .

When they demonstrate a functional movement vocabulary in which they can consciously manipulate the elements of time, space, force, and flow . . .

When they achieve greater control of their bodies in order to cope with a wide variety of practical challenges . . .

When they successfully create their own movement sequences . . . then go on to the next grade level.

BIBLIOGRAPHY

1 Allenbaugh, Naomi, "Learning about Movement," *NEA Journal*, March 1967.

2 Andrews, Gladys, *Creative Rhythmic Movement for Children.* Englewood Cliffs, N.J.: Prentice-Hall, 1954.

3 Angell, George, "Physical Education and the New Breed," *Journal of Health, Physical Education and Recreation* **40,** (6), (June 1969).

4 Barrett, Kate Ross, *Exploration: A Method for Teaching Movement.* Madison, Wisconsin: College Printing, 1965.

5 Bilbrough, A., and Jones, P., *Physical Education in the Primary School.* London: University of London Press, 1963.

6 Bloom, Benjamin S. (ed.), *Taxonomy of Educational Objectives, the Classification of Educational Goals. Handbook I: Cognitive Domain.* New York: McKay, 1956.

7 Boyer, Madeline, *The Teaching of Elementary School Physical Education.* New York: J. Lowell Pratt, 1965.

8 Broer, Marion, *Efficiency of Human Movement.* Philadelphia: W. B. Saunders, 1966.

9 Brown, Camille, "The Structure of Knowledge of Physical Education," *Quest* **9,** 53–67 (1967).

10 Brown, Camille, and Cassidy, Rosalind, *Theory in Physical Education: A Guide to Program Change.* Philadelphia: Lea and Febiger, 1963.

11 Brown, Margaret, and Sommer, Betty, *Movement Education: Its Evolution and a Modern Approach.* Reading, Mass.: Addison-Wesley, 1969.

12 Brownell, William A., "Problem Solving," in *The Psychology of Learning.* Chicago: University of Chicago Press, 1942.

13 Bruner, Jerome S., "The Act of Discovery," *Harvard Educational Review* **31,** no. 1, 1961.

14 ———. *On Knowing.* Cambridge, Mass.: Belknap Press of Harvard University Press, 1962.

15 ———. *The Process of Education.* New York: Vintage Books, 1963.

16 ———. *Toward a Theory of Instruction.* Cambridge, Mass.: Belknap Press of Harvard University Press, 1966.

17 Cameron, W., and Pleasance, Peggy, *Education in Movement School Gymnastics.* Oxford: Basil Blackwell, 1964.

18 Charters, W. W., and Gage, N. L., *Readings in the Social Psychology of Education.* Boston: Allyn and Bacon, 1963.

19 Combs, Arthur, *Perceiving, Behaving, Becoming.* Washington, D.C.: American Society for Child Development, 1962.

20 Corbin, Charles B., *Becoming Physically Educated in the Elementary School.* Philadelphia: Lea and Febiger, 1969.

21 Cratty, Bryant, J., *Movement Behavior and Motor Learning,* 2nd ed. Philadelphia: Lea and Febiger, 1967.

22 Cronbach, Lee J., *Educational Psychology,* 2nd ed. New York: Harcourt, Brace and World, 1963.

23 Delacato, Carl H., *The Treatment and Prevention of Reading Problems: The Neuro-Psychological Approach.* Springfield, Ill.: Charles C Thomas 1959.

24 Dewey, John, *How We Think.* Boston: D. C. Heath, 1933.

25 Diem, Liselott, *Who Can.* Frankfurt, Germany: Wilhelm Limpert, 1965.

26 Fenton, Edwin, *The New Social Studies.* New York: Holt, Rinehart and Winston, 1967.

27 Getzels, Jacob W., "Creative Thinking, Problem-Solving, and Instruction," in *Theories of Learning and Instruction.* Chicago: University of Chicago Press, 1964.

28 Getzels, Jacob W., and Jackson, Philip W., *Creativity and Intelligence*. New York: Wiley, 1962.

29 Gilliom, M. Eugene, "Structure and the History Curriculum," *The Social Studies* **59,** No. 2 (February 1968).

30 Glass, Henry, *Exploring Movement*. Freeport, N. Y.: Educational Activities, 1966.

31 Goodlad, John I., *School, Curriculum, and the Individual*. Waltham, Mass.: Blaisdell, 1966.

32 Guilford, J. P., "The Structure of the Intellect," *Psychological Bulletin,* July 1966.

33 Hackett, Layne, and Jensen, Robert, *A Guide to Movement Exploration*. Palo Alto: Peek Publications, 1966.

34 Halsey, Elizabeth, and Porter, Lorena, *Physical Education for Children: A Developmental Program*. New York: Henry Holt, 1958.

35 Hilgard, Ernest, *Theories of Learning*. New York: Appleton-Century-Crofts, 1956.

36 Hilgard, Ernest R. (ed.), *Theories of Learning and Instruction: The Sixty-third Yearbook of the National Society for the Study of Education*. Chicago: University of Chicago Press, 1964.

37 James, William, *Talks to Teachers*. New York: Henry Holt, 1929.

38 Jewett, Robert E., "The Problems Approach and the Senior High School," Mimeographed. Columbus, Ohio: Ohio State University, 1960.

39 Krathwohl, David R., Bloom, Benjamin S., and Masia, Bertram B., *Taxonomy of Educational Objectives: The Classification of Educational Goals. Handbook II: Affective Domain*. New York: McKay, 1956.

40 Kuhn, Alfred, *The Study of Society, a Unified Approach*. Homewood, Ill.: Dorsey Press of Richard D. Irwin, 1963.

41 Laban, Rudolf, *Modern Educational Dance*. London: MacDonald and Evans, 1948.

42 Laban, Rudolf, and Lawrence, F. C., *Effort*. London: MacDonald and Evans, 1947.

43 LaSalle, Dorothy, *Guidance of Children through Physical Education*. New York: Ronald Press, 1957.

44 Libby, W. L., "Tools for Discovery of Problems and Their Solutions (Heuristics)". Mimeographed Chicago, Ill.: Center for Programs in Government Administration at the University of Chicago.

45 McBride, Wilma (ed.). *Inquiry*. Washington: National Education Association, 1966.

46 MacKinnon, D. W., "What Makes a Person Creative," *Theory into Practice* **5,** no. 4 (October 1966).

47 Maltzman, Irving, "On the Training of Originality," *Psychological Review* **67,** (July 1960).

48 Mauldon, E., and Layson, J., *Teaching Gymnastics*. London: MacDonald and Evans, 1965.

49 Metheny, Eleanor, *Movement and Meaning*. New York: McGraw-Hill, 1968.

50 Mooney, Ross, and Razik, Taher (eds.), *Explorations in Creativity*. New York: Harper and Row, 1967.

51 Mosston, Muska, *Developmental Movement*. Columbus, Ohio: Charles E. Merrill, 1965.

52 ———. *Teaching Physical Education: From Command to Discovery*, Columbus, Ohio: Charles E. Merrill, 1966.

53 Murray, Ruth Lovell, *Dance in Elementary Education*. New York: Harper and Row, 1963.

54 Ohnmacht, Fred W., "Achievement, Anxiety and Creative Thinking,"
    American Educational Research Journal **3:** 131–139 (March 1966).

55 Pallett, G. Doreen, *Modern Educational Gymnastics.* Oxford: Pergamon
    Press, 1965.

56 Paterson, Ann, and Hallberg, Edmond C. (eds.), *Background Readings
    for Physical Education.* New York: Holt, Rinehart and Winston, 1965.

57 Phenix, Philip H., "The Architectonics of Knowledge," *Quest* **9,** 28–41
    (1967).

58 Polya, G., *How to Solve It.* New York: Doubleday, 1957.

59 Porter, Lorena, "Movement Patterns in the Young Child," *Theory into
    Practice* **3,** no. 3 (June 1964).

60 Randall, Marjorie, *Basic Movement: A New Approach to Gymnastics.*
    London: G. Bell and Sons, 1961.

61 Rarick, G. Lawrence, "The Domain of Physical Education as a Discipline,"
    Quest **9,** 49–52 (1967).

62 Razik, Taher, "Recent Findings and Developments in Creativity Studies,"
    Theory into Practice **5,** 160–168 (October 1966).

63 Rogers, Carl R., "Significant Learning: In Therapy and in Education,"
    Educational Leadership, January 1959, pp. 232–242.

64 Rosenblith, Judy F., and Allinsmith, Wesley, *The Causes of Behavior:
    Readings in Child Development and Educational Psychology.*
    Boston: Allyn and Bacon, 1962.

65 Russell, Joan, *Creative Dance in the Primary School.* London: MacDonald
    and Evans, 1965.

66 Sax, Gilbert, *Empirical Foundations of Educational Research.*
    Englewood, Cliffs, N.J.: Prentice-Hall, 1968.

67 Schwab, Joseph H., "Problems, Topics, and Issues Related to the
    Structures of Knowledge," *Quest* **9,** 2–27 (1967).

68 ———. "Teaching and Learning as Inquiry and the Contributions
    of Television," in *Inquiry,* edited by Wilma McBride. Washington:
    National Educational Association, 1966.

69 Scott, M. Gladys, *Analysis of Human Motion,* 2nd ed. New York:
    Appleton-Century-Crofts, 1963.

70 Simpson, Elizabeth, *The Classification of Educational Objectives:
    Psychomotor Domain.* Washington: U.S. Department of Health,
    Education, and Welfare, Office of Education, 1967.

71 Smith, Hope M. (ed.), *Introduction to Human Movement.* Reading, Mass.:
    Addison-Wesley, 1968.

72 Sweeney, Robert, *Selected Readings in Movement Education.* Reading,
    Mass.: Addison-Wesley, 1970.

73 Taba, Hilda, *Curriculum Development: Theory and Practice.* New York:
    Harcourt, Brace and World, 1962.

74 ———. *Teachers' Handbook for Elementary Social Studies.* Palo Alto:
    Addison-Wesley, 1967.

75 Taba, Hilda, Levin, S., and Elzey, F. F., *Thinking in Elementary School
    Children.* U.S. Office of Education, Cooperative Research Branch
    Project No. 1574. San Francisco: San Francisco State College, 1964.

76 Torrance, E. Paul, *Guiding Creative Talent.* Englewood Cliffs, N.J.:
    Prentice-Hall, 1962.

77 Torrance, E. Paul, "Nurture of Creative Talents," *Theory into Practice*
    5, 168–174 (October 1966).

78 Tyler, Ralph W., *Basic Principles of Curriculum and Instruction.*
    Chicago: University of Chicago Press, 1950.

79 Waetjen, Walter B., and Leeper, Robert R. (eds.), *Learning and Mental Health in the School.* Washington: National Education Association, 1966.

80 Wellington, C. Burleigh, and Wellington, Jean, *Teaching for Critical Thinking.* New York: McGraw-Hill, 1960.

81 Wertheimer, Max, *Productive Thinking.* New York: Harper, 1959.